TO
Sally,

Richard
Parker

Stomp and Shout!
The All-Too-Real Story of
Kenny and the Kasuals
and the Garage Band Revolution of the
Sixties

By Richard Parker and Kenny Daniel

Copyright 2015, Richard Parker

Stomp and Shout!
The All-Too-Real Story of Kenny and the
Kasuals and the Garage Band Revolution of
the Sixties

by Richard Parker and Kenny Daniel

Published by Oomph Media, LLC
Fort Worth, Texas

First Printing 2011
Revised Version First Printing 2015

Printed in the United States of America

Dedication

This book is dedicated to all the garage bands who made it, who almost made it and who never even made it out of the garage.

Contents

Introduction

What follows is the story of one band – Kenny and the Kasuals of Dallas, Texas. More successful than the average garage band, less successful than some others, this group's story seems to sum up the births and deaths, the experiences and dreams of garage bands in every state of the country. In telling this story we will also be telling the story of the entire "Garage Band" era from 1963 to 1967.

In those years the top teen band in North Texas was Kenny and the Kasuals. To earn the distinction of being number one was no easy task in those days as the competition in the area was fierce. The hot R&B band The Nightcaps, were still rockin' the city in the mid-sixties and younger rock bands were also filling local clubs and dances. Jimmie Vaughan was leading The Chessmen while his younger brother Stevie Ray was just starting to be noticed in a band called The Cast of Thousands. With competition from The Novas, The Briks, The Sensations, The Chaparrals, The Outcasts, The Five Americans and so many other talented groups in town, it meant that the choices when booking a band were huge. But the top choice was always Kenny and the Kasuals.

They were the kings of the proms, frat parties and dances, drawing full houses and demanding top dollar. The first LP for Kenny and The Kasuals was "The Impact Sound of Kenney and the Kasuals Live at The Studio Club". This mouthful of a title was rarely used, and almost everyone referred to the album simply as "Impact." Only 500 albums were pressed, with the band thinking that it might be difficult to sell even that many. It wasn't. The album sold out (except for a few dozen copies which were warped beyond salvation in the heat while in manager Mark Lee's car one summer day).

"Impact" has been cited by Rolling Stone as one of the most collectible American albums ever, and original copies have sold for over $2000. The LP was reissued on vinyl in the seventies and is now available on CD. After a couple of additional single record releases, in 1966 they hit on the song that would be picked up for national release. It was called *Journey To Tyme* and has been labeled as the very first "psychedelic style" recording.

Local airplay and positive sales caught the attention of the successful national record label United Artists, which negotiated with manager Mark Lee for the American rights. The song received good radio station play around the country, making the top ten in its hometown and reaching number one in Buffalo and Pittsburgh. Kenny has stated that the band's unwillingness to sign exclusively with United Artists kept the song from breaking into the national hit charts.

Record collectors rediscovered the "Impact" album in the early seventies, and eventually all of Kenny and The Kasuals recordings were re-released. In 1966 the band released what has been called the first psychedelic record, *Journey To Tyme*, an "almost national hit."

The band has been featured in write-ups in Rolling Stone (which called them one of the only true sixties bands left in the world), Texas Monthly, D Magazine, Creem, Bomp and Goldmine Magazines and has been featured on television news and variety shows.

Today in the North Texas area, Kenny and the Kasuals still perform, regularly featuring three of the original members (and on certain fun occasions, the entire original band). Two other top-quality musicians round out the current line-up. The music they play is still a high-energy mix of the hits and album dance songs that filled the dance floors in the sixties.

Some chapters in this book will deal exclusively with The Kasuals and their leader Kenny Daniel. Some chapters will explore the garage scene that was occurring across America. And other chapters will look at other local Dallas bands of 1963 – 1967, and the rock music scene that existed in the area.

By the time it's all said and done, hopefully you will have not only a good idea who Kenny and the Kasuals were (and are) but also what weird and seemingly unrelated factors crashed together to create a five-year period of madness wherein regular nobodies from down the street could dream of becoming famous...and maybe just get there.

The majority of the book comes from the memories of Kenny Daniel and co-writer Richard Parker, and from Richard's extensive study and research into the popular music of the area and the era. Other contributions were made via interviews with several of the Dallas area rockers of the time, including members of the Kasuals and other local bands. The memories and stories, although many are shared between the authors, will all be told from the point-of-view of Kenny, to keep the narrative in a readable order.

At the end of the main text is a large chapter containing discographies, commentary, fun lists and histories of the garage bands and the North Texas rock scene of the sixties.

Every effort will be made to tell the truth, the whole truth and maybe a few lies that we have come to believe as the truth. So read on. Here comes the story of sex, drugs, rock and roll, three chords and a cloud of dust.

"I grew up thinking art was painting until I got into music and I found I was an artist and didn't paint."
Chuck Berry

ARE YOU A CRETIN?
(a bit of backstory to help set the scene…)

*"…Rock and roll is music made for and
by mindless cretins…."*
- Frank Sinatra

I am a mindless cretin. At least according to Frank Sinatra. Rock and Roll was the music of my youth, my middle age and now as I creep toward senility, it continues to orchestrate my life. I will take the music to my grave. "I don't care what people say, rock and roll is here to stay" (*Rock and Roll is Here To Stay*, Danny and The Juniors, 1958).

Now in its fifth decade, rock and roll continues to be the most popular form of recorded music worldwide. Not bad for a bunch of mindless cretins.

I really don't believe that Frank Sinatra felt that rock and roll was all that cretinous. I do believe that he felt…threatened. Here was a new music style in which he had no place whatsoever. He didn't like it, he couldn't perform it and he sure wouldn't embrace it. The cretins had taken over the Cretinatorium and the superstars of the past were being driven off the charts by a stampede of young, naïve and often untrained musical performers. Most of these new performers couldn't even read music for cryin' out loud. Their guitars wailed with three chords and a threat. Drums pounded loud and ruthlessly, the sound of the jungle, now in the streets of America.

Saxophones no longer crooned; they bleated, honked, screamed and testified. These new voices were not trained, not classical, not traditional and not at all like Frank Sinatra's. The voices of rock and roll were the voices of the street. They were real. They were voices that were accessible to the millions of baby boomers, many of whom were still babies at the time.

Rock and roll was not cretinous, but it was dangerous. It was in fact deadly to the careers of many crooners and musicians who had crafted their art in the thirties and forties. In the early fifties, a few rock and roll style songs crept onto the pop charts. By 1955, there were more than just one or two. But it was 1956 when the music charts changed dramatically and the pop-style hitmakers of the previous years seemed as old hat as old hats. They were suddenly dirigibles in the space age, floating slowly and going nowhere as the jets of a new generation screamed around them.

<u>Check this out:</u>

1955: The year of pop chart success for THE FOUR ACES, PERRY COMO, JONI JAMES, THE FONTANE SISTERS, TERESA BREWER, TENNESSEE ERNIE FORD, JOHNNY DESMOND GEORGIA GIBBS, THE MCGUIRE SISTERS, LES BAXTER, FRANK SINATRA, EDDIE FISHER, JUNE VALLI, NAT KING COLE, DINAH SHORE and so many more.

1956: The year of pop chart success for FATS DOMINO, CHUCK BERRY, LITTLE RICHARD, ELVIS PRESLEY, GENE VINCENT, THE CHARMS, FRANKIE LYMON & THE TEENAGERS, CLYDE MCPHATTER, THE PLATTERS, THE JAYHAWKS, BILL HALEY & HIS COMETS, THE SIX TEENS, SHIRLEY & LEE, THE G-CLEFS, THE FIVE SATINS, LAVERNE BAKER and so many more.

Even with the influx of the rockers, the 1956 pop charts still were predominately pre-rock sounds by Sinatra, Jo Stafford, Perry Como, Frankie Laine, Gogi Grant, Julius LaRosa and others. But the writing was on the wall and by 1957 the charts were dominated by rock and roll. In the more than 40 years since then the overall genre known as rock has never surrendered the domination of the record charts, not even for a week. The newest hit musical styles are still basically rock and trace their roots directly from r&b-pop. Even today's "easy listening" radio stations program music that in 1957 would have been labeled "the music of mindless cretins."

Rock and roll may have attacked and captured the hit charts in the mid-fifties but the music didn't begin there. Some music historians may claim the roots of rock stretch back to the caveman days, but I see it as a purely 20th Century phenomenon.

Here are just a few of the various elements that created the sound of rock and roll: Blues, hillbillies, gospel, World War II, manpower shortages, radio cross-pollination, electricity, honky-tonks, recessions, swing, automobiles, voodoo, television, Les Paul and Frank Sinatra. We mindless cretins owe our music to a weirdly diverse grab-bag of influences, including old blue eyes himself.

Rock and roll was not invented – it just happened, spread and dug in. It had no earthly creator, no architect or plan. The music did not begin in New York or New Orleans or Memphis or Mars. There was no musical invasion or overnight success story. It simply grew from the earth like an audible weed, appearing everywhere at once – loud, mean and impossible to stomp out.

And of all the mindless, cretinous, crash-bang, rock 'n' rolling, musical sounds that ever existed, my favorite is what they now label "garage band music." Raw, rugged, a big beat and a bad attitude. Music we dug simply because we did. We had "Nothin' Better To Do" and we were doing it as loud as we possibly could. In the mid-60s the AM radio reached out of our dashboards, grabbed us by the ears and screamed:

"Mindless cretins of the earth, here is your music!"

15

Preface
"One Night at DreamAires"

HARRY STONE PARK
RECREATION BUILDING

September 1963: A gymnasium in East Dallas called Harry Stone Recreation Center. Saturday night. A dance named "DreamAires". Three hundred high school kids, mostly from Bryan Adams High, filled the huge gym.

This Saturday and every Saturday during that year. Some nights there was a "big name" local band playing. The Dallas rock kings – The Nightcaps – had even played there. Other nights Denny Freeman, a recent graduate of "BA" as the high school was usually called, led his group, The Corals through their paces at DreamAires. The band featured most often was a fifties-style combo named Johnny Gee and the G-Men who were enjoying their last year of real local fame in these few remaining pre-Beatle months.

There was no stage at DreamAires, not even a set of ten-inch risers like you'd find in most gymnasium dances. They just set the band up along and in the middle of one of the longer of the gym walls. The bands were literally at the same level as the crowd, socially and physically, though as all bands do – they enjoyed a special status simply because they were actual paid musicians.

How much they were paid is another matter. The pay scale was the same at teen dances all over town: "Not much". Tonight the band was called The Illusions, and they would have played for free or even less, but they didn't tell the DreamAires promoters that. The band comprised three guitars and a set of drums. The "bassist", Charles Beverly, was playing the lower strings of a regular electric guitar. No one seemed to notice or care. Blaine Young, the drummer, was having a problem with his kit. He usually had a carpet scrap under the set, but had not brought it tonight. The carpet kept the drums from moving around on slick floors. No floor was slicker than the gym floor at Harry Stone, so every time Blaine stomped the kick-pedal to whack the bass drum, the entire drum set inched forward just a bit. Every few beats he would have to grab the runaway bass drum and haul it back toward him, never missing a beat.

On lead guitar and vocals, Tommy Nichols was rolling through a rambling medley of *Bo Diddley*, *Hey Bo Diddley* and *Hand Jive*. Again no one noticed or seemed to care that the lyrics were a jumbled mess concocted from all three songs at once. The words didn't count for that much anyway. This raw and rugged dance music was all about the beat and the attitude.

17

Johnny Gee and the G-Men

On rhythm guitar was a skinny, curly haired kid named Kenny Daniel. He sang too, although Tommy handled most of the vocals in the band. Kenny took the lead on the next song, an older early-Motown hit by Barrett Strong called *Money*, although this version came to the band by way of The Kingsmen, a northwest band that was most famous for *Louie Louie*, the ultimate in crash-bang rock and roll.

Out in the overheated gym, the equally overheated crowd danced around madly, performing no actual steps and mostly just bouncing around to the beat. Ever since The Twist had come and gone, no one danced together for a fast song. This was just fine with the boys, most of whom could never master that pre-Twist fast dance style which had descended from the Lindy Hop down through the Jitterbug and finally to a dance just called "fast dancing". This new style freed the guys who could just bounce and wiggle and flail their hands and still be referred to as "a real good dancer."

Slow dancing had always been easier for the guys. You just grabbed one hand and the back of a girl and sort of moved back and forth. Even guys with absolutely no sense of rhythm could do that. Recently however some local joker had tossed a wrench into the dance works. In the early '60s, a new dance developed at Bryan Adams. It was called the Low Life and by 1963 it was THE slow-dance in East Dallas. (The dance had spread to the next high school over, Woodrow Wilson, and stopped there. It was never known to be danced anywhere else in the world but these two schools.)

The Low Life was a sort of a one-step-one-step-two-step-and-spin affair, and covered a lot of ground. Sometimes Low Lifers would form what amounted to a race track along the outside perimeter of the dance floor, with couples slow dancing as fast as humanly possible around and around the room. Those who could not do the Low Life or would not participate in a dance-race, stayed to the safety of the inner areas of the dance floor.

In between the music, the teens necked and fought and pitched pennies, three activities which were frowned upon by Officer Friendly. (In Dallas, the rent-a-cop at any teen dance was always referred to as "Officer Friendly", after the host of a local TV kid show.) The rent-a-cop's job was a lot easier while the music was playing.

As the DreamAires dance began to near its closing, The Illusions romped through a few Chuck Berry songs, the hits of The Nightcaps (*Wine Wine Wine* and a couple of others) and ended up with a

19

slow fifties ballad called *We Belong Together* which had recently become a local hit by Jimmy Velvit. In 1963 in Dallas, if one member of a couple said to the other "Listen, they're playing our song", it was almost always *We Belong Together.*

The lights came up, the kids left and The Illusions split 15 bucks, loaded up Tommy's old car with what limited equipment they had, and the night was over.

On that Saturday night, the same basic event was being played out in a thousand gyms and VFW halls across America. It was the beginning of an era that wouldn't be identified as even existing until many years later. It was time for The Garage Bands to run screaming through the music business. It was an era that could not have happened and yet it did.

Bryan Adams High School — the home of Kenny and the Kasuals. The Rafters, The Five of a Kind, Jimmy C. and the Chelsea Five, The X-Tremes, The Countdowns, The Demolitions, The Rain Kings, The Madras Men, The Embers and The Vibrations.

Chapter One
C, F, G And An Attitude

"Anything that is too stupid to be spoken, is sung."
- Voltaire

High Hopes In Lo-Fi

Before we can begin to look at who Kenny and Kasuals were (and are) we need to find out how and why they existed at all. Because their story is one of – not just a single band – but basically every band that made it (or never quite made it) in the sixties. To do this we must go back a few decades to even before the mid-20th Century.

It Started With a Bang

Rock and Roll music began when the Japanese attacked Pearl Harbor. Really. Even though that is an oversimplification, it is nevertheless true. Here is how that happened.

Prior to World War Two there was jazz, blues, country, western (not "country and western" but "country" *and* "western"), pop, marching band tunes, classical pieces and regional-ethnic dance music. But there was no rock and roll. The term may have existed, and even appeared in song lyrics and titles from the '30's on...but the music was not rock and roll. Real mid-fifties rock grew from several sources, each of which was itself a hybrid of previous styles.

In fact, none of the musical styles listed above came to exist fully grown. Each of these styles was the fruit of that many-limbed musical tree. So, set the wayback machine for the far, far distant past...

Classical Gas

Roll over Beethoven and tell Tchaikovsky the news! Rock and roll began in the big, fat orchestras you guys led. OK, that's not quite true. But one genealogical line from Elvis does lead directly back to the classical composers and the big orchestras of the way, way distant past.

Big orchestral ("classical") music was *not* the music of the people. It was the music of the upper class and the royalty. That's who commissioned it and that's who showed up at the concerts. The average working stiff of the 17th Century could no more pay to attend a concert by a large orchestra than he could juggle ten Kings. The Kings (and the dukes, barons and all the high and mighties) *could* afford it and tapped their royal toes to the tempo of a dozen drums and a hundred horns whenever they could.

But the common folk were not to be denied the band music, even if they couldn't afford the band. So the bands shrunk in size and in musical scope, if not in the sheer power of the songs played. Brass bands became the working class orchestras, often including a few woodwinds, a snare and a big bass drum. Imported to the States, this music became the marching and military band, along the lines drawn by John Philip Sousa and others.

In New Orleans, the birthplace of jazz, the marching brass band tradition took a strong hold. (Even today the amazing brass marching bands of New Orleans can be heard, although usually during funeral parades.) The brass band tradition in the city began to merge with the bordello-based ragtime and boogie piano sounds coming out of the notorious

Storyville red-light district. Add to these elements the up-tempo acoustic blues dance-tune style and voila! Jazz.

That New Orleans and deep-south Jazz was of course influenced by and slowly merging with a form of field-holler blues that had been imported from Africa. It began as the pounding of sticks on logs and rhythmic dancing around campfires. Chants of lost tribes from centuries past. Simple stringed instruments not all that different from the early ones created in England. Handed down from generation to generation, in languages unknown to most Americans, these tribal chants were performed as religious rituals, war songs and sometimes just for the fun of it.

Imported to the New World, the rhythms remained, even as the language of the chants was lost. Those rhythmic "field hollers" of the early enslaved workers evolved slowly into bluesy "call and response" work songs. The field workers worked to the rhythm of the accapella music. Decades passed and the chants became more musical, although the call and response format continued.

Eventually, the songs took on a recognizable form. The first line (with a response). The second line was a repeat of the first, with the same response. The third line was different, though rhyming with the first and second. Often the third response was different. This was still the basic format of blues songs into the industrialized era.

And way back, in England and the Nordic states, string music was evolving from a form featuring one strolling balladeer, to trios and quartets. This "string band" style was then transported into America via immigrants from those areas, many of whom settled into the Eastern mountain areas around the south. There, isolated in the hills, the music grew only a little and changed only a bit for two centuries. Lutes, violins and lyres evolved into banjos, fiddles, zithers and guitars, but the heart of the music remained untouched. These were story-telling songs, songs of love and faith, told to the twang of three or four hand held string instruments. By the mid-twentieth century it was called Hillbilly music.

In the North, especially in New York City, a much broader group of immigrants brought a wider scope of musical influences. The English and Irish brought the story-telling string instrument concept. Middle Europeans brought a horn-based band style to the area. Piano based light classics and Baroque styles were introduced by the new society folks of the area, many of them Dutch. These three styles began to blend into a recognizable fourth style – Pop music (although it wasn't called that then.) By the late 19th Century this "Tin Pan Alley" style of easy-going popular music was all rage in the big cities.

Rock of Ages Past

The blues, jazz, northern pop and southern hillbilly traditions began to crash wildly into one another in the early part of the 20th Century primarily because of technology. Several inventions led to an amazing amount of cross-pollination across the board in American society in the first thirty years of the century.

Railroads. Electricity. Paved roads. All from the nineteenth century. Then Records. Radio. The automobile. All from the early 20th Century.

Prior to these developments, the culture, language, music and morals of one section of the country almost never crossed into another section of the land. So, the hillbilly tradition of the Appalachians never made it over those mountains to the north. The pop tunes of New York City, were not easily transported to the south. The New Orleans deep-dixie "jass" music (as it was originally spelled), the brass bands with a beat, were basically unheard of once you were out of earshot of the actual band itself. Blues was a deep south phenomenon. These styles each developed from other specific styles, but then were allowed to germinate in a void, untouched by the culture of the next state over, much less influences from another country.

Ah, but the march of time kicked all that into yesteryear. Electricity cometh, and with it radio and record players. And with radio and record players came the opportunity to hear the music of another world, even if that world was only a few hundred miles away. And with railroads and automobiles came true mobility for the first time in our history. Musicians from one part of the country could hop a train and be someplace else overnight.

Jazz went north. Pop went west. Southern bluesmen took their acoustic rhythm to Chicago where it merged with the poppy-jazz of the inner city, forming a happy hybrid called amplified urban blues. Hillbilly string bands merged their sounds with northern urban blues bands and New Orleans Dixieland jazz and boogie-woogie. Jug bands began to sound like jazz groups and big orchestras became big swinging bands. Swing music combined elements of everything but kazoo tunes.

World War, Too

Then came World War II and the need for servicemen from all over the country to be shipped all over the world causing a further spread of the musical styles, as they each took their regional and ethnic music with them. Suddenly after two centuries of solitary development, the different sounds were everywhere, mingling with each other and creating beautiful bastards like Jump, Jive and Western Swing. These three genres weren't apart very long either. The Tin Pan Alley popsters noticed all the hub-bub, and stole mightily from each style. Which in turn caused the bluesy hillbillies and jazzy boogie bands to pay more attention to the pop recording industry, where after all, the money was.

By the forties, wartime manpower shortages combined with a public thirst for bigger, better, newer and louder music, but
with fewer people in each band. Smaller groups began to make louder music in the era of the Jump Bands, The Honky Tonk String Bands and the smaller jazz combos. Then these styles began to cross-pollinate as the radio stations began picking up on the various sounds being recorded. Jazzmen started to dig the jump band sounds. Blues bands began to amplify and go more uptempo to match the honky-tonk frenzy of the string bands. Southern string bands began to get jazzier and bluesier while the Texas and Southwestern hillbillies developed a jazzy-bluesy-country style eventually tagged rockabilly.

Before you could say "V-J Day", the musical taste of a large part of the American public was a wonderfully confusing mish-mash that could only be described as "Jive Urban Hillbilly Black-White Boogie Jump Bop". Or something.

27

By the early fifties the music industry charts, which for so long had so jealously guarded the gates between pop music, hillbilly hits and rhythm and blues, were at a loss to keep the bastard-forms out. Hillbilly wild men began appearing on the pop charts along with southern rhythm-and–boozers. Smooth pop vocalists began doo-wopping up their sound to compete with the gospel groups who had switched over to rhythm-and-pop. Big bands got smaller, but their sound got louder and their beat became bigger.

A single amplified guitar could replace all the strings and woodwinds and one saxophone kicked out the entire horn section. Keep the piano, the bass and the drums. Send the
harpist and the flautist and the clarinet player back to the classical orchestras. Singers, you better shout or you won't be heard at all. And plug in, get electric if you want to get loud.

Thus the styles all came together and around the mid-decade of the fifties we started calling it rock and roll.

It was all over but the shouting,
but the shouting went on for years.

The real 'rock and roll' story - at least on a nationally recognized level - starts in the mid-fifties when this truck driver named Elvis Presley made a bit of news with his deep south combination of blues, country, pop and gospel. They called it rock and roll, but it was more than that, because that implies it was just music. It wasn't. It was a social, cultural, political and entertainment revolution that continues to revolve madly into the 21st Century.

One (and only one tiny little) piece of the social puzzle that Elvis contributed was the basic line-up for a rock and roll band. Singer with rhythm guitar. Lead guitar. Bass. Drums. (No trumpets, no flute, no trombones, no frills.) You could add a sax or a keyboard, but get that clarinet player back to the marching band!

A couple of years later, Buddy Holly solidified it all in the hearts and minds of high school boys across the country. You didn't have to look like Elvis to be in a rock and roll band. Buddy looked like the absolute anti-elvis of all time. Skinny, with bad teeth and thick glasses, from someplace named Lubbock (somewhere in Texas, they said), he had nothing going for him but talent. And a band. Two electric guitars, bass and drums. We knew that was his band's line-up because we saw him on The Ed Sullivan Show, and that was the same honor as if he had beenknighted by the king. He played live, and all that music came from just those four guys. No orchestra hidden behind the curtain, just Buddy, Jerry, Nikki and Joe.

Gangly, jangly Buddy Holly from somewhere else, USA! If he could be in a band on The Ed Sullivan Show, then anyone could be in a band and at least appear at the high school gym or the National Guard Armory Dance. No matter what kind of rock and roll you dug, you could get three other guys and get on stage somewhere and do it. In the late fifties, in every city that had electricity, at least one band of pimple-faced pals plugged in and got loud.

In Texas by the early sixties, the trend was represented by The Nightcaps. In the Northwest it was Ron Holden and the Thunderbirds. In Florida it was The Blazers. In New York it was The Starlighters.

In the deep south it was Wayne Cochran and the CC Riders. Around the country sprung up r&b, rockabilly and blues-rock popsters with two guitars, a bass and a drum set. The Corals, The Exotics, The Embers, the list went on. Since most of them were in high school, they would play cheap, anywhere, for as long as you wanted them to. They had no rent to pay, no food to provide, and all their girlfriends cost them nothing, because after all, these guys were in a rock and roll band. (In those days "Money for nothing and your chicks for free" was not exactly true. It was more like "the money is nothing, but your chicks are free".) So if you offered the band eight dollars and soft drinks, you had four hours of entertainment at your dance. (Four hours of a band playing usually offered about two hours of non-repeated entertainment, since the band only knew about 30 songs and would do each one twice.) By 1960, there was still not exactly a band on every corner, but there were twice as many as there had been in 1955. The next five years changed everything. By 1965 there were two bands on every corner and at least one more in a car parked down the street.

There was not a high school anywhere in America that could not afford a live band for each dance of the school year. My old high school had two dances each week with live bands, plus one for every special occasion (Sweetheart's Dance, Sadie Hawkins Day, Homecoming, National Potato Week, any excuse for a dance, since the school charged about 50 cents for admission and made a bundle off of soft drink sales.) The St. Valentine's Dance (which we always referred to as the St. Vitus Dance, based on the dancing prowess of our high school classmates), was a major event in most schools in most areas of the country. In 1965, my school started having before school dances too, five days a week, just to make sure the income didn't dry up (details follow in a later chapter.)

By the mid-sixties not only were there thousands of local bands, but these bands were being recorded. Played on the radio. Filling dance halls. Written about in the paper. The Garage Bands had arrived and owned the damn place.

That's what was happening. That's how it started. But why did it have the opportunity to start in the first place?

How could these bands possibly compete with the established professional bands that had been working the circuit for years? The pro bands had all the things that a working band was supposed to have – matching stage outfits, professional equipment, a booking agent, business cards, equipment guys to set up the stage, portable lighting equipment. How could a bunch of kids in one Chevy with half a drum kit, two amps and one microphone steal away business?

Was it simply because they would play for peanuts, or free Pepsi or nothing at all? That was a part of it but just a small part. It was, is and will continue to be about the music.

The fact is, the established bands were not playing the music that their audiences wanted to hear. The garage bands were.

Booking agents were mostly from a previous generation, learning their trade in the forties and fifties and merrily rolling on quite successfully until the mid-sixties. They had learned a valuable lesson in the late fifties when teens demanded true rock and rollers for their dances and the bookers and promoters were still offering "Lance Hargrave and

His Syncopated Serenaders" or some such band. After a rocky few years the booking agents adapted and signed up the talent that the kids wanted to hear, but only after allowing the door to stay open long enough for a new breed of young, hungry rock and roll promoters to get in.

But lessons may be learned, even though they may not be remembered. Once all was well again, the young promoters blended into the establishment of seasoned promoters and all of them signed up groups with names like "The Kool Kats". By the early *Louie Louie* era, The Kool Kats had become The Old Guys, and the teens knew it. Fifties rock was still cool enough, and would continue to be the foundation for sixties rock, but things were changing fast.

Every generation of the century brought new sounds to the bandstands. Every ten years or so popular music was buried and a new popular music ascended the throne. By the late fifties this ten-year trend became an eight-year trend. Then it became a six-year musical turnover. By 1964, the musical-trend acceptability level of teens began to turn in about a five year cycle. The trend-following promoters could not keep up with the trend-setting teens who were their bread and butter.

The introduction of hedonistic dance hits like *Louie Louie*, *California Sun*, *Surfin' Bird* and others came right before the mass musical turnover called The Beatles. Everything the promoters thought they knew about trends and trendsetters went out the window. The lessons they had so painfully learned in 1957 also flew out the window on the cool breeze from Britain.

The bookers continued to place the fifties and early-sixties rockers in nightclubs, of course. Without these clubs, which catered to the over-21 set, the established performers would have been waiting on tables of patrons instead of playing to them. But the teen dances were essential to music promoters, and they could not turn their backs on them. Most nightclubs paid less than a huge gig at the National Guard Armory or the "Teen Valentine Blast" at the VFW hall. In 1964 trying to place "Johnny Bop and the Twisters" into a high school dance was like trying to put toothpaste back into the tube. The musicians got the message first, and the youngest of them left the old bands and drifted together to form new groups with names like "The Demolitions" or "The Dark Screams".

These semi-pro groups and the totally amateur high school combos that surrounded them had no management, no organization and virtually no chance to work, and yet somehow they were stealing all the gigs. Some of the "promotion" of these bands was purely word of mouth.

Somebody knew the bass-player for The Demolitions because he was in the same English Lit class with him. So the band was booked in the school hallway in between classes and played the Groundhog Day Hop that Saturday night.

Fingers can fly over this guitar's fast-action neck.
You can see how slim it is...
how strings sit just a soft squeeze above the fingerboard
...how frets are spaced close
to make even hard chords easier

Guitar Amplifier
Big 12-inch speaker
$68⁹⁵

Big speaker delivers your music clean and clear. And 18 watts of tonic power assures plenty of volume and tone. Built-in vibrato adds exciting sound effects to your playing ... can be turned on or off instantly with foot switch.
Built-in preamp boosts sound coming from guitar pickups. Uses 4 tubes, rectifier 20-9,000 CPS response. Volume, tone, vibrato speed and intensity controls. 2 channels, 3 input jacks. Gray leatherette, white grille. About 17x20x8 in. $5 monthly.
57 N 4821...Wt. 36 lbs. Cash $68.95

The Electro-Harp
Amplified...easy to play
$79⁹⁵

Powerful amplifier and big 6-inch oval speaker fixed you to mono-filling sound... and both are built conveniently into the case.
Anyone can play it... just press one of 18 chord buttons and strum strings to accompany songs. And you can create guitar, banjo or harp-like music with proper picking.
Three-octave range, 36 strings. Includes instructions with 26 popular tunes. pick, tuning key. Leather-ette-covered plywood case. About 23x16x4½ in. For how-to-play record, see Big Catalog. $3 monthly.
57 N 1890L...Wt. 23 lbs. Cash $79.95

NOTE: Amplifier and ... Photos Rack ... 60 cycle AC.

Solid-body Electric Guitar
$89⁹⁵

So easy to play. And you enjoy powerful "all-steel strings" sound only solid-body guitars give. Dual pickups assure right tone for chords and solo playing. True vibrato-tailpiece adds exciting "Hawaiian guitar" effects.
Two tone, 2 volume controls; 3-way pickup switch. Adjustable reinforcing rod in neck, rosewood fingerboard. Adjustable rosewood bridge. About 39x13x3 in.
57 N 1478L...Shpg. wt. 10 lbs. $5 monthly. Cash $89.95

Leatherette-covered Chipboard Case for above.
57 N 7401...Shipping weight 8 pounds............ 10.98

Save $5. Above guitar and guitar amplifier at left.
57 N 14971.2...Shpg. wt. 38 lbs. $8.50 month. Cash $153.90

Autoharp and Case. Easy to play... no fingering needed. Just press any of 15 chord buttons and strum. Great for folk songs, western music accompaniment. Three-octave scale, 36 strings. Plywood body about 23x16x5 in. With 4 picks, tuning key, music holder, songbook, instructions and leatherette-covered plywood case.
57 N 1844C.2...Shpg. wt. 16 lbs. $4 month. Cash $38.90

Autoharp without carrying case. $4 monthly on Terms.
57 N 1845C...Shipping weight 8 lbs.... Cash $28.95

SEARS 381

Some of the booking process was just luck of the draw and waiting your turn. If a high school kid had a band (and about one out of five did), sooner or later he would get his chance to play in the gym or at a supermarket opening or a battle of the bands at the shopping center. Live bands were playing everywhere – schools, churches, gas stations, furniture stores and pool parties. Everyone's turn came.

But established music-management tradition dies hard, even if the practitioners of the tradition began dying every five years. Soon a few teenage promoters became the "managers" of the better of the local bands. The most clever of these teen entrepreneurs made loads of money for their bands and themselves simply by working the telephones, printing up ten bucks worth of business cards and talking a good game.

These new, young turk bands soon became the professionals, the equivalent of Johnny Bop and The Twisters from only four years previous. And these bands soon met the same fate as Johnny Bop and his boys. 1967 came rolling over these groups with a tidal wave of new styles, and overnight the *Louie Louie* era garage bands seemed as quaint as a Dixieland jazz group.

Psychedelic music, hard rock, metal, country-rock and an early form of disco/funk took hold and the garage bands were history. The more talented of garage players drifted together to form bands with names like "Crystal Moves" or "The Orange Membrane" and continued on with the secure knowledge that this particular new wrinkle of rock and roll was here to stay.

Yeah, right.

There's A Market To Our Madness

In 1962, some rock and roll fans would have said that popular music really sucked. It was music and it was popular in that it sold a bunch of records and therefore people were buying it. But to a generation raised on Little Richard, Carl Perkins and Chuck Berry, it may not have seemed like real rock and roll.

Where was the rock attitude? Where was the grit-and-grunge sound that was the hallmark of teen rebellion? Where were the tunes that were indelibly stamped with street-smarts and sounds that your parents hated? They had all gone to the garage to rethink their strategies.

The powers-that-were had recaptured the rock mountain from the wild rebels who had taken it. Peace had been restored to the music world and nice young men in matching jackets were once again at the microphone and on the record charts.

A sampling of top ten hits in 1962: Folk songs like *If I Had A Hammer* by Peter Paul and Mary. Teeny-pop like *Bobby's Girl* by Marcie Blane. Drippy love songs like *Johnny Angel* by Shelly Fabares. Old fashioned pop vocals like *Ramblin' Rose* by Nat King Cole. The hit charts were filled with performers like Pat Boone, Connie Francis, Andy Williams, Jimmy Dean, Johnny Crawford, Bobby Vee, Bobby Vinton and The Lettermen. Even pure popsters of the past like Patti Page, Burl Ives, and Perry Como were regularly being heard on the "rock and roll" radio stations. Rock and Roll? Rex Allen, Walter Brennan, Tony Bennett and Hayley Mills? It may have been good music to some, but it sure as hell was not rock and roll.

Pretty people with pretty voices singing pretty songs. It was a pretty bad situation for a generation of teens hungry for raw, rambunctious rock and roll. (There were of course some rock and r&b hits in that pivotal year of '62: Ray Charles, The Isley Brothers, Gary U.S. Bonds and others provided relief from the stream of pop pap programmed on rock radio. But a huge amount of music on teen radio was from performers with traditional pop styles.)

So the stage was set for a revolution – a horde of hungry, ignored and disaffected fans looking for some relief. The recording industry powers had a firm grip on the output of music. Radio station executives had a firm grip on the past. Radio programmers and deejays had a firm grip on payola money from the big companies who had axes to grind and product to move.

Only five years before, unknown performers recording in basements and living rooms were enjoying top ten hits. Needless to say, in those early-rock days the record company honchos envied the local entrepreneurs and hated this trend of homegrown hits, mainly because the honchos were being left off the gravy train. By 1962 all was back to normal. It seemed impossible for a wild young band to walk into a studio, pay fifty bucks to record a raw rock song and get it released at all, much less see it become a hit.

And then that's exactly what happened. The Kingsmen recorded *Louie Louie* in one take using one microphone at a cost of about one buck and had one huge hit in 1963. Then rugged, twisted local scream-fests and frat-blasts like the above-mentioned *California Sun* and *Surfin' Bird* came wailing out of the woodwork and the industry hotshots found themselves back at square one (or at the most, square two).

To compound the problem for the traditional money-changers, The Beatles hit in early 1964, and what was left of everything the industry thought it knew about teen tastes disappeared overnight. Bad-ass sounding bands came attacking from overseas, fueled by the need of American teens for real rock and roll. Groups with names like The Animals, The Zombies and The Yardbirds scared hell out of mid-American parents, and electrified their kids. When the lead singer of Them appeared on the hit charts with vocals that sounded like his tongue was permanently swollen from some strange accident, the way singers sang and sounded was given a direct boot in the chops. Van Morrison made every local band singer want to sound like he had hot marbles in his mouth.

Mick Jagger of The Rolling Stones, Eric Burdon of The Animals and Paul Jones of Manfred Mann brought a guttural growl back to rock vocalizations. These bands, along with The Yardbirds, The Beatles and The Spencer Davis group reintroduced good old American r&b to American teens, who thought it was new and used it like a drug.

Thousands of U.S. teens (mostly pimply-faced boys like me) bought guitars, learned those three chords and began forming bands. They saved their paper route money, plus any cash they received from playing gigs at the high school hops or supermarket openings and invested wisely in one hour of recording studio time at a local facility which had previously made its living recording church choirs and school marching bands.

These recordings were released by the ton on local labels too naive to realize that it simply wasn't done that way. The rewards for this naiveté were local hits, national hits and sometimes enduring fame. It couldn't have happened and yet it did.

Most of these recordings went nowhere in a mad rush, only to be discovered twenty years later, labeled as "garage band classics" and reissued world-wide (and thank God for that). By the '80's, bands who couldn't afford business cards in 1966 were gracing the covers of albums released in Paris, London and New York City! The bands still could not afford business cards, but at least they were enjoying a brief measure of fame denied them in their teens.

That's how and why it happened. Home grown bad-attitude bands and records created indirectly by the industry that tried to prevent them.

Back To The Garage

Like I said, we were only one of thousands of garage bands who tried to make it in the mid-sixties, and kind of did. What happened to those bands that stood in line to play at the local high school hop?

Only one garage band out of a thousand made any impact on the record charts, even locally. One band out of ten thousand had a certified national hit. Pretty lousy odds considering all the work that went into the creation and continuation of a rock band, then and now.

And even though each band harbored a secret fantasy of having a hit, appearing on The Ed Sullivan Show and touring the country as the opening act for The Rolling Stones, it rarely happened. The real appeal of being in a band was simply in being in a band. Standing on stage, playing, screaming and basking in the admiration of the audience (although this admiration was to some degree only in the performers' minds.) After a year or two of limited fame within the neighborhood, the bands broke up. What happened to the members?

Well, there seems to have been some sort of cosmic mathematical formula for dealing with the weakest and slowest members of the band, perhaps tied in somehow with Darwin's theory of natural selection and the survival of a species. If you had five members in your band in 1965, when you broke up, two of these members would move on to another band. This second band was then composed of two members of your old band, two members of another broken band and one other guy who came from across town somewhere.

This means that natural selection has taken care of at least six of the smallest creatures, leaving them out of the biz, and leaving five standing. But then this new band broke up as well, because suddenly psychedelic music was the rage and most of the band simply couldn't play it. So two members of this band left and formed "The Lemon Merry Go Loud" with two members of another failed garage band from way, way on the other side of town. (Note: Survivors had to begin looking further afield for other survivors, sometimes even looking in the next city over!)

Now all was well, even though if you look back on the family trees of this new band, you'll see about fifteen abandoned souls for the four survivors. But The Lemon Merry Go Loud (now called simply Lemon Gong after merging with the band previously known as The Everpresent Gong of Truth) was the opening act at a new nightclub called Fogg City, even though the band members were all still under the age of 21. Fogg City lasted about two years, and Lemon Gong lasted a considerably shorter period of time. One member joined a white soul band led by an ex-jazz saxophonist and was happy for the work. Another member formed a band called The Cumberland Stargazers and began playing a mild form of country rock inspired by Poco and The Flying Burrito Brothers. The rest of the band went on to college, a year late.

By 1968, these two bands had disbanded and only one of the original players from the original twenty garage bands that had gone into creating them, was still in the music business. He was probably the nerdy bass player from The Meatloafs, who while in high school was voted the most likely to pick his nose on national television. (He is now a successful producer of music videos, lives in Malibu and is married to the cover girl of a recent Sports Illustrated swimsuit issue.)

Everybody else in each of the untold number of garage bands that fed the everflowing stream of crushed dreams went to school, or work, or joined a commune or disappeared altogether. Most of them are now insurance salesmen, clerks, gardeners, corporate honchos and/or hopeless drunks. In other words they merged with mainstream American society.

The system works. Long live the system.

"The wise musicians are those who play what they can master."
Duke Ellington

41

Chapter Two
Journey Back In Tyme

Just across the Trinity River from downtown Dallas is a section of town called Oak Cliff. In the early days it was its own independent town, but back in 1903 it was annexed to the city of Dallas. These days if anyone thinks of Oak Cliff at all, they usually associate it with Lee Harvey Oswald, who lived there (and was captured there at the Texas Theater) on the day he killed President Kennedy. But some folks know it as a source of blues and rock performers. In the Twentieth Century a lot of rockers and bluesmen were from Oak Cliff. T-Bone Walker (originally called

"Oak Cliff T-Bone") wasn't born there but he grew up and adopted the place as his home town. Stevie Ray Vaughan and his brother Jimmie were born and raised there, along with drummer and Vaughan collaborator Doyle Bramhall.

Edie Brickell (Mrs. Paul Simon) of New Bohemians, B.W. Stevenson, Michael Martin Murphy, drummer Mickey Jones, and guitarist Rocky Athas were all born in that section of town. So was guitarist Rollie Anderson (more about him later).

Now, I don't put myself up with T-Bone Walker or Stevie Ray Vaughan, but nevertheless back on May 1, 1946, I, too, was born in Oak Cliff, Texas. And I lived there until the ripe old age of five months, when the family packed up and moved to Manhattan Beach California, settling in at 660 27th Street. My father and his brother Ed started a hardware manufacturing business on the west coast, and in their spare time, they hung around with Lawrence Welk and his orchestra at the Aragon Ballroom.

Left to right: Uncle Ed Daniel, Alice Lon (The Champagne Lady),
Pop and Lawrence Welk in California

My dad, George Kenneth Daniel (who most everyone called Budda and I called Pop), was a drummer who had played big band music in The Century Room of the Adolphus Hotel in Dallas and other hotspots in the late '30's and '40's with my Uncle Ed. They were the mainstays in the Ed Daniel Orchestra, a thirteen piece "big band". (Hey, thirteen pieces WAS a big band in Dallas at the time!) The Ed Daniel Orchestra was a popular club band too, enjoying a long association with the Sylvan Club on Greenville Avenue. Pop played drums, Uncle Ed played piano, accordion and trumpet and several other hot local players filled up the bandstand including Fred "Mac" McCord (later the owner of the well-known Dallas music stores, McCord Music.)

Athletic Club Is Host At Annual Junior Dance

Many members of the college set home for the holidays joined with the high school students Friday evening at the Dallas Athletic Club for the club's annual Christmas junior dance. Horns, noisemakers and paper hats added to the hilarity of the group, who danced from 9 to 12 to the music played by Ed Daniel and his orchestra.

Pop and Uncle Ed Made the news now and then

44

In California we lived very near the beach and yet we rarely went there except when family came to visit. Then we packed up towels and umbrellas and picnic baskets, went straight to the beach and acted like we did this all the time. I remember wishing we would have more company, more often. But when I was ten, we moved back to Dallas and that was the end of my beach boy days.

My Dad always thought I would be a drummer, like him, and when I was around eleven years old, he bought me a set of Premier drums. I practiced every day and was told that I was doing all right too. I had grown up with big band music playing in the house and I was trying to master that genre. I also was a big fan of country music and would play along to the local country radio station.

Pop had always felt that if the drums didn't work out for me, that I would become a trombone player like Glenn Miller, who was one of my his idols. Once during World War II, while Dad was in the Army Air Corps in England, The Glenn Miller Orchestra came and played for the guys stationed in the area. Glenn Miller was the leader of the Army Air Corps Band during the war and traveled the world entertaining the men. On this particular day, after the concert, Dad asked Glenn for his autograph and as he was signing it, Dad stepped back and took his photograph. It was one of the last (if not THE last) ever taken of Glenn Miller, who died in an airplane accident shortly after that day. Years later, Dad gave me that photograph. I still have it today.

I never did become a drummer or a trombonist because one day in the fifties there came a life changing event. Now, in a lot of biographies you will read about various "life changing experiences" –

The last photo ever taken of Glenn Miller.
Taken by my Dad in December of 1944

floods, earthquakes, World Wars and so on. My life
changing experience shook the earth too…at least the
earth under which I stood. It was October 7, 1957
and the event was an episode of "Ozzie and Harriet".
Really. It was a regular episode entitled "Fixing Up
The Fraternity House" in which David and his frat
brothers live up to the episode title.

If I remember correctly, Ozzie and Harriet somehow got involved with helping Dave and the frat boys get the place ready for a an episode-ending dance. It was a standard "Ozzie and Harriet" program – easy-going to the point of drowsiness, funny, light-hearted and over in a half hour. At least for the first twenty-seven or so minutes of that half hour it was that way.

And then at the end for the Frat House dance scene, Ricky Nelson, only 18 at the time, came out with a hot back-up band featuring future guitar legend James Burton, and performed *Be Bop Baby*, an up-tempo rockabilly classic. That was it. I was a guitarist and a rocker from that moment, even though I had never even attempted to strum a guitar. (Decades later I had the opportunity to play with the great James Burton. Yeah, I'm a shameless name-dropper.)

So anyway, I picked up an old Kay acoustic guitar that seemed to have always been lying around the house, and began to destroy the tips of my fingers with endless practicing and experimenting. By mid-junior high I had learned *What'd I Say*, the Ray Charles dance classic and was driving my mother crazy by playing it constantly.

At that time we lived in the Casa View section of East Dallas, a part of town that fed the new Bryan Adams High School, which opened in 1958. I was still a punk kid at Gill Elementary getting ready for the move up first to Gaston Junior High and then to the brand-new Robert T. Hill Junior High. Back then Hill being new and in a newer section of the neighborhood, was considered to be the classier of the two schools. But many of us who went there harbored a jealousy of the Gaston kids. You see,

Gaston's school nickname was "The Warriors" and their mascot was a cool, mean-looking Indian brave brandishing a wicked tomahawk. At Hill, our school nickname was "The Highlanders" a tribute to the Scottish fighting men of a previous century, and our mascot was a guy in a plaid skirt playing the bagpipes. We suffered from "mascot envy"

The rivalry between the two Junior Highs was immediately forgotten in the 10th grade as both schools fed into Bryan Adams High, home of the Cougars, a mascot we could all get behind.

By the time I was a sophomore we had moved to a nice big house near Hill Junior High and I had room to get away from the family to practice. I had mastered at least those three essential chords – C, F and G, and was itching to perform in public. As Don McLean said a few years later in the song *American Pie*...

"I can still remember
How that music used to make me smile.
And I knew if I had my chance
That I could make those people dance
And maybe, they'd be happy for a while."

Being up on a stage (or at least up on a one-tier riser) playing guitar, singing, making people dance, watching the girls sigh – being Ricky Nelson – that was my dream at age 15. And being a relentless self-starter, I went out and just flat made it happen.

In 1962 my dad bought me a 1962 Sunburst Fender Stratocaster guitar. The guitar cost less than two hundred dollars then. If I had that guitar today I'm told it would be worth around $100,000.

One of my closest buddies, Tommy Nichols, was a guitar player too and he harbored the same "local hero" dreams as I. So we got together and practiced and harmonized and convinced each other we were stars.

Tommy and I were taking guitar lessons at McCord music in downtown Dallas on Elm Street from Terrell Gardner. Fred McCord played guitar with my Uncle Ed's big band back in the 30's. Fred was called Mac by his good friends and was a

Cousin Gregg on the left, little brother Rusty on drums, and me on the right with my 1962 Strat

wheeler dealer of many sorts. He and his wife Juanita would come over to our house for dinner a lot and encouraged our early attempts at performing. However in high school in 1962, there was absolutely no market for a band with no drummer or bassist, so we began to scout around. All we could come up with was another guitarist, a really good guy named Charles Beverly. Even though at that time we were all about equally adequate on the guitar, Charles agreed to take the position of bassist, but had no intention of buying a bass. (Just as I had no intention of being a bassist — I mean, did you ever see Ricky Nelson playing a bass guitar? I think not.) So Charles just plucked the lower strings of his electric guitar and by golly, it sounded like a bass or close enough.

Still no drummer. That meant still no gigs. Then I remembered that a buddy of mine who lived across the creek behind my house at least had a drum kit. Having a drum kit meant that you were a drummer, even if you couldn't actually play the drums. So Blaine Young was in the band and we got lucky, because he could actually play the drums. It was pretty easy to talk Blaine into joining the band, since he was madly in love with my younger sister Martha at that time, and spending time at my house practicing (and showing off in front of her) was a positive in his mind.

So now we had three electric guitars, drums, two microphones and a couple of amplifiers about the size of matchbooks and we were on our way.

We became "The Illusions" and most of our early performances were illusions too. Our first gig was in 1963 at a party at classmate Beth Stricklin's back yard.

She lived across Peavy Road from our high school. We played for several hours and her dad gave us $1.50 per man and bottle of Alfred Dunhill cologne. We were professionals! Of course, counting the time it took to load the car, drive over, unload, set up, play three one hour sets, tear down, reload the car and drive home, we could have made five times that much in tips carrying out groceries at Jimmy White's Supermarket. We didn't care. We felt like rock stars.

Anything we may have lacked in repertoire we made up in stage outfits. We oten wore black slacks, black shirts, white ties, and black dress shoes. It had been a high-style for local bands, mostly rockabillies, in Texas in the fifties and the style still stuck. At least until November of 1963 when The Beatles hit and just blew everything away including how you looked and acted on stage.

The Illusions rock the gym

We traveled in style too, or at least we thought so. We drove Tommy's 1942 black Plymouth coupe, with red and white tuck-and-roll interior. A chick magnet if ever there was one. We had such limited equipment that it would all fit into the car along with us and room to spare for a girlfriend or two. A classmate at BA named Larry Olson was our make-shift manager and was always there to make sure we had whatever we needed. Musically we became surprisingly good very quickly, though our appearances were still hit-and-miss affairs. Sometimes we were called The Illusions and sometimes we were The Ken Daniel Combo. Neither Tommy nor I can remember why we changed the band name now and then. We weren't all that great yet, but we weren't so bad that we had to keep changing our name to get jobs.

Descriptions of those first gigs would match those of almost any beginning high school combo in any city, anywhere at that time. Somebody's cousin's birthday party. A free gig at a supermarket opening just for "the exposure". A junior high dance at "The Big Thicket", a tiny, rustic party-place for hire at nearby White Rock Lake. For our first four appearances we probably earned ten dollars total, to split four ways. Luckily for us and every other start up band, the money was not the issue...at least not yet.

It was, I admit, all about girls. They came to dance and ended up lining the front of the stage looking up...at us! At me! Kenny "Ricky Nelson" Daniel. I was the three-chord king of rock and roll, at least in that particular location at that particular moment. Girls, girls, girls! This was a "pre-sex" era and so contact with girls was mostly limited to flirting with a little bit of lip-wrestling thrown in. Later came the "sex and drugs" portion of our story.

The admiration of the girls was more payment than any local gig could have provided anyway. The way they looked at you, dreamy-eyed, flush-cheeked, with odd little smiles that even they didn't understand. We would have paid for the opportunity to play and bask in that warmth.

By that time (late 1963), Tommy and I (with Charles and Blaine) were pretty glad we were in a band.

"Thinking back now, I think that if Kenny and I hadn't taken lessons together at the beginning, there may not have been a band." Tommy Nichols remembers. "Before the lessons we were pretty much playing E, A and B7 over and over. The lessons taught us a bunch of new chord progressions to build on and taught me the lead to "Johnny B Goode". For a while I built most of my leads around that song, changing it just enough to get away with it. The lessons and the endless hours practicing in Kenny's room gave us a jump-start and a little musical credibility that may not have happened otherwise. Or a least taken a lot longer."

Bands were harder to find in the early '60's and we played all over the place, mostly private parties and school events. About this time we started a tradition at Bryan Adams High School.

The school had dances in the girls' gym on a regular basis. Every Friday night during the fall there was a "Victory Dance" after the school football game. It was called that whether the BA Cougars were victorious or not. The school's real goal was to make a buck. It cost 50 cents to get in and soft drinks were a dime, sold by the school's "fraternity" called The Key Club. The place was packed every Friday. By this time the school was also having other dances on a regular basis, no matter how lame the excuse was for doing it. Thus we had a Sadie Hawkins Dance, a costume "twirp dance", Homecoming Dance, The Military Ball, fund-raising dances for practically every club in school from the French Club to the Future Homemakers, and of course one for every holiday. Since the school fund kept a portion of all proceeds, I'll bet that if the school could've found an open weekend night they would have squeezed in a dance for National Pickle Week and "Remember The Maine Day"

In 1964 or so, the school realized that they were missing an opportunity to soak the students for a few more quarters and began having before school dances too, sometimes several times a week, just to make sure the income didn't dry up. (I bet they had at least considered canceling classes altogether and just charging for dances three times a day.) We helped start that early-morning dance trend by volunteering to play the first before-school dance for free. Half the school showed up and before you could say "gimme a quarter kid", we were playing at least once a week in the girl's gym, usually every Friday morning at 7am. It was of course a "sock hop" because everyone had to kick off their shoes so as to not scuff up the gym floor. Piles of shoes lined the walls around the gym and watching the students scramble to find his-or-her own pair at the end was one of the most fun parts of the dance. After the dance, kids went to first period class tired, sweaty and ready to take a nap as soon as the teacher started droning on about the Punic Wars or something.

Other local bands played at the BA dances in the girls' gym too. A few of the BA bands of that era that appeared as gymnasium heroes included The Five of a Kind, The Rafters, The Rain Kings and Jimmy C. and the Chelsea Five. Bands from other high schools soon got in on the gravy train too. The Briks, The Sensations, The Chessmen, The Warlocks, Kit and the Outlaws, The Novas and The Outcasts just to name a few. (In a later chapter we will cover in detail the large Dallas-area band scene from 1963 – 1967.)

The Sensations

The Rafters

Chapter Three
What the Hell?

As described in Chapter One, traditional bands had begun to collapse of their own weight by 1963. Combos like The Illusions were springing up everywhere. Stores in Dallas like McCord's Music, Whittle, Brook Mays and Arnold & Morgan sold guitars by the hundreds on a pay-as-you-play basis. What little money a high school band might make mostly went right back to the store to pay for amps, microphones, drum kits, Farfisa or Vox organs and Fender guitars and basses. Profit not being the main motivating factor, these upstarts were forcing the "real bands" out of existence.

It was almost two decades later before anyone thought to name these combos "Garage Bands." Why? Obviously because most of the rehearsing (and sometimes all of the actual playing) occurred in someone's dad's garage. That's how the bands were named but....

What was garage band music? Of course Garage Band Music was an actual musical style, easy to identify even fifty years after the fact. But it was more than just music. It was an attitude.

Bad Boys

The attitude was "don't tread on me" (which became a title of a grungy garage classic song by the Dallas band Kit and the Outlaws). The bands from only one year before had matching stage outfits, choreographed dance steps, happy smiles and cute names like The Rhythm Toppers. A garage band wore whatever clothes were the most wrinkled, scowled a lot, slurred their vocals and had names like the aforementioned Outlaws.

Or names that sounded fast and dangerous (The Demolitions, The Chevelles, The Sonics). Or names that implied that the band was on the outside of society (The Outcasts, The Rovin' Kind, The Knaves). Or names that sounded just plain evil (The Bad Seeds, The Roots of Evil, The Trolls.) Or spooky names (The Haunted, The Warlocks, The Headstones). Or names that were just weird or confusing (The Grodes, The Briks, The Thingies). Or names that clearly stated that they were from the upcoming generational takeover of the world (The New Breed, Our Generation, Things To Come.) Or names that meant nothing to most people but implied a kind of a what-the-hell mystique of their own (The Unrelated Segments, The Movin' Morfomen, The Lemon Fog, The Rain Kings.) One of the exceptions to this rule in Dallas was Kenny and the Kasuals, who although we dressed in matching outfits and had a name that was strictly from 1962, we became THE Garage Band in Dallas.

Easy To Play

The music was three-chord rock and roll, usually C, F and G (for the experienced garage band of the world, you may add G7 and even an E where applicable.) *Louie Louie, Gloria, Farmer John* and *Twist and Shout*. The vocals did not require actual "singing" as in the forties or fifties, but more of a tuneful growl. Most garage singers adapted the vocal stylings of the two most important singing influences on local teen band singers – Mick Jagger and even more importantly, Van Morrison. This style required the singer to sing as if his tongue were slightly swollen in some mysterious bee-sting-to-the-mouth episode, and to sound angry about it.

Harmony was almost unheard of, so one microphone would put you in business. Almost every song you added to the playlist was a variation on the songs above. (*Hang On Sloopy* was a combination of *Twist and Shout* and *Louie Louie* with new words.)

The lead guitar breaks were mostly whanging against one or two strings, so the rhythm guitarist from most bands could easily become the lead guitarist in a garage band (until you tried to add any song by The Yardbirds into your set, then you better be able to play.)

Drumming was mostly a matter of owning a drum set. All of this meant that almost anyone who could afford the down payments on the instruments (guitar, bass, drum, and perhaps a portable Farfisa or Vox organ for the top-level bands) could form a band and get work.

Dance Without Thinking

The song list may have been pretty easy to learn, but it was absolutely set in granite. (See "playlist" later in this book.) Why? Because the teenage audience did not want surprises. They came to dance without having to think about it. The music started and a free-form style of grooving to the music was what dancing was about in the school gyms and frat houses. There were no steps, there were no rules and there was no stopping once they started. Anyone could dance to this music, just as almost anyone could perform it. It was the ultimate grass-roots expression of dancing for the sheer hell of it.

Deliver Us From The Days Of Old

What mattered most was that it was not at all like the music your older siblings danced to just three years before. The fast dance which forever had been called the jitterbug had finally died hard in 1962. The touching hands, swaying back and forth, spinning under each others arms were entirely gone by 1964.

"This is our generation" every generation says, convinced it has invented youth. "And we know what's good." What was good in the three years of American garagedom was loud, fast, raunchy, ominous and rebellious.

Or at least it had to sound rebellious, even if it was being played at the Lions Club Hall in Des Moines, Iowa. Most of all, it was new. It was yours and yours alone. And it would last forever! (And it almost did, until 1967, since three years seemed like forever back then.)

It wasn't called garage music then. It was just "music" as if nothing else musical existed on the planet. And it was good.

"None of us wanted to be the bass player. In our minds he was the fat guy who always played at the back."
Paul McCartney

Chapter Four
Kasualized

Kenny and the Kasuals in the Bryan Adams
High School Gym, 1965

In 1964, three things happened that stick with me. The first was a truly mind-blowing experience, the second a very bad decision, and the third worked out pretty well.

First, along with a few million other people, I watched The Beatles appear twice on The Ed Sullivan Show. Dang! This was even bigger than Ricky Nelson on "The Adventures of Ozzie and Harriet".

Secondly, I traded in my beloved Fender Sunburst Strat for a white teardrop Vox 12 String like the one Brian Jones of the Rolling Stones played.

And finally, The Illusions became Kenny and the Kasuals. The Illusions Combo had by early 1964 lost Blaine Young to the Marines. (Tragically while stationed in Hawaii on his way to Viet Nam, Blaine was struck with acute lymphatic leukemia and died.)

He was replaced by David "Bird" Blachley, one of Tommy's best friends, but someone with whom I just never connected. However he was a better drummer than Blaine and had a better and more complete drum set, and he stuck with the band for the rest of the sixties. The Illusions continued with Charles still on bass, playing dances in the school gym and other local teen venues.

In Dallas, there was a club called The Lantern Club in the Lamplighter Motel on Highway 30 near Big Town Mall in Mesquite, where I had met future Kasual Jerry Smith when we were both lifeguards at the swimming pool. (Jerry was also a BA Cougar, in my class of '64.)

The Lamplighter also had a nice restaurant and huge pool. With my connections there as lifeguard I talked the management into booking The Illusions in the Lantern Club. Our price was right (meaning it was a lot less than the pro bands they had had been booking) and so we became regulars there. Often on Friday nights we would play out by the pool for a teen swim party and it was there at poolside that we turned a page in our story.

A woman who was at the Lamplighter for a regular Friday night bridge party heard us playing and wandered out to the pool area to take a look. Not too long before that she and her son, Mark Lee, had also watched The Beatles on the Ed Sullivan Show and that memory was fresh in her mind as she listened to us.

The next day she mentioned to Mark that she had just seen a band that was "better than those guys" meaning The Beatles. The next night, Mark Lee came to a party at the Fontana Apartments where we were playing. He sat and listened politely. During a break he came up to us and asked what we called ourselves and we told him we wereThe Ken Daniel Band. (Why we were using that name on that night I still can't remember, because most of the time we were The Illusions Combo.)

I don't know if Mark also thought we were "better than The Beatles", but he must have liked us somewhat because he said, "That's not your name anymore. From now on you're Kenny and the Kasuals and I'm your manager." Mark was still in high school himself, attending Hillcrest High in a much tonier part of town than we hailed from. He looked older, wearing a stylish suit and everything, and he acted older too. He thought of himself as sort of a Brian Epstein, and he told us in no uncertain terms that he was going to make us stars and we were all going to be rich. Needless to say he made a great first impression with us and became our manager that very night. We considered ourselves lucky that his mom had seen us at the Lamplighter.

(As a side note, The Lamplighter Motor Hotel played an odd role in the Kennedy assassination, or at in least one conspiracy theory about the assassination. According to one book, the "self-confessed killer" claims to have stayed at the Lamplighter the week prior to the assassination, met Lee Harvey Oswald there along with a CIA operative who was their "handler". It would have been about a year later when Kenny and The Kasuals were regulars on the Lamplighter bandstand.)

We made the transition from Illusions to Kasuals in two ways. First, Charles Beverly left the group. He was never really a bassist and was not the rock and roll type. We knew another could-be bassist – a guy who played guitar in another Bryan Adams combo called The Vibrations. He didn't actually have a bass guitar, but was willing to buy one to join our band and we were sure that he would be able to master the bass quickly and play it better than Charles. He was another Bryan Adams student, one year behind me in the same class as both Tommy and Charles, named Lee Lightfoot.

It was during this transitional time that I began to take on almost all of the lead singing. Tommy being a great guy with an easy going personality, never voiced his objection, so I just took over the microphone. (And, hey - we were now called Kenny and the Kasuals, not Tommy and the Kasuals!)

We (Tommy, Bird, Lee and I) had been playing as Kenny and the Kasuals for a few months when Bird suggested adding an organist. He knew a guy who had been in the BA marching band with him, who tooted the bass clarinet, but who could really play the organ. We weren't sure at that time that an addition was necessary. The band had really gelled with the addition of Lee, Bird and our ever-sharpening skills on guitar. However the sound of a cool organ like Alan Price played in The Animals seemed like a good idea so we decided to give the guy an audition.

"I would guess we were The Kasuals for maybe six months or so before Paul joined," Tommy recalls. "Bird recommended him and said that he could play standing up like the organist in The Dave Clark Five. Well, that's pretty cool. We could sound like The Animals and look like The Dave Clark Five? So, Bird called him and we set up an audition at – of all places – the pavilion at Flagpole Hill."

Paul remembers: "In 1965, 'Bird' was a drummer in the marching band where I played bass clarinet. He persuaded me to come and audition for Kenny and the Kasuals. At that time the only keyboard that I had access to was a big Thomas console organ that my parents had at home. I convinced my mom that I would be really careful with the organ if I could figure out a way to get it over to the audition. So Bird showed up to take me to the audition. He was driving an old Pontiac that had been souped up and making a lot of noise. We picked up the organ and had to end up putting it into the trunk as my mom watched with a look of horror on her face – welcome to rock n roll!"

Flagpole Hill at White Rock Lake Park was a major party place, for official gatherings (those sanctioned by the Park Board) and for impromptu gatherings which could swell to a hundred BA and Woodrow Wilson students in about ten minutes. The covered (but open air) pavilion was wired for electricity and it was not uncommon for bands to just hook up and start playing to attract a crowd.

"We set up the stuff up there in the pavilion and were noodling out a practice when Paul showed up," Tommy continues. "He set up this big old organ. We kinda looked at him and said something like 'well, what d'ya know how to play?' He launched into the organ intro to *Money* and we joined in. I remember Kenny and I looking at each other with big smiles while we were playing. We hired him on the spot."

"When I first joined the band in the 1965, I was a total nerd - a high school marching band nerd to be exact," Paul adds. "The manager, Mark Lee, was only a year older than me, but he convinced us all that he was, as they say, 'wise in the ways of the world'. At first he had the band playing wholesome gigs at party rooms in apartment complexes and the like. But once early on, Mark surprised us all by booking us into a strip club. I lied to my parents about where I was going to play and headed off into the great unknown.

"In the '60's, strip clubs were not nice places and this club was no exception. I walked into the club and immediately didn't like it. The building and the interior were seedy and the joint just screamed 'low life'. Then I looked over and saw this gorgeous Hammond B3 organ with a Leslie speaker. I couldn't believe my eyes. I had learned how to play on a Hammond and played one in church and now here was the finest of instruments sitting in this strip club waiting for me to play on it. I wasn't sure what to make of this development but I sat down, cranked the organ up and played.

"We lasted one night at that club. There were no strippers, so the usual crowd didn't show, and our regular crowd either couldn't or wouldn't come down to the dump where we were playing, so we played to an empty room. But I did get to play on that big beautiful Hammond B3. It wasn't church that's for sure, but I still enjoyed it."

The personalities in the band were very different, but seemed to mesh somehow. Bird and I were very different. He liked to discuss things that others in the band didn't know or care about. He was (and probably is) a true genius, high IQ sort of a guy, while the rest of us were bright and educated, but not on his level. I'm not surprised that Bird went on to get two doctorate degrees and become a success in medicine. He was always too smart for rock and roll. But he did keep a good beat.

Tommy recalls: "Kenny and I were a little wild and unpredictable while Paul and Lee were quiet and laid back. Bird was always upset with our behavior. That bothered Kenny, while I was so used to it I never gave it a second thought. Bird and Kenny are both great guys, but they just never got along with each other. Such is life."

TRES JOLIE Dance Club has planned an exciting agenda for 9 p.m. Saturday at Northwood. Mal Fitch will present music for dancing, and Kenny and the Casuals will provide entertainment. Giant balloons in pinks and oranges will add to the color of the evening planned by Mr. and Mrs. William Gribble. Mr. and Mrs. William D. White Jr. are president couple of the club.

They misspelled "Kasuals". Seems like the newspapers just couldn't accept the "K". Maybe it was due to some early form of "spell-check."

It was about the time of Paul's joining the band that we decided to get some really different stage outfits. Mark Lee suggested it actually, and we went along with it. But we really weren't sure about the odd choices Mark would make about our wardrobe. He took us to an upscale local menswear shop called Irby Mayes and bought us the clothes. First of all we began wearing white pants, not a common sight on guys in the mid-sixties. Then the other four guys wore white turtleneck sweaters, with dark black, button-front sweaters over that. To top it off, we wore black and white saddle oxford shoes. In contrast I wore a black turtleneck and a white sweater over. If our faces hadn't been teenage pink, we would have looked like we stepped out of an old black-and-white movie. As I said, we were not at all convinced that the look was right, but it was similar to the stage outfits that The Dave Clark Five wore and so we agreed to wear the outfits at least for a while.

The clothes became our visual trademark, especially the two-tone saddle oxfords. Soon several other Dallas bands were wearing them too, including one from our school who called themselves The Madras Men, wearing multi-colored madras shirts and the two-tone black and white saddle oxfords. A weird clash of styles, but nevertheless a tribute to the Kasuals. At one time the Kinney Shoe Stores in Dallas had our black and white jobs in their store windows, advertised as "Kinney's Kasuals" an obvious and flattering nod to us.

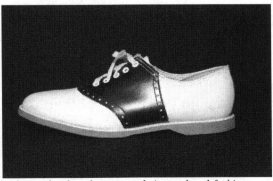

Yeah, this is the shoe that we made into a band fashion statement in Dallas in the mid-sixties.

Chapter Five
Dazed in Dallas

"Anything worth doing is worth overdoing."
Mick Jagger

Perhaps this would be a good time to talk about Bryan Adams High School and the other bands which were from there. Starting in the early sixties, BA became a hotbed of musical talent. Perhaps this is because it was the largest high school in the city, (second largest in the state of Texas), and therefore had more students to draw from. Perhaps it's because the school was just weird, and weirdness promotes creativity. But in those pre-Illusions Combo days there were three Bryan Adams bands that kicked butt.

The earliest band was The Corals, under the direction of lead guitarist Denny Freeman (still an internationally known guitar hero.) The second hot band in school was The Diminshuns (yes that's spelled right) led by guitarist Jimmy Herbert. Tim Cooper and the Dynamics were the third most popular band at the school. This was in the day before there were ten bands at every junior high, and having three really talented combos in one high school was unusual. These high school bands (and most others in Dallas – Fort Worth) were heavily blues and R&B influenced, though straight up rock and roll was always a feature of their sets.

These three BA bands played at all the standard venues, gas station openings and backyard parties, and also were regulars at a White Rock and Casa

Linda area legendary weekly dance known as "Teen Timers".

As Mary Elizabeth Goldman writes in her book "To Love and Die In Dallas":

The Diminshuns circa 1961

"....Teen Timers. Home of the original dirty dancing, the birthplace of the Casa Linda Low Life, Teen Timers was so full of smoke, noise, and packed bodies, that we could barely see, hear, or breathe. Amateur bands imitating Jerry Lee Lewis, Jimmy Reed, and Buddy Holly played nonstop for the dancers and listeners alike. It was a blissful sanctuary where rumors not only circulated wildly, but originated right there in the girl's room. In short, Teen Timers was a dimly lit haven with parental blessing."

Teen Timers – the name makes it sound like a harmless Andy Hardy kind of an affair, and that may be why as Goldman writes, it had "parental blessing." The fact is that it was a place where local teens from both sides of White Rock Lake would go to get drunk, stoned, laid or in a fight all to the tune of *Wine Wine Wine*. The one rent-a-cop (yes he was also called "Officer Friendly") could not control the hundreds of hormonally raging teens who packed the inside and spilled out into the alleyway behind the Casa Linda Plaza location. In fact he rarely attempted to keep complete order, and would only intervene to break up the most violent of fights.

Many of these fights originated when rivals from the two area high schools – BA and Woodrow Wilson – would square off. Other times battles would ensue when the younger members of a notorious Dallas... uh ... "youth social club" – The Lakewood Rats – would mix in with the high schoolers. The Rats had been around since the post war years, and like any other gang, new members joined and others graduated each year. The Lakewood Rats were well-known for winning most of the fights they started due to the fact that the members all carried canes. These were just regular walking sticks until the fracas broke out and then the heavy wooden canes became almost lethal weapons. The Rats were not to be trifled with.

Everyone at Teen Timers smoked cigarettes including me – even if you were a non-smoker – and you could barely see across the room for the smoke which hung like a curtain from the ceiling to the floor. The most popular song at Teen Timers was The Nightcaps' *Wine Wine Wine*, maybe the best dance song ever, from anywhere. Every band played it at every teen dance in Dallas in the early 60's.

The Nightcaps were the most regular band at

Teen Timers and were there any Friday night that they had no better paying gig. Billy Joe Shine, leader and lead singer of the band remembered the night when legendary bluesman Jimmy Reed played at Teen Timers with the Nightcaps as opening act. On this night the regular 25 cent admission price
went up – maybe as high as 75 cents. Billy Joe recalled having to sit beside a heavily drinking Reed and whisper the lyrics of the bluesman's own songs to him. Billy Joe would know those lyrics, that's for sure. In Dallas in the late 50s through the late 60s if a band did not play Jimmy Reed songs, that band did not play.

When The Nightcaps took the stage and broke into their local hits, the dance floor was packed. After *Wine, Wine Wine*, their second most popular song was *Thunderbird*, another tribute to the fruit of the vine.

"Get high everybody get high
Get high everybody get high
Have you heard, what's the word?
It's Thunderbird!"

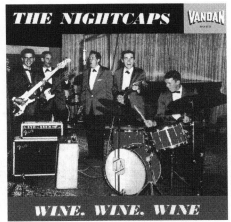

This album inspired a generation of Texas rockers

Denny Freeman and The Corals, a few years younger than The Nightcaps and still in school at BA, were one of the other most popular Teen Timers attractions, though the admission price to their shows was a quarter. If The Corals were there, I was there. Denny Freeman was my idol in those days.

At that time I would haunt any dance I could find, studying the guitarists and soaking in the rhythm and blues. Usually I had to go no further than the BA girls' gym. Jimmy Herbert had a hot BA band called The Diminshuns. They were the first combo from our school to make a record, and were semi-stars in the halls of BA in those days. In 1960, when I was still in Junior High and trying to learn which end of the guitar went in which hand, they cut a double sided instrumental – *Firewater* and *Slippery When Wet*. Jimmy wrote *Slippery When Wet* and James Anderson wrote *Firewater*. Jimmy was the lead guitarist on both songs. He later played with Johnny Gee and the G-Men and The Chessmen.

The other members of The Diminshuns were Mike Davis on drums, Vic Stewart on rhythm guitar and the bassist was James Anderson, all BA students. Mike Davis was a heck of a good drummer, a jazz enthusiast and a big fan of Dave Brubeck's group. Mike could play any style of music you could throw at him, and Brubeck's drummer Joe Morello was his ideal. James Anderson went on to a long career as a bassist with several groups like The Guys Five and The In Crowd as well as a long-time association with local guitar legend Bugs Henderson.

Denny Freeman was the leader and lead guitarist in The Corals, who were regulars at the local school dances, both junior and senior highs. I don't think they ever recorded, but they were the band that every White Rock area band wanted to be. Denny and Jimmy are both still red-hot pro guitar-slingers and well-respected world wide.

The third early sixties BA band to compete for time in the gym was Tim Cooper and the Dynamics, who broke up when Tim joined The Diminshuns. Tim is still in the music business in Dallas as a producer and engineer.

Top: The Diminshuns at the State Fair
Below: The Dynamics at the Fair the previous year.

"The Dynamics were formed back in the late '50's when I was fourteen years old," Tim Cooper recalls. "I was sitting on my porch playing guitar when Steve Cohen walked past. He came up and told me he played guitar too. So, we walked down to his house and discovered that we both owned the exact same style guitar – a $29 Sears Silvertone."

Steve and Tim became the mainstays of The Dynamics with Phil Cannon on sax and Chuck Cheshire on drums. They played all the local events including DreamAires at Harry Stone Rec Center.

Tim Cooper and the Dynamics, around 1963. That's Tim kneeling on the far right. Chuck Cheshire on drums, Phil Cannon on sax and Steve Cohen kneeling on the left

"We were playing at Harry Stone one night probably in early 1962, when Jimmy Herbert and James Anderson came up to me during a break," Tim continues. "Vic Stewart, the second guitarist in The Diminshuns was leaving the band and they offered me the job. Needless to say, I took it since The Diminshuns played more often and made more money. The Dynamics were pretty upset though and broke up right after."

Tim and I were in the same home room class for three years at BA, but for some reason never connected in bands. He was and is an excellent guitarist who went on to become a Grammy winning recording engineer.

The city of Dallas was hoppin' in the late 50s and early 60s. Great bands from Dallas and Fort Worth crossed back and forth along the thirty miles between the cities to fill clubs, gyms and social halls. Here's just a brief idea of the bands and performers rocking the area at the time (in alphabetical order)...

The Atmospheres – This was Jack Allday's band prior to The Nightcaps. They had a local record called *The Fickle Chicken*. Also in the band: Bill Kramer, Clarke Brown, Steve Voekel and Ben Hill.

The Big Beats – A traditional 50s-sytle rock band with plaid jackets and bow-ties, they rocked pretty darn hard. They are credited with being the first rock band to sign with Columbia Records.

Tommy Brown and the Tom Toms – This was one of the ace bands in Dallas in the late 50s, the house band at The Guthrey Club. After Tommy Brown left, they backed up Gene Summers and then split off to become Sam The Sham and the Pharaohs.

Gaylon Christie and the Downbeats – Country and rock performers, they cut a string of local records and were big in the area nightclubs.

The Continentals – They recorded songs like *Kangaroo Hop* on the local Vandan label. Led by Bobby Charles.

Bobby Crown and the Kapers - In 1959 they recorded *One Way Ticket* and were a very popular club band.

Ronnie Dawson – He started as a rocker in the fifties, moved to banjo bands and folk singing in the sixties and back to hot rocking when his career took off again in the 90s.

The Don Hosek Band – Formerly called The Jokers, they played dances and clubs. Jamie Bassett of The Chaparrals says that in the late '50's Hosek's band was one of the most popular in town.

Don Hudson and the Royal Kings – Filled clubs all over town.

Jesse Lopez – With two different groups in the late fifties – The Knights and the Misters – Trini's brother was a sax player and singer who played on the Nightcaps' classic *Wine Wine Wine*. The Misters were a popular group from North Dallas High School.

Trini Lopez – Became famous after leaving for the coast but was a popular entertainer in area in the late 50s.

The Martels – Longtime Dallas band, made many club and TV appearances.

Scotty McKay – His real name was Max Lipscomb and he began his career as a back-up singer and guitarist with Gene Vincent. Kenny and the Kasuals recorded Scotty's great song *Rollin' Dynamite* in the late '70s. All told Scotty probably recorded 50 or more singles in the '50s, '60s and '70s. Even he couldn't remember them all.

Buddy Miller and his Rockin' Ramblers – A rockabilly outfit that could flat tear down the house. They had a local hit with *Little Bo Pete*.

Vince Murphy & the Catalinas – Club and dance rocking combo from Oak Cliff. He recorded a great rocker called *Speechless* way back in 1956.

Vince Murphy and the Catalinas

The Nightcaps – With local super hits *Wine Wine Wine, 24 Hours* and *Thunderbird*, these guys were the hottest thing in town in the late '50s and early '60s. Billy Joe Shine was the vocalist, Mario Daboub was the leader and bassist, Jack Allday was on drums,

Gene Haufler on rhythm guitar and David Swartz played the lead guitar. They influenced every young player in town from Denny Freeman to Jimmie and Stevie Ray Vaughan.

Bobby Poe and the Poe Kats – A top local bar band and hot rockabillies. After leaving the area they became The Chartbusters and scored a hit with *She's The One.*

Gene Rambo and the Flames – From high school dances to recording studios around town, Gene and the Flames were serious rockers.

Bobby Rambo – With and without his brother Gene, Bobby Rambo was a great guitarist who was with several successful local bands through the sixties (The In Crowd, Jimmy Rabbit's band, even The Five Americans for a while.)

The Straightjackets (with Delbert McClinton) – This Fort Worth band played all over the area and backed up Bruce Channel on the national hit *Hey Baby.*

Kirby St. Romain – Hit in the early 60s with with *Summer's Coming.*

Gene Summers and the Rebels – The local hits kept coming for Gene from *Straight Skirts* through *Big Blue Diamond*s.

Ray Sharpe – Fort Worth blues rocker had a national hit with *Linda Lu* in 1959.

Jimmy Velvit — Local blues-crooner who immortalized the song *(You're Mine) We Belong Together* for a generation of North Texas kids.

Joe Wilson and the Sabres — Another well-known hot local club band.

And a host of high school bands — not one at every lunch table like the mid-sixties, but at least one at every high school.

Jimmy Velvit and Gene Summers were local stars.

LOCAL HERO:
Spotlight On Jimmy Reed
(1925-1976)

Jimmy Reed, although recording concurrently with the early rockers, had as much if not more influence on the rock and roll scene than the straight blues artists who preceded him. His easy-rocking tunes and lazy swamp-harmonica stylings put a little needed rhythm into slow dancing songs. Often unofficially accompanied by his wife "Mama", Jimmy's slurred vocals and sexy guitar stylings captivated young rockers primarily through the American South and Southwest. He had more and larger-selling blues hits in the fifties and sixties than probably any other artist.

As we've said, most southern club and dance bands had a whole series of Jimmy Reed songs in their repertoire, straight through the sixties. They had to. If they didn't play at least some of Jimmy's songs, they probably couldn't have found work. In Dallas, Jimmy Reed was the absolute boss of them all.

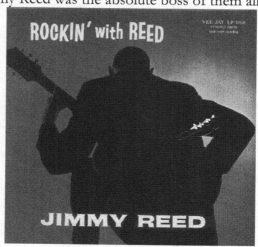

Here is a good sampling of the Big Boss Man's recordings from 1953 to 1964:

Ain't That Lovin' You Baby
Aw Shucks Hush Your Mouth
Baby What You Want Me To Do
Big Boss Man
Boogie In The Dark
Bright Lights Big City
Can't Stand To See You Go
Caress Me Baby
Down In Mississippi
Goin' To New York
High And Lonesome
Honest I Do
Hush Hush
I Don't Go For That
I'll Change My Style
I'm Gonna Get My Baby
I'm Nervous
Little Rain
Oh John
Shame Shame Shame
Take Out Some Insurance
Too Much
What's Wrong Baby
You Don't Have To Go
You Got Me Dizzy

(Jimmy Reed was not from Dallas, but was almost deified by the locals.)

Chapter Six
Looking Back

BEFORE THE GARAGE
The Bobbys - Born To Be Mild

Teen idols were not a 1950s creation. In the forties Frankie Sinatra had the bobby-soxers panting in the aisles. Rudy Vallee was the king of the teen flappers in the twenties and thirties. I'm sure that some caveman thousands of years ago had the teenage cavegirls in a twitter over the way he smacked two rocks together.

But the fifties and sixties took the concept of the teen pop idol to a new and unbelievably profitable level. The first of the artificially created pop stars appeared in the mid-late-fifties, on the heels of a new wave of cute-as-a-button singers who were making a fortune for someone. These late-fifties boys-next-door were the industry's response to the raucous, wild-eyed musical sex symbols of the mid-fifties.

By 1957 or so, the slick, pomaded pompadours and sexy, sneering leers of Elvis, Gene Vincent, Chuck Berry and others were being partially replaced by the nicer and more adult-acceptable styles, attitudes and gentle smiles of Frankie Avalon, Bobby Rydell and Jimmy Clanton.

Even Elvis began to be styled-down into a more acceptable nice boy product, and his record sales soared to ever higher levels. Gone were the sideburns, gold lame suits and surly smiles, replaced by a "gee, he's really a good boy" type of attitude, which was duly reflected in his post-army movies and music.

Although Elvis continued to be idolized by teenage girls, he never really slipped into the Teen Idol mold, popularized by "The Bobbys" of the late fifties through the mid-sixties. These popsters, not all named Bobby of course, were often talented young singers who slipped gratefully into the pop genre that gave them the best chance of recording success. A few, like Fabian, were pretty-boy creations of the system that fed the hunger of teenage girls for fantasy figures who were not as dangerous appearing as the wild ones of the rock

Fabian Forte would undoubtedly admit this himself – he was not a professional singer or musician, but was an incredibly good looking guy who could make the girls swoon just by standing on stage smiling. He was discovered not as a musical artist but as a "looker" – he was simply movie star pretty and possessed a sincere, nice-guy attitude. He was the perfect late-fifties musical teen idol except for one thing. The music. Fabian's vocal range was incredibly limited, though his voice was not nearly as bad as some would have you believe.

He could find and hold the right key if the song was not too vocally demanding. He could also move on stage, perhaps not with the uninhibited naturalness of Elvis, but in a simple, smooth manner that the girls liked. He seemed to be a really nice guy (which music historians usually agree was actually true in his case.) He was not perceived as a sexual threat by the moms and dads of the fifties, and was much more of a romantic figure than a sexual one to his legion of teenage female fans.

But, could he sing? Well, who cares? His songs like *Tiger* didn't demand much in the way of vocal chops, and he handled them as well as any guy off the street could have. One of his hits, *Turn Me Loose*, was actually a pretty good rock and roll song, though no one confused his voice with that of Elvis or Little Richard.

Ultimately his future success was in movies, not music, and once again he handled himself with humble grace there, too.

A simple, unpretentious acting style served him well for over a decade, appearing in several big budget Hollywood films from "North To Alaska" to "Mr. Hobbs Takes a Vacation" and into the surf and sand movies of the sixties. No one considered him for acting awards, but many studios considered him for the role of the "handsome young guy." And why not? He *was* handsome, he *was* young and he *was* a guy. He never claimed to be Elvis or Brando, he only claimed to be Fabian. And he made a good living at it.

Other bobbys appeared as actors in movies too. I can't tell you how relieved I was while watching "The Longest Day" when Fabian, Paul Anka and Tommy Sands all landed on the shores of Normandy to save the world for democracy. Bobbys to the rescue!

Many of the bobbys actually had musical talent to go with the good looks. Although few would be vocally compared to Caruso, they often had vocal talent at least equal to the Rudy Vallees of previous decades.

Frankie Avalon and Bobby Rydell, two of the most successful bobbys of the fifties, began as instrumentalists — playing the trumpet and drums respectively — and then moved into vocals as they discovered that a) they could sing, and b) the money was made at the front of the stage, not the back.

Frankie was more of a traditional crooner, even though at first he was forced into a whiny little-boy vocal delivery by his early producers. *De De Dinah* and *Gingerbread*, though both huge hits, didn't feature his real voice, but a more "accessible" imitation of an adenoidal teen from next door. His later hits featured a smoother, crooning style. It wasn't exactly rock and roll, but it really wasn't all that bad either. Like so many bobbys after him, his songs and his looks were more the culprits than his voice in landing him in the sappy syrup pool with the rest of the teen idols.

Bobby Rydell had more of a big-band, jazz-vocalist style than the run-of-the-mill bobbys of the era. His voice was big compared to the thin vocal stylings of other bobbys and he had a Copacabana nightclub style to his performances even in his earliest appearances. It could be easily argued that he had no place at all in rock and roll, but was a pure pop vocalist. A decade earlier and he might easily have slipped onto the charts alongside the male vocal stars of the era. Again, his music may not have been real rock, but it really wasn't bad. A series of sappy songs and finger-snappin' Vegas-style appearances on TV has permanently sealed him in the bobby-barrel of the fifties, but his continuous successful nightclub shows for the last four decades reveal him to be a pop music survivor.

Also a major-league bobby of the fifties, Jimmy Clanton was a model of pure bobbyness. He had a naturally nasal boy-next-door twang, and a bit of genuine rockabilly-r&b legitimacy to his roots. But his good looks and impossibly cool pompadour hair style directed that he should go straight to the bobby charts after scoring a good r&b New Orleans style legitimate rock ballad with *Just A Dream*. Some talent-svengali or other probably said "we can make a million bucks offa this kid" and set about doing just that. Paving the movie-road for Fabian, Frankie and Bobby Rydell, Jimmy made a couple of forgettable films, a few memorable songs and a place for himself on the bobby-list, whether he wanted to be there or not.

Some singers like Pat Boone and Neil Sedaka, who began their successful bobbyness in the fifties, continued strong into the sixties. In fact it could be argued that Pat Boone was the very first fifties bobby, and one who continues successfully today. Frankie Avalon, Bobby Rydell, Paul Anka and others also continued their ride into the early sixties.

Moving further into the sixties, a whole truckload of up and coming bobbys put whatever musical legitimacy they had on the line as they cashed in on the teen idol status that was offered them.

Bobby Vee may hold the record for the wimpiest hits, even though the bar is not all that high in the category of bobbysongs. Vee was actually a pretty good rocker in his earliest incarnation, prior to chart-topping success. As Robert Velline he possessed a good and interesting voice with just a tiny hint of the grit that could have earned him some rock hits, had he gone that way. But he was blessed (or cursed) with a cutie-pie teen idol face, and went the way of many pretty boys with pretty good voices. He became THE "bobby". The bobby from whom all former and future bobbys got their name. He became...Bobby Vee.

Bobby Vee's early sixties four-part salvo of sappy songs is the ultimate statement in Wimp Rock. Not that Robert Velline himself was a wimp. He may have been and continue to be a studly dude. But his alter ego, Bobby Vee, recorded the four wimp classics that define the genre.

First Vee whimpers *Take Good Care of My Baby* as some obviously cooler guy makes off with his woman. And he tells the girl that if she loves the guy, she should *Run to Him* which she does with some haste. Totally wimped out by the experience, he tearfully begs his friends *Please Don't Ask About Barbara*. And when the girl decides to give him another chance, he comes bouncy-bouncing back to her just like a *Rubber Ball*. Typical bobby behavior. You wouldn't find a rocker acting like that. A Chuck Berry or Gene Vincent probably would've punched his rival out and hauled the girlfriend off in his caddy. End of story.

But the bobbys were a different breed, at least in their song selection. True to the genre, Bobby Vinton, Bobby Sherman, Bobby Goldsboro, Dickie Lee, Johnny Crawford, Johnny Tillotson, Brian Hyland and others continued the individual cutie-pie teen idol era into the sixties. However, these solo stars began to feel heat from the trend in the mid-sixties toward musically complete bands.

The Monkees, The Cowsills, Gary Lewis and the Playboys, Herman's Hermits and Dino, Desi and Billy became some of the biggest of the wildly successful teenybop-groups of the sixties, as the bobbys started to run in packs.

The teen-pop, "bubblegum" musical train has never even slowed down much less been sidetracked. Through the remainder of the twentieth century, boy-bands such as New Kids On The Block, through Hanson, The Jonas Brothers and forward, continue to feed the frenzy and seemingly endless fantasy needs of teenage girls.

Bobbys never go away, they just change outfits.

Above: Frankie Avalon, Bobby Rydell
Below: Bobby Vee, Jimmy Clanton

1964 – Everything Just Changed

By the time we became the Kasuals, a lot had changed...for some it had changed for the better. For others it was a time of dreaded change. The Beatles records hit America in late 1963, but it was in February of 1964 that the fifties really ended, musically. The Beatles appeared live on the Ed Sullivan Show. As described in Chapter Two, everything went out the window and rock and roll was at a start-over.

Dallas rockabilly king Gene Summers had a huge local hit *Big Blue Diamonds* poised to go national at that time. "The Beatles came out at that exact time and the whole ball game changed," Summers remembered. "They were dominating the airplay and that just killed *Blue Diamonds* deader than a doornail."

In Dallas and every American city, local high school combos sprung up everywhere. In 1964 -1966 there were at least ten rock bands of various quality at Bryan Adams High School alone, not counting Kenny and the Kasuals. Count 'em: The Rafters, The Five of a Kind, Jimmy C. and the Chelsea Five, The X-Tremes, The Countdowns, The Demolitions, The Rain Kings, The Madras Men, The Embers, The Vibrations and probably a bunch more that I don't remember.

The British Are Coming

All of those bands above were inspired to pick up guitars and learn three chords and take to the risers in the BA girl's gym, by what they heard on KLIF and KBOX radio starting in January 1964, and tidal-wave rolling over Dallas by Spring of that year. A bunch of long-haired sissy-looking "blokes and chaps" from England, of all places. When we first saw pictures of The Beatles in a January 1964 issue of Life Magazine, we laughed. Two days later, we heard *I Want To Hold Your Hand* on the radio and we stopped laughing. This was special. This was semi-magical. This was indeed life-changing. In one instant we all wanted to be long-haired sissy-looking blokes and chaps. That is the moment that the sixties began for us, regardless of the date on the calendar.

The Five of a Kind live on the stage at Bryan Adams High School

But how did it begin in England? As crazy as it sounds, rock and roll in England began in America. The British beat industry started in the late fifties as a pop idol phase, inspired by Elvis, Bill Haley and Ricky Nelson. It took the cleanest and least-threatening elements of American rock and presented it to the supposedly mild-mannered British teens. It started so innocently yet by 1963 there were more angry young garage bands in England than there were garages. The British beat boom, as it's called, was a backlash movement, caused by the same type of suffocating pop stranglehold that the American powers-that-were had over stateside pop music in the early sixties. In Britain it was an underground movement going on simultaneously all across the empire. Young men grew tired of the pop pap on the airwaves, picked up guitars and began to bash out the same three chords that they had heard on a handful of true American rock and roll records that had entered the country.

The earliest British rock and roll records were from well-scrubbed, not-too-threatening young men who may have adapted Elvis' hairstyle but not his attitude. Tommy Steele set the stage for the type and set a trend for surnames like "Steele". Before long England was overrun with singers named Marty Wilde, Adam Faith, Johnny Gentle, Duffy Power, Rory Storm, Dickie Pride, Vince Eager, Georgie Fame and Billy Fury. John Lennon once referred to them as the guys with the "superman names."

George, John, Ringo and Paul – Apparently these guys were in a musical group from England…or somewhere.

By 1963 the pop idol era in England was overwhelmed by a surge of "beat bands" led of course by The Beatles. Although individual performers didn't simply disappear from the charts in the mid-sixties, it certainly – and suddenly – helped to be considered a part of a band. When The Beatles captured America in January of 1964, every American label sent scouts to try to beat the Brit bushes for beat groups. Many of these discoveries were already big in England, but some made a bigger splash in the states than they ever did in their homeland.

In The Beginning – Brit Pop and Brit Rock

Most early British rockers weren't necessarily rockers at all. They were teen idols, cut from the mold of the American "bobbys". (Bobby Vee, Bobby Vinton, Bobby Rydell, et al.) Soft white boys who, even with their Elvis-style pompadours and a bit of a sassy strut, still couldn't pass as rock and roll rebels.

A few genuine rockers emerged at the time, even a few of the super-surnames. Marty Wilde showed an occasional urge to rock, Adam Faith interspersed bobby-songs with rockers and Duffy Power had a good bluesy-rock voice and style. But most of the Brit teen idols spent most of their chart time being cute, cuddly and successful.

By the late fifties and into the sixties English television featured a few series dedicated to rock and roll. Programs such as "Oh Boy" and "The 6.5 Special" featured not only home grown hit makers but also a few American wild men such as Little Richard, Jerry Lee Lewis and Gene Vincent. This taste of real rock whet the appetites of English teens who wanted more.

A handful of British acts stepped up to appeal more to the rock side of the English youth. Singers Tony Sheridan (later to record with the very early Beatles) began to offer slightly more straight-up rock and roll to TV audiences. Instrumental groups such as The Shadows and Sounds Incorporated started to offer some fairly serious rock, though most of their output was still "happy-pop" just without words.

The Roots Scene

In London and in isolated areas of the Empire, an appreciation of rootsy blues, r&b and good ol' country music began to take hold in the fifties. "Trad" jazz, a New Orleans style of British dixieland became a major trend. And Lonnie Donegan headlined a true craze calle "Skiffle", a kind of combination of jug band, folk music and country blues styles. It was a down home music which any schoolboy believed he could master. All it appeared to require was a guitar, three chords, a couple of friends to pound on pans or washboards, and maybe someone plucking on a one-string washtub bass. The sound was raw, unpretentious and easy to master, though perhaps not to the professional level of Donegan and the other skiffle groups who followed.

Lonnie Donegan became a huge national celebrity scoring hits like *Rock Island Line* in 1956 and causing thousands of British boys to take up the guitar (not unlike the impact of Elvis in the States.) This guitar frenzy led to the creation of hundreds of skiffle outfits in every town, which in turn evolved into dozens of rockin' garage bands in the early sixties, all pounding out r&b, rockabilly and rock and roll.

In the larger cities, the guitar-based roots movement took a slightly harder turn, toward the urban blues of Chicago and the American south. In London, blues groups like Blues Incorporated (featuring Charlie Watts, Alexis Korner, Long John Baldry and Jack Bruce), John Mayall's Bluesbreakers, The Graham Bond Organization and Cyril Davies' All Stars, popped up playing the songs of Howlin' Wolf, Muddy Waters and Jimmy Reed. Future sixties superstars like Eric Clapton, Mick Jagger and Keith Richards salivated at the sounds of electric blues guitars, pounding drums and wailin' harmonicas.

By 1962, the musical styles had all crashed together, forming a weird hybrid of blues, rock, pop and hillbilly that was about to take America by storm.

Meanwhile, Back In The States

Although the radio playlists in the states were fairly sappy in 1962, there were still some great rock songs being recorded and purchased (like *Twist and Shout* by The Isley Brothers, *You Better Move On* by Arthur Alexander, and hits by Ray Charles, The Everlys, Sam Cooke, James Brown and Elvis). But the charts were being dominated by Neil Sedaka, Bobby Rydell, Connie Francis and other straight pop performers, causing a slight tremor of unrest among American teens.

This second wave of American rock and roll consumers were growing ever more tired of the slick mass-produced pop they were exposed to, longing instead for something harder, hotter and edgier than Frankie Avalon or The Four Seasons. By the end of 1963, this group of disenchanted teens was growing desperate and dreading the idea of listening to "rock radio" featuring Perry Como, Little Peggy March,

Sammy Davis Jr., Steve Lawrence, Eydie Gorme, Wayne Newton, Jack Jones, Andy Williams and The New Christy Minstrels – all of whom had big hits during the year.

Then, along came The British with a "brand new sound". This brand new sound was of course a pastiche of American rock, blues, r&b and rockabilly served up in a new and attractive package. Suddenly the English rockers became "the real thing" by reheating real rock and roll and feeding it to the starving masses in the States.

And we ate it up. The music and the refreshing "new" attitude. We had almost forgotten that rock and roll was supposed to be raw, unrehearsed and covered with acne. The spontaneous sounds that came flooding into the States were a powerful blend of cockiness, humor and a big beat presented with an unpretentious, take-it-or-leave-it attitude. Parents distrusted The Beatles, feared The Rolling Stones and didn't like their kids dancing to bands with dangerous names like The Zombies, Them, The Animals, The Kinks and The Yardbirds.

This breath of life flowed across the Atlantic and out of our stereos just in the nick of time. A mere two years later and The British Invasion was all but over, as the pop powers once again seized control of the asylum from the maniacs, and replaced them with nice young men in matching jackets.

But in those two years, American kids re-learned what it was like to discover a raw style of music that was theirs and theirs alone. Never again was there no alternative to pop-pap radio, as we always anticipated a newer wave of wildness just around the corner. Following The Invasion, the garage bands, the psychedelics, metal maniacs, punks, slackers and grungers were waiting for their turns to shock and shake the music industry.

Little Boy Blue and The Blue Boys

This is how the first version of The Rolling Stones was christened, though this band may have been the most ignored in all of southern England (see photo below). Mick and Keith (the mainstays of The Blue Boys) were later "discovered" by Brian Jones, who was a successful London blues band sideman (at least successful in Mick and Keith's eyes, as they were roaringly unsuccessful and practically starving.) Brian, who had been using the nom-de-stupido Elmo Lewis in gigs around London, formed a group with the two, calling it Brian Jones and the Rolling Stones. Brian was the founder and leader – as it was common in England for a band's leader not to be the lead singer.

They added Charlie Watts from Blues Incorporated and Bill Wyman of The Cliftons to the line-up and eventually became the hottest r&b outfit in London. Signed to a record deal, they specialized in remakes of obscure American rhythm and blues songs until Jagger and Richards realized they had songwriting talent. From that time on the great Stones' hits *(The Last Time, Satisfaction, Get Off My Cloud, Jumpin' Jack Flash* and so many more) were Jagger-Richards compositions.

After a few years Mick and Keith wrested the leadership from Brian, whose legendary excesses had drained him physically and emotionally.

The earliest known photo of The Rolling Stones, then called "Little Boy Blue and the Blue Boys"

Brit R&B and BritPop

From its earliest days the English rock scene has been divided into two main camps – r&b and pop. The popsters often played rock and roll, even tinged with a bit of blues, but the style and the approach was still very poppy. The r&b guys sometimes drifted into love ballads, but their style and approach was usually firmly based in the blues tradition.

The most successful band ever to emerge from England was of course The Beatles, arguably a great straight-up rock and roll ensemble who appreciated the rawer aspects of rootsy rock. But the reality of their recording history shows a more pop oriented musical taste. Show tunes, soft love ballads and covers of the softer hits of r&b demonstrate this. In their own songwriting it was rare to find them drifting toward hard-edged blues sounds. The Beatles rocked, of course, but in a modified pop style. In their recordings of the songs of America, they tended toward Chuck Berry, Little Richard and Arthur

Alexander, true rockers, but with a smoother pop approach than the straight-ahead bluesmen.

Other pop-oriented hitmakers from Britain included The Hollies, The Searchers, Billy J. Kramer and the Dakotas, The Seekers, Lulu, Petula Clark, Sandi Shaw, Gerry and the Pacemakers, Freddie and the Dreamers, Cilla Black, Wayne Fonta and the Mindbenders, The Swingin' Blue Jeans, The Hullablloos, The Honeycombs, The Tremeloes, and so many more. The Dave Clark Five was much more successful in the States than in England, putting seventeen pop-rock songs on the US top 40 in four years.

Meanwhile, a few British lads were eating rhythm and blues for breakfast, lunch and supper and these guys were the prototype for American garage bands. The Rolling Stones were the most successful Brit r&b outfit, a group that has stayed true to their hard-edged brand of rock for decades. Although heavily influenced by Chuck Berry, the more rootsy bluesmen were represented in their early records. By recognizing the contributions of Jimmy Reed, Howlin' Wolf, Muddy Waters and others, The Stones helped energize the blues revival movement in the States in the mid-to-late sixties.

Other successful blues-based Brit rockers of the era included Them, The Animals, The Yardbirds, The Spencer Davis Group, The Kinks, The Pretty Things, The Zombies and others.

Then there were the hardcase blues bands and the pure-pop ensembles of England. John Mayall's Bluesbreakers were the keepers of the flame in England as far as true-blue blues is concerned. They kept company with the afore-mentioned Alexis

Koerner's band Blues Incorporated, The Cyril Davies All Stars and The Graham Bond Organization. Graduates of these bands include Brian Jones, Mick Jagger, Keith Richards, Charlie Watts, Long John Baldry, Jack Bruce, Ginger Baker and many more top names of British beat. Much more well-known in England, these bands had more influence on our influences than they did directly on us.

The pure pop-stars in Britain included Herman's Hermits, Chad and Jeremy, Brian Poole and the Tremeloes, Cilla Black, The Bachelors, Peter and Gordon and many others, performers who had little if any impact on the hard rocking gymnasium bands in America.

Top: The Searchers
Lower: Gerry and the Pacemakers

Above: The Zombies and The Who
Below: The Nashville Teens and Wayne Fontana & The
Mindbenders

The Beatles

Probably about a hundred billion words have been written about The Beatles, so there is very little left to say. The Beatles not only changed music in 1964, but changed the lifestyle, attitudes and lives of an entire generation. They had a massive and lasting impact not just on fashion and hairstyles, but the world's culture itself — politics, religion, the peace movement, television, movies, drugs, sex and rock and roll.

Musically they had more influence upon the last half of the 20th Century than any other act with the possible exception of Elvis Presley. They sold more records than anyone during their years together. They placed an astounding 29 songs on the American music charts in one year alone (1964).

Chuck Berry — one of the major influences on British rockers.

"If you tried to give rock and roll another name,
you might call it Chuck Berry."
John Lennon

John and Paul became the most successful songwriting team in the history of music. The list of superlatives, achievements and awards could go on, but since you've heard all about these things so many times, I will just skip to the one area that has not been as widely covered or understood. The songwriting of John and Paul.

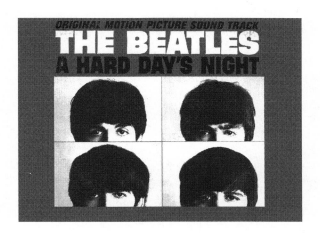

Lennon And/Or McCartney

When fans complimented him on the song *Yesterday*, John Lennon would usually smile politely and say "That was one of Paul's". It seems that there were and are major misconceptions about the writing of Beatles hits. John was often assumed to have written the moody pieces, like *Yesterday*, while Paul was often thought to have written all the nostalgic love songs like *In My Life*. In these two cases, the exact opposite is true. John wrote *In My Life* and Paul wrote *Yesterday*.

"It was Elvis who got me hooked on beat music. I heard
'Heartbreak Hotel' and I thought – this is it."
Paul McCartney

Sir Paul McCartney (back when he was just Paulie, the Liverpool scruff) began seriously writing songs with John Lennon in the early sixties. When they signed their first publishing agreement, the two were still writing together even though one or the other usually had the concept for a song before they began collaborating. So, the two decided to become one, at least for the purposes of songwriting credits and royalties payments. Every Beatle era song written by either of them (or as a team) was credited to both songwriters. The term "Lennon/McCartney" seen in parentheses under so many Beatle song titles really should have read "Lennon And/Or McCartney".

This may have been confusing to Beatle fans, but it was a pretty effective way of establishing the songwriting team in the public's minds, and an easy way to keep track of royalties. As it turns out, the final tally of who wrote what on the hit singles and the album cuts, came out fairly even, so neither songwriter got totally shafted financially.

Even today, this combined credit method continues to cause confusion about who really wrote what. A good rule of thumb is to simply listen to the recorded song. If Paul sings it, he probably wrote all or most of the song. And if John is the vocalist, it's equally likely that he was the primary composer. This rule of thumb applies mainly to songs from 1964 on, when they began working more on songwriting apart from each other. As with all good rules of thumb, it is not 100% effective, but will usually suffice.

When listening to Beatle originals, remember that it simply wasn't true that John was the moody lyricist and Paul was the happy-go-lucky tunesmith. If Paul wrote a song, he wrote it all, lyrics and music, and the same is true for John Lennon. And it's not true that John wrote all the introspective or "serious" songs, and Paul wrote the "silly love songs." Both wrote some of each.

But it is true that there is a usually a discernible difference between the styles, subject matter and attitudes of the two songwriters. The songs each wrote usually reflected his personality and general attitudes toward life.

Even in John Lennon's love songs, there is almost always a touch of anger, frustration or a sense that the relationship is probably doomed going in. Paul's love songs – whether sad laments or "I-love-my-woman" rockers – all seem to have a more positive outlook. Even when he is crying over a lost love, Paul seems to feel that somehow, someday, all will be right again.

In *You Can't Do That*, John jealously tells his girlfriend to quit talking to other guys, or else. He seems to look for the black cloud in front of the silver lining. But *And I Love Her* (a Paul song) is unabashed positive thinking all the way. And when Paul sings "It's getting better all the time", John adds "it can't get much worse." Optimism vs. pessimism.

I Should've Known Better seems like a happy love song, but still the singer/songwriter (John, of course) feels like he's been trapped into falling in love with the girl. Paul's rocking love song, *She's A Woman*, sings the praises of love and the one he loves, with no regrets or worries about the future.

John in his bitter, angry and pessimistic style seems to assume that he is heading for an emotional train wreck. Paul, in his satisfied, happy and optimistic style usually assumes he's heading for blue skies and butterflies, even in introspective songs like *Fool On The Hill*.

But in perhaps the greatest Beatles love song, *Something*, neither Paul nor John has anything positive, negative, optimistic or pessimistic to say. That's because the song was written by George Harrison.

"The Quiet Beatle" – George Harrison

"The Beatles will exist without us."
George Harrison

THE LIVERPOOL SOUND

"The Liverpool Sound" itself has been described in detail above. A weird hybrid of American country music, pop, rock, R&B and rockabilly stirred in with the Skiffle sounds that had taken England by storm.

What set Liverpool (and the towns right around it) apart from other places in England was the unwhetable thirst for fun, uninhibited, rugged dance music among the locals.

Far away (it seemed) from London, and the heart of British entertainment, Liverpool just created its own entertainment, and once the kids got wind of of it, they couldn't get enough.

If you think the list in this book of all the bands in Dallas in the era - coming up in a few pages - includes a lot of names, you ain't seen nothin' yet. Below is a list of just *some* of the bands playing regularly in the area. It seemed every bar, coffee house, restaurant, meeting hall, church basement and open lot had a band and a dance. This many venues were needed to keep the incredible number of bands even working part time.

The top bands in the city were (from 1962 on) The Beatles, Gerry and the Pacemakers, The Big Three, Rory Storm and the Hurricanes, The Foremost, The Undertakers and The Merseybeats. Some made the big time in the states, and some remain unknown here.

Two of the "second tier" bands actually made a bigger splash in America – The Searchers along with Billy J. Kramer and the Dakotas. It came down to management, promotion and that all-important first record. Dozens of Liverpool bands recorded in that first mad rush to try to find another Beatle-sized success, few made any impact on even local charts, much less nationally or internationally.

Tommy Quickly appeared on national American TV, to a resounding yawn from the audience. The Swingin' Blue jeans had a mid-size hit with *Hippy Hippy Shake*. Ian and The Zodiacs had a minor hit or two in various regions of the U.S.

But only The Beatles, Gerry and the Pacemakers, The Searchers and Billy J. Kramer had any lasting impact among the Liverpool lads competing for American's attention.

BANDS FROM THE LIVERPOOL AREA
1962 - 1966

The Alphas
The Apaches
The Argonauts
The Asteroids
The Barons
The Beatcombers
The Beatles
The Blackjacks
The Blue Beats
The Breakdowns
Cass and the Casanovas
The Casuals
The Centremen
The Chants

The Chessmen
The Citroens
The Chevrons
The Colts

The very early Beatles with Tommy Moore on drums

The Big Three

The Big Three
The Corals
The Corvettes
The Cuban Heels
Lee Curtis and the All Stars
The Daleks
The Decibels
Mike Dee and the Detours
The Dee Jays
The Demons
The Dennisons
Derry and the Seniors
The Lee Eddie Five
The Elektrons
The Escorts
The Everests

Faron's Flamingos

Faron's Flamingos

The Ferrymen
The Fireflies
The Five Aces
The Five Stars
The Flames
The Fourmost

The Foremost

The Gamblers
Gerry and the Pacemakers
The Good Times
The Gunrunners
The Hawks
The Hustlers
The Hy-Tones
Ian and the Zodiacs

Ian and the Zodiacs

The Incas
The Inmates
The Interns
The Invaders
JJ and the HiLites
The Jaguars
The James Boys
The Jaywalkers
The Jensons
The Jet Blacks
The Jokers
The K-Ds
Sonny Kaye and the Reds
The Kegmen
The Kilroys
The Kingpins

The Kinsleys
The Kinsmen
The Knights
The Kobras
The Kordas
Billy J. Kramer and The Dakotas
The Krestas
The Krinks
The Kubas
The Lancastrians
The Lavells
The Leesiders
The Legends
The Liverbirds

The Liverbirds

The Liverpool Express
The Locations
The Martinis
The Masqueraders
The Masterminds
The Mastersounds
The Matadors

The Medallions
The Merseybeats

The Merseybeats

The Mersey Five
The Mersey Four
The Mersey Monsters
The Metronomes
The Minits
The Mojos
The Moonstones
The Mops
The Motifs
The Mustangs
The Nightwalkers
The Nocturnes
The Notions
The Nomads
The Nutrockers
The Odd Spots
The Onlookers
The Outkasts
The Oxfords
The Paladins

117

Pharoah and the Exiles
Mark Peters and the Sillouettes
The Pilgrims
The Poets
Earl Preston and the Realms

Earl Preston and the Realms

The Pontiacs
The Questions
Tommy Quickly and the Remo Four
The Raiders
The Rapides
The Rebel Rousers
The Rats
The Rebels
The Remo Four
The Renegades
Rhythm and Blues, Inc.
Rick and the Delmonts
The Riot Squad
The Roadrunners

Cliff Roberts and The Rockers
Robin and the Ravens
The Rondels
The Ron Tons
The Runaways
The Sabres
The Saints
The Santones
The Scaffold
The Scorpions
The Searchers
The Secrets
The Sensations
The Sinclairs
The Shades
Sounds Plus One
The Soundtracks
The Spekeasys
Freddie Starr and the Starr Boys
The Lee Stewart Quartet
Rory Storrm and the Hurricanes The Strangers
The Star Combo
The Stormers The Strollers
The Subterranes
The Sundowners
The Sunsets
The Swingin' Blue Jeans
Kingsize Taylor and the Dominoes

*Rory Storm and the Hurricanes
(a young Ringo Starr on the right)*

The Swingin' Blue Jeans

Kingsize Taylor and the Dominoes

The Thunderbirds
Tommy and the Satellites
Tony and the Quandros
The Travelers
The Tributes
The Tridents
The Triffids
The Tudors
The Undertakers

The Undertakers

The VanDunes
The Verbs
The Vigilantes

The Vigilantes

Vince and the Volcanoes
The Vulcans
The Wanderers
The Whipcords
Vance Williams and the Rhythm Four
The Zeniths
The Zephyrs

AND MANY, MANY MORE!

Chapter Seven
Dallas Surrenders Unconditionally

The music came back to us from England, where we had sent it. And now, if anything, it was even better. And within a few months, across the Dallas-Fort Worth metro area there were well over a hundred teen bands all scrambling for the same small stage. We would play anytime, anywhere for as long as you'd let us, for free. And for the groups getting paying jobs, the list of local bands is staggering in its length. Here are a few of the working Dallas area combos that I remember from 1963 -1966:

The Accents, The American Blues (with Dusty Hill), The Bards, The Barons (with John Nitzinger), The Bear Fax, The Beefeaters, The Benders, The Big Sounds, The Boards, The Boys, The Briks, The Brimstones, The British Colonels, The Buccaneers, The By Fives, The Caretakers, The Cast of Thousands (with Stevie Ray Vaughan), The Cavemen, The Changing Times, The Chaps, The Chaparrals, The Chaunteys, The Chessmen (with Jimmie Vaughan and Doyle Bramhall), The Chevelle 5, CharlesChristy and the Crystals, The Chosen Few, The Cicadelics, The Coachmen, The Com'n Generation, The Counts, The Court Jesters, The Crowd + 1, The Cult, The Cynics, The Demolitions, The Derbys, The Embers, The Esquires, The Excels, The Exotics, The Felicity (with Don Henley), The Five Americans, The Five of a Kind, The Floyd Dakil Five, The Four Dimensions, The Four Speeds (who became Felicity), The G's, The Galaxies, The Gentlemen, The Gnats, The Images, Johnny Green

and the Green Men, The Gretta Spoone Band, The Guys Five, The In Crowd, The Intruders, The Jackals, The Jades, The Jinx, Just Us Five, The Karats (with Jimmy Rabbit), Kempy and the Guardians, Kit and the Outlaws, Knights Bridge, TheKnights, The Kommotions, Lady Wilde and The Warlocks
(with Frank Beard), Larry and the Bluenotes, The Livin' End, The Lynx, The Madras Men, The Malibus, The Marksmen (with Steve Miller and Boz Scaggs), The Scotty McKay Band, The Menerals, The Mods, Mouse and the Traps, The Mystics, The Noblemen, Nobody's Children, The Nomads, The Novas, The Offbeats, The Orphans, The Other Half, The Outcasts (with Marc Benno), The Pagans, The Pendulums, The Penthouse 5, The Pitmen, The Plague, The Playboys Five, The Rafters, The Rain Kings, The Reasons Why, The Redcoats, Reekus the Rat and the Rubber Ducks, The Reverbs, The Revolvers, The Roamers, The Rogues, The Roks, The Rondels (with Delbert McClinton), The Roots, The Sensations, The Sensors (with Bugs Henderson), The Shadows, The Sirs, Sounds Incorporated, The Squires, The Styks and Stones, The Sticks, Theze Few (with "England Dan" Seals, and John Ford Coley), Those Guys, The Tracers (aka The Trycers), The Upper Class, The US Britons, The Visions and The Wilshire Express.

Rollie Anderson (who I was later to be with in "The Next Band From Texas") remembers the specific gigs that his band – The Com'n Generation – played in 1965 and 1966:

September 19 - Wheelchair Bowler's Association
        meeting, Bronco Bowl
    October 17 – Wheelchair Bowler's Association
        meeting, Bronco Bowl

October 24 – Church social, Gail Watkin's house
December 31 – New Year's Eve Party,
    Glen Fowler's house
March 1 – Audition for DeSoto High School
    talent show
March 4 – DeSoto talent show,
    DeSoto Elementary
April 9 –   Hobby Shop, DeSoto
May 20 –   Private Party, DeSoto
June 3 –   Private Party, DeSoto
June 25 –   Private Party, DeSoto
July 8 –   JayCee dance, DeSoto
July 15 –   Lion's Club Carnival, DeSoto
August 13 – Rollie's sister Marlene's Park Party,
    Anderson house
November 4 – South Oak Cliff High School
    Spanish Club, Cedar Canyon Club
November 5 – Battle of the Bands, Gibson's
    Department Store, Oak Cliff
December 2 – Wynnewood Movie Theatre lobby

*Rollie Anderson's first band The Com'n Generation in the high
school gym. Notice the bassist on the right (Glenn Fowler) is sporting
a pair of the two tone saddle oxfords we made famous in Dallas.
(That's Rollie on the far left wearing the high-water
pants and white socks.)*

125

<u>Rollie remembers how it all happened for him:</u>

"Once I witnessed the phenomenon that was The Beatles when they performed on The Ed Sullivan Show in February of 1964 I became an 'altered' boy. Until then I had harbored dreams of becoming popular and making a name for myself as a star athlete or at least as an admired member of the prestigious school cheerleading squad. In the case of the former I was too much of a runt and nowhere near being dedicated enough to bulk up by working out. As for the latter I was just not equipped with the necessary charisma or stunning good looks to qualify. But there, on TV in gorgeous black and white, was my salvation. The answer to my prayers. My ticket to fulfillment. The purpose for my being born. It became crystal clear to me that I was conceived in order to be a famous bass guitarist just like Paul McCartney!

"The fact that I couldn't put together two notes of music on a guitar that made any sense didn't present a problem in my mind. I was able to pick out a few chords on the upright piano but nothing that actually sounded like a song. Nonetheless, I soon found out that other teenage boys like the friends I hung out with at Kiestwood Baptist Church had also been instantly afflicted with the same 'Mersey Beat' fever that I had contracted. We realized that we had the necessary four members for a combo and, in quick order, assigned each other the various positions in the band that we were going to occupy.

"It went on like this for months as I tried to make the B Honor roll (this was the stipulation for getting a bass and amplifier from my folks.) Meanwhile, our imaginary combo had yet to come up with the most important ingredient for success. We had to have a cool name. Our moniker was probably more vital than having instruments or talent. "Rollie and the Roundmen", "The Roundabouts", "The Rondells", "The Landells", "The Shastas", "The Shastells", "The Shondells" and "The Hubbubs" were the impressive front-runners early on.

"To my parents shock, I made the B-Honor roll and asked politely for my bass. Following a hasty huddle held in private, they solemnly informed me that, due to unforeseen financial difficulties, they wouldn't be immediately able to buy the bass guitar and amp as promised. However, they could scrape together enough loose change to afford a nice Silvertone electric guitar from Sears & Roebuck. At first I was highly indignant and outraged. But once I calmed myself down I had to admit that a standard electric guitar and amplifier was better than nothing and I shouldn't look a gift horse in the mouth.

"On June 21, 1965 I got my first electric guitar, a double pickup black and white Silvertone solid body model that cost $54.95 plus tax. A few days later my Dad took me downtown to The Melody Shop and bought me a low-powered Kent amplifier. Words cannot describe the feeling of accomplishment and excitement that washed over me. I was now equipped to take on the rock and roll universe. All I had to do was learn how to play the dern thing."

"I never studied anything, really. I didn't study the drums. I joined bands and made all the mistakes onstage"
Ringo Starr

Back to Kenny...

While Rollie and his yet unnamed band were starting to learn their instruments, all of those other bands listed above and a bunch more were all scrambling for the same gigs in town at the time. We were all playing dances, and parties and the same kind of oddball gigs like when Rollie's band played at that hobby shop in DeSoto. It was the same for us when we first started. Anywhere. Anytime. For two bucks and a bag of chips.

So, although the heightened interest in the "new breed" rock meant that there were more dances and music venues than ever, the sheer number of bands outweighed any increase in opportunities. It actually makes me proud that we were constantly booked, with so much competition in the area. And many of the bands in the above list were good...really good. Some others were just working for chips and soda like we had been only a year before.

The very style of the new sound made it easy for a group of guys with almost no real musical experience to form a band and play somewhere, every now and then. Two guitars, three chords and a drum set would get you in the door. Beginning players could learn ten to twenty songs in a couple of weeks and be playing at someone's pool party within a month. In fact after you learned those three chords, the hardest part was memorizing the lyrics.

The songs had gone back to the roots. British groups like The Beatles, The Animals, and especially The Rolling Stones help us rediscover American rock-and-rhythm. Here (in alphabetical order) is a typical playlist from a high school combo in Dallas in 1964 with a description of the artists that brought the song to our attention...

The Essential Playlist

Ain't Got You – The Yardbirds
The Yardbirds tried hard to be a blues band, but never quite made it. Instead they were recognized for their great garage rock and early psychedelic contributions. This grungy great was solidly in most teen bands repertoire.

Baby Please Don't Go – Them
Originally a John Lee Hooker song, this version was the a-side of the greatest b-side of the sixties, *Gloria*. This was the big hit of the record, though *Gloria* had the eternal staying power. Both sides benefited from Van Morrison's ultimate garage vocal and Jimmy Page's uncredited guitar solos.

Beautiful Delilah – The Kinks (from Chuck Berry)
An album cut for The Kinks, from a Chuck Berry rocker. The tempo was frenzied and the slurred, nasally vocal was ideal for the garage set. The Kinks also placed hits and another album cut – *So Mystifying* – on many garage playlists.

Doo Wah Diddy – Manfred Mann

Although they were primarily a bluesy-jazzy-pop band from England, one of their songs (this one) was on almost every garage playlist. From 1964.

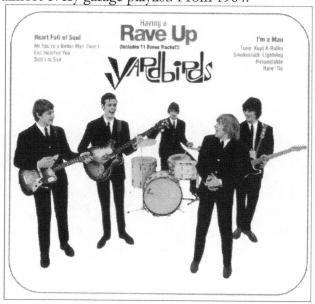

Get Off My Cloud – The Rolling Stones
One of the many Rolling Stone songs that filled the playlists of the raving amateurs, this song was a pure "bad attitude" song.

Gloria – Them
Along with *Louie Louie*, this was the essential garage band song. If you couldn't play it, you couldn't find work. In other parts of the country the song was a hit by The Shadows of Knight, but in Texas and the Southwest, this was the ONLY version.

Above: Manfred Mann
Below: THEM – featuring Van Morrison

I Can't Explain – The Who
Sheer modness from The Who, one of the few mod-rocker bands of England who were embraced by the garage guys.

I'm A Man – The Yardbirds
Although Muddy Waters and Bo Diddley each did an earlier version of this song, it was The Yardbirds who firmly placed it on the must-play list for garage bands. It helped if you had a harmonica player, but if you played it loud enough no one seemed to miss the harp.

I'm Cryin' – The Animals
Eric Burdon's growling vocals and the sound of Alan Price's big fat Hammond B-3 organ helped make this English band one of the most-copied of sixties hitmakers.

I'm Movin' On – The Rolling Stones
Originally a country song by Hank Snow, rockers picked it up from a version by Ray Charles.

I'm Not Talkin' – The Yardbirds
This choppy super-fast song had a tricky guitar lead and was therefore only attempted by bands with a decent lead guitarist.

It's Alright – The Rolling Stones
A simple and very danceable song that could and often did get played for ten or fifteen minutes non-stop, it was a good "last set" song, when the dancers just did not want to stop even for a minute. (Also known as "I'm Alright")

Last Time – The Rolling Stones
1965. With a mean guitar riff that wouldn't quit and a solid dance beat, this song filled many a gym floor with dancers.

The Animals

Louie Louie – The Kingsmen
This is the unquestioned anthem of garage rock.
Originally written and recorded by Richard Berry, it
became a staple of Northwest garage and frat bands
in the early sixties. The Kingsmen recorded it in one
take in one room with one microphone – the ideal
conditions for a garage classic. Over two thousand
covers and remakes later, it still makes people dance.
A hit twice – in 1963 and again in 1965.

Mona –The Rolling Stones (from Bo Diddley)
Simple, mean-sounding and danceable, this was a song that a garage band would play whenever they couldn't remember what song they were supposed to play next.

Money –The Beatles (from Barrett Strong)
The Stones and other bands also recorded this classic. In the The Kingsmen's muffled grungy version of this Motown rocker was a line that became immortal in the pantheon of punk-sixties bands. "Stomp, shout and work it on out!"

The Nazz Are Blue – The Yardbirds
Here's an interesting song. Inspired no doubt by the slide guitar style of Elmore James, the title may have been inspired by a very different source. According to many, the term "Nazz" is jazz-lingo referring to Jesus (of Nazareth), and came from a bebop comedy record called The Nazz, by Lord Buckley. Then again maybe it was just a word somebody made up. Hard to know for sure. This song was an up-tempo blues rocker and became a staple of any garage band that had a lead guitarist capable of playing the Jeff Beck guitar breaks.

Route 66 – The Rolling Stones
The Stones didn't do the original version of this song, not even close in fact. Written by jazz songwriter Bobby Troup it was a hit in the fifties for Nat King Cole and recorded by dozens of performers. The Rolling Stones' rock version from 1964 was easy to

play and easy to dance to, the perfect combination for a high school combo to perform. The real trick in singing this song was to remember that list of cities from Chicago to Los Angeles. The line "don't forget Winona, Kingman, Barstow, San Bernadino" usually came out something like "don't forget manonna, big wheel, Moscow, San Bernadino." That was the way Mick sang it so it was good enough for us and close enough for a gymnasium dance.

Satisfaction – The Rolling Stones
Once Mick Jagger and Keith Richards realized they could write songs, they really wrote some songs. This one, an early anthem of sixties dissatisfaction, had an insistent fuzzy guitar riff and some angry lyrics about a guy who can't get everything that he wants instantly and is ticked off about it.

Nothing appeals more to a self-centered group of American teens than a song that demands every pleasure on a silver platter. Therefore this song became a moral anthem for a generation who only asked for instant gratification at no cost and with no repercussions. Rock on.

She's Not There – The Zombies
The breathy, desperate vocal pleadings in this song added a grunge feeling to the fairly jazzy arrangement.

Tired Of Waiting – The Kinks
Even though this medium-tempo tune wasn't easy to dance to (neither fast nor slow), it was a regular part of the song set. It gave dancers the chance to sit and catch a breath, or go outside and catch a smoke.

2120 South Michigan Avenue – The Rolling Stones
Every band had a break song, and most bands had this one. We certainly played it at every dance. It was an instrumental (as all good break songs should be) usually accompanied by me saying something like "we're gonna take a little break now, be back in about 15 minutes. Don't forget to tip the waitresses." The title of the song came from the address of Chess Records in Chicago.

The Train Kept A Rollin' – The Yardbirds
A much older song than this version, it was introduced into rock and roll through a wild and fuzzy rockabilly riot by the Rock and Roll Trio in the mid-fifties. By the mid-sixties it was a grungy, pre-pyschedelia blues-rock festival of noise and attitude. With the hardest-to-translate lyrics since *Louie Louie*, the song usually required two singers singing two different vocals at the same time to approximate the double-track double-talk of Keith Relf. A little too weird for the mid-sixties frat set, it was still an anthem to the high-schoolers of the era.

Twist and Shout – The Beatles (from The Isley Brothers) The original by the Isleys was a screaming gospel-style r&b classic. The Beatles 1964 version was much more garagatic in style and was immediately accepted by the locals. This song was often played in a medley with *Hang On Sloopy* and *La Bamba*. (And to hear anglo teens trying to imitate the vocals to La Bamba was quite an experience: "Balooda bada la bamba, pola seela maroon in the paco la gabba.")

The original by the Isleys was a screaming gospel-style r&b classic. The Beatles 1964 version was much more garagatic in style and was immediately accepted by the locals. This song was often played in a medley with *Hang On Sloopy* and *La Bamba*. (And to hear anglo teens trying to imitate the vocals to La Bamba was quite an experience: "Balooda bada la bamba, pola seela maroon in the paco la gabba.")

Walkin' The Dog – The Rolling Stones (from Rufus Thomas) Another easily performed song, and one that propelled dancers onto the floor. "The Dog" was a dance that began innocently enough but eventually became a bump and grind exercise in hormones-gone-wild.

We Gotta Get Out Of This Place – The Animals
1965. Even middle-class kids who would never again be in a better place than they were, embraced this song as a generalized goal for life. We got out of that place, and eventually we wanted back in.

You Make Me Feel So Good – The Zombies
This was the b-side to The Zombies big hit *She's Not There*. Even though most garage bands including The Kasuals specialized in up-tempo ravers, this was a feel-good slow-dance song. In 1965 at a dance in the gym, we would get countless requests for this one.
(While we were playing at the BA Class of 1966 40-Year reunion in 2006, co-author Richard Parker requested it and he and his wife danced like it was 1966.)

You Really Got Me – The Kinks
Sorta like *Louie Louie* played inside-out, this was a
screaming power-chord pounder from Ray Davies
and the guys.

Did you notice something about the above list?
Every song except one was introduced to American
Garage bands by British groups, though many of the
songs were originally American R&B recordings. The
sole U.S. exception is *Louie Louie*, which was a must-
play song at every club or dance.

LOUIE GOES GOLD

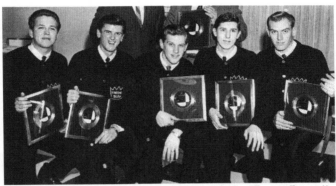

The Kingsmen accepting their gold records for "Louie Louie".
Only two guys in this photo were actually playing on the record
— Mike Mitchell, second from the left and
Lynn Easton, in the middle.

The actual lead singer, Jack Ely was forced out of the group by
the time the record sold a million copies.

OK now, here's something else you must know about garage bands...the songs we would never, ever play.

The Anti-Playlist of the Garage Bands

Although garage bands played mostly covers of hit songs and great album cuts from the stars of the genre, few of them could be described as "cover" bands. A cover band played the hits of the day, including songs that a true garage-frat combo wouldn't touch with an insulated lightning rod. The garage playlist above is composed of raw r&b rockers, variations on *Louie Louie* and a few originals that had been "blessed" by the international garage kings like The Rolling Stones or The Animals.

The songs below were all big, big hits in the garage era (1963-1966), although not on any garage band playlist. Even attempting one of these songs would have caused a band to be impolitely escorted to the back exit of the frat house or VFW Hall in short order. These songs were reserved for the happy smilers who populated the cover bands, playing for packed houses at weddings, hotel lounges and cocktail parties. If you were in a garage band and played any of these songs, well no wonder you remained undiscovered and unsuccessful.

Title	Year	
Ballad of the Green Berets	1966	Barry Sadler
Blame It On The Bossa Nova	1963	Eydie Gorme
Call Me	1966	Chris Montez
Chapel of Love	1964	The Dixie Cups
Cherish	1966	The Association
The Days of Wine and Roses	1963	Andy Williams
Dominique	1963	Singing Nun
Downtown	1964	Petula Clark
Elusive Butterfly	1966	Bob Lind
Everybody Loves Somebody	1964	Dean Martin

The Girl From Ipanema	1964	Getz / Gilberto
Go Away Little Girl	1963	Steve Lawrence
Hello Dolly	1964	Louis Armstrong
Hush Hush Sweet Charlotte	1965	Patti Page
I Will Follow Him	1963	Little Peggy March
It's My Party	1963	Lesley Gore
King of the Road	1965	Roger Miller
Lady Godiva	1966	Peter and Gordon
Make The World Go Away	1965	Eddy Arnold
The Men In My Little Girl's Life	1965	Mike Douglas
My Boy Lollipop	1964	Millie Small
Shangri-La	1964	Vic Dana
Strangers In The Night	1966	Frank Sinatra
There I've Said It Again	1963	Bobby Vinton
Two Faces Have I	1963	Lou Christie
We'll Sing In The Sunshine	1964	Gale Garnett
You Were Made For Me	1965	Freddie and The Dreamers

The Singing Nun – definitely not a Garage Band.

The Biggest Local Threats To
Us Making a Buck

Let's take a brief look at the top Dallas area bands in 1964 -1966, other than Kenny and the Kasuals and The Chessmen (who are described later.)

In no particular order:

<u>The Novas</u>
If you didn't know better, you'd have thought they were The Byrds, The Hollies or one of the other vocal-based rock bands of the era. Their singing and harmony was top-notch and they had some of the best players around. The Novas filled dances and were on local TV (Ron Chapman's "Sump'n Else" program) more than any other band. Members: David Dennard, John Salih, Gary Madrigal and David Brown.

The Briks

Led by Richard Borgens, who graduated from Bryan Adams the same year I did, The Briks were blessed with a terrific rock voice in Cecil Cotton, who could sound almost exactly like Mick Jagger, Eric Burdon or Van Morrison, depending on the song. Richard was one of the most accomplished guitarists on the scene in those days. The other members were Mike Meroney, Lee Hardesty and Steve Martin. Later on Richard joined the Kasuals for our New York adventure.

The Briks, 1966

The Chaparrals

Jamie Bassett (yet another BA graduate) was bassist for this band who played mostly at clubs geared toward young adults (in other words – places where the booze flowed.) They were basically the house band at a rowdy club called The Pirate's Nook. The Chaparrals were also huge on the frat circuit, mostly at North Texas State up the highway in Denton. The band also featured Steve Karnavas, Chuck McKay, Wayne Rossee and Tommy Cashwell.

Kit and the Outlaws

Led by Kit Massingill, this north Dallas band released a cool version of *Midnight Hour* on the BlacKnight label. Other members were Joe Jesmer, Jerry Caldwell and Alan Rafkin.

Kit and the Outlaws

The Nightcaps

By the mid-sixties, The Nightcaps were still rockin' but were playing to an older crowd. By this time three originals (Billy Joe Shine, Jack Allday and Gene Haufler) were joined by Gary Mears, who as leader of a group called (ironically) The Casuals had a big national hit record called *So Tough* back in 1958.

Floyd Dakil and the Pitmen

A good old fashioned show band brought into the sixties rock era. The late Floyd Dakil was an extremely talented vocalist and was known locally as "the human jukebox". You simply could not stump him on a request. It was as if he knew every rock song ever written. The band was sometimes known just as The Floyd Dakil Combo, and was made up of players from Highland Park and Thomas Jefferson High

Schools. The group featured Ronny Randall, Geoff West, Terry Billings, Andy Michlin and later Dennis Mills and Chris Brown. "The Pitmen" got their name from being the house band at a local teen club called "The Pit". Their big local hit was *Dance Franny Dance*.

The Outcasts
Another top draw at the Studio Club, they were led by Marc Benno who went on to fame in L.A. This band morphed into The Blues Bag and then into the wacky show band The Bennie Darvon Revue. In this last incarnation, Benno was known as "The White Tornado" and was famous for his James Brown impression

The Cavemen
Hard rocking band from Oak Cliff, who were the house band at a west side teen club called "Surfer's A Go Go". The club did not feature surfers or much

go-go, but it *was* a hot spot for the type of down-home bluesy rock that flourished in Oak Cliff. (Also spelled "The Kavemen".)

The Warlocks
This group was headed up by Rocky Hill and his brother Dusty (later of ZZ Top). Rocky was an excellent guitarist and of course Dusty was the bassist and (as I remember it) the main vocalist. The Hill Brothers went to Woodrow Wilson high school, just across White Rock Lake from BA. Frank Beard (also of ZZ Top) was the drummer for the Warlocks.

The Jackals
Mike Neal, Billy Lawson, Ronny Sterling, Phil Campbell and John Talley. Garage rock and soul dance hits were the staples of this band. (Campbell and Sterling had previously been in The Pendulums with Jimmie Vaughan.)

The Excels
From McKinney, just outside of Dallas. Members: Danny Goode (bass), James Goode (rhythm guitar), Roger Bennett (lead guitar) and Gibson Harris on drums. Their record of *Let's Dance* and *Walkin' The Dog* is a very cool bit of garage grunge greatness.

The Excels

Theze Few

From Samuel High School just across the highway from BA territory, these guys were a very talented band whose vocals were softer and more melodic than most of the screaming punkers in the area. Members Dan Seals (England Dan) and John Colley (John Ford Coley) went on to a series of national hit records in the seventies like *I'd Really Love To See You Tonight* and *Nights Are Forever Without You*.

Theze Few evolved into Southwest FOB

The Marksmen

They went to St. Marks private school, hence the name "Marksmen". Both Steve Miller and Boz Scaggs were in this band, and how they kept from being the biggest thing in Dallas, I don't know. Another Marksmen alumni, Bob Haydon, had a local hit in 1965 called *Hey Suzanne*.

Mouse and the Traps

Ronnie "Mouse" Weiss had a voice that was very reminiscent of the mid-sixties Bob Dylan, and he played those similarities up. The band released several records, two of which – *A Public Execution* and *Sometimes You Just Can't Win* – became regional hits.

The band minus Mouse plus KLIF DJ Jimmy Rabbit hit locally with *Psychotic Reaction* as "Positively 13 O'Clock". North Texas guitar ace Bugs Henderson was in this band.

The Sensations
Featured Roe Cree on lead vocals and rhythm guitar, Mike Nelson on lead guitar and vocals, Mike Cooper on bass and vocals and Richard Schulzeon drums and vocals. In the 90's, Mike Nelson became a semi-regular with Kenny and the Kasuals.

The Briks

And..."The Com'n Generation"
Back to the story of Rollie Anderson and his first band. Rollie continues:

"I had seen various bands at school dances and sock hops like Seab Meador's The Gentlemen and Jimmie Vaughan's The Pendulums, but in that Summer of '65 I finally saw my first professional group. The Nightcaps of *Wine, Wine, Wine* fame played a concert inside the Lancaster-Kiest shopping center and all of my wide-eyed comrades and would-be band members took in the show. I knew from the first song that I wouldn't be satisfied until it was me performing up there on the stage.

"One of my school and church-mates - Gene Banks - also had a guitar and amp and his equipment was vastly superior to mine (a red Gibson guitar and a Fender amp). As a bonus, Banks could really play! He taught me more than any professional guitar teacher could have in half the time and for a price that couldn't be beat. Free. (All the guys I knew who paid for formal lessons were being taught useless old folk songs and campfire sing-along ditties so I never had the desire to go that route. I was only interested in learning the rock and roll tunes I heard on the radio.) I picked up loads of clues and pointers by watching Gene play and by observing guitarists like Ray Davies and Keith Richards on TV shows like 'Shindig' and 'Hullabaloo'.

The Mel Bay chord book I purchased at Watkins' music store became my bible and I learned how to make bar chords by studying the picture of David Crosby on the back of the first Byrds album.

"Banks' father had been a member of the Wheelchair Bowler's Association for some time and got us our first gig at their Convention to be held at The Bronco Bowl (home of The Pit Club). We only performed three songs in the small meeting room but the young girls who crowded their way into the doors and made a noisy fuss over us gave us boatloads of confidence. (In my mind, the whole thing was working as advertised: play music, meet girls.) Our drummer Gene Fowler had gotten a sparkling red trap set of drums and his cousin Glenn Fowler was on bass. Eventually Jim Dawson joined as our lead singer and we were a real band...sort of...with a real name...finally. We were "The Com'n Generation".

"Our scarce bookings consisted mainly of playing for private living room and garage parties, Jaycee fairs and community-center dances. We were fortunate if we gigged twice a month and luckier still to make $5 per man when we did. After a year of this, we changed our name to 'Dust', lost Gene Banks and added a keyboard player. Our gigs steadily got better and so did we.

"When I look back on those youthful, formative years I treasure the wonderful moments that will stay with me forever. As we made our way through our teenage years we doggedly pursued our rock and roll dreams while other boys who picked up instruments following the British Invasion of the mid '60's put them aside after a few months of lessons or finding out that steel guitar strings really hurt the fingertips. For us it was a way to release our energy and passion and to express ourselves in ways that others could relate to. We were all doing the best we could during the topsy-turvy events of that revolutionary decade, looking for our own individual path that would lead us into adulthood. Rock & Roll was our pressure valve and our muse. We constantly turned one another on to new music and different ways of thinking. We helped each other to expand our horizons of what was possible. And the fraternity that was the band became the glue that held us together. The band was what we could depend on to be there when the rest of the world let us down or presented us with problems that seemed insurmountable.

Rollie's high school band "The Com'n Generation"

More from Rollie later... meanwhile let's turn on the radio.

Charlie, Harrigan, Weird Beard, Rabbit, The Cool Fool and Jolle.

No, you're not expected to know those names unless you grew up in Dallas - Fort Worth in the sixties. Those guys were some of the top DJs in Dallas at the time. KLIF and KBOX slugged it out for years as the top two rock stations in Dallas. It was a constant argument among local teens – which was better KLIF or KBOX? It was sort of like the Beatles vs. Stones debate or the Pepsi Challenge a decade later. KBOX called itself "Wonderful KBOX" and KLIF was the self-styled "Mighty 1190".

KLIF was one of the very first (if not THE first) Top 40 Radio stations in the country, owned and operated by the legendary Gordon McLendon. During the rise of rock in the '50s every kid in town was glued to KLIF. The only competition it had in those early days was a weekend-only show on WRR called "Kats Karavan" The Karavan was hosted by a local blues fan named "Old Jim Lowe"

who called himself "The Cool Fool". Most Dallasites of a certain age today will tell you how important and influential this show was to them. Lowe played primarily blues and R&B with a sprinkling of rock and roll. He was to Dallas what Alan Freed was to Cleveland. He was uncommonly good to local bands and singers and promoted them freely on his show. The Nightcaps, Jimmy Velvit and many others will tell you of Jim Lowe's boost to their careers.

KBOX got into rock and roll in the sixties and gave KLIF a run for its money. Frank Jolle, Bill Ward and Dan Patrick were the top three KBOX jocks in the mid-sixties era of Kenny and the Kasuals. Dan was the urbane and funny morning drive guy (who had been "Charlie Brown" of KLIF's Charlie and Harrigan until KBOX lured him away.) Bill Ward was another clever and fun guy, who looked much older than he really was. Many kids thought "This old guy is Bill Ward??!" but he was actually about the same age as the other local DJs. Bill is remembered for running outrageous fake contests where to the grand prize winner, Ward was going to "send a big ugly man to come and look in your window."

The night guy on KBOX was a high-energy wild man named Frank Jolle (pronounced "Jolly"). He was a Dick Biondi Chicago-style DJ – constant chatter and wacky sound effects with as much rock and roll crammed in as humanly possible. Other KBOX personalities of that time included Bill Holley, Ron Rice, Terry Byrd and Ken Scott.

Over on KLIF Ron Chapman was the king morning guy using the name Irving Harrigan. He later hosted the local TV rock show "Sump'n Else". The evening star on KLIF was Jimmy Rabbit who was also a singer and bandleader in his own right. The night guy who Rabbit replaced was an incredibly creative man named Russ Knight who called himself "The Weird Beard". His shows were a crazy quilt of noise and impromptu monologues with The Weird Beard going off into loony-land for minutes at a time. Oh, he also played rock and roll. Other important KLIF personalities of the day included Johnny Dark, Ken Dowe and Rex Miller.

KBOX Survey from March 1962. Local singer Jimmy Velvit
was at Number 3 with "We Belong Together". Local band Big Bo
and the Arrows were at Number 16 with "The Big Bo Twist".
Dallas rockabilly star Gene Summers was at number 25.
Local talent received good airplay in Dallas in those days.

KLIF and KBOX were big, big stations in a very important market. Record pluggers from all over the country brought their records, stars and under-the-table goodies to both stations in large numbers. So it was unusual that local kids like us could even consider asking the big on-air personalities to play our records, but guess what? We did ask and they did play them. Both stations were very supportive of the local music scene and many local bands got regular airplay.

KBOX Jocks with Peter and Gordon. L to R: Bill Ward, Peter, Frank Jolle, Gordon, and J. Morgan VanBuren

Our records fared well as did the releases of Gene Summers, The Exotics, The Briks, The Chessmen, The Mystics, Scotty McKay, Kirby St. Romain and many others. Today if your record is not on the approved list sent down by corporate headquarters, it will not be played, ever. You can forget about handing your record through the station's window and getting it played like we did in 1965 with Frank Jolle on KBOX (more about that story later.)

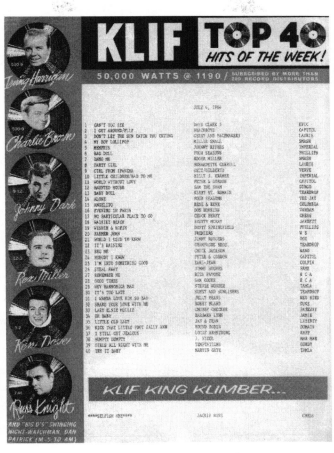

A KLIF Top 40 Survey from 1964.

Chapter Eight
Rebels Without Applause
(The Anti-Kasuais)
An Irritating Interruption By Richard

After Kenny and I have given you an idea of what
being in a *good* garage band was like, I feel I have to
interrupt to offer the opposing view and make the
following confession: in the mid-sixties I was also in a
musical outfit, this one called The Rain Kings.

Well, "musical outfit" may not be the correct
term. We weren't very musical, even though we
looked good in our outfits.

Perhaps that term "garage band" *is* better. Then
again the word "band" implies an "organized group
that rehearsed and then worked at paying gigs". We
weren't very organized. "Rehearse" to us was a word
like pholajanxion – it simply had no meaning. And
"work" was never in our plans either and therefore
"paying gigs" were pretty much ruled out too.

That only leaves the word "group". We were that.
Sometimes the number in the group would be four or
five and other times it would swell to ten or twelve.
We never knew how many of the group would show
up, or which ones of us would be among the present.
If we were playing at a birthday party or gas station
grand opening or some other gala event, and four
guys showed up, it would sometimes be just the bass
player, the harmonica blower, the tambourine rattler
and the guy who carried the amplifiers. We'd play
anyway, and no one in the audience seemed to notice
the eerie silence where the guitar breaks should have
been or where the drum solo was supposed to go.

That's probably because most of our audiences never seemed to notice us at all. At one extravaganza in someone's backyard our audience consisted of two little kids, one stone-deaf old lady in a lounge chair and a small terrier giving us the dreaded "dog head move". (See "The Dog Head Move" below for a complete yet worthless explanation.) Everybody else was gathered around the barbecue pit, the six-inch deep plastic pool or had gone home the minute we began tuning up.

They should have stayed, because tuning up was what we did best. It was the highlight of our shows and was usually requested again after each number. Even the deaf woman enjoyed the tuning up portion of our elaborate stage performances. The tambourine player was a delight to watch as he tuned up his instrument and the drummer, when he showed up at all, was constantly tuning up the radio that he listened to in between our sets.

During our illustrious career we also played in a high school gym, a church basement, an orphans' home and a gas station. And for some unknown reason and by a weird trick of fate, we held the all-time attendance record at The Studio Club, a popular local venue, outdrawing bands like The Yardbirds and Kenny and the Kasuals. (I am *not* kidding, although I admit I can offer no logical explanation.)

Yes, we were among the musical elite in the area, being hailed as the "best band north of Garland Road and west of Peavy Road yet southeast of Rustic Circle, bounded by Sylvania Drive to the east and Timmy's house on the southwest." Quite an honor.

In The Rain Kings' performances, we not only began to enjoy getting strange audience reactions, we courted it. After all, the only reputation we had was one of weirdness interrupted by occasional music, so we decided to maximize
our public image and go for it all. We set our goal on "Stupid". Our reasoning was that merely being bad was not enough to bring in the patrons, and being bad and weird was somehow even worse. But being "stupid"...now that had possibilities. There's logic in there somewhere. People will gather to watch the clean-up of a train wreck. They will stop at an empty field and say "Look, here's where old Henderson's barn used to be." They will watch mimes perform. Therefore, if it is presented right, people will watch anything. Especially if it is stupid.

Crowds of curious and disappointed fans flocked in the high single digits to our Stupid Show. We played one song while lying on our backs. We sang a rock version of a radio commercial for pies. We sang a hillbilly ballad from the 1930s accompanied only by the sound of tire tools pounding on wooden objects. We sang our hit records, of course, since they were incredibly stupid even before we planned to be that way.

We changed the words of all the standard garage band songs to fit our personality. So the great song *Gloria* became *Gorilla* about a woman who is "6 foot 8 with hair down to the ground". And the line in *Farmer John* that goes "I'm in love with your daughter, the one with the champagne eyes" became "I'm in love with a logger, the one with the chow mein thighs." Stupidus Maximus with a beat.

We didn't just stop being stupid with the music, either. One satisfied customer described our stage outfits as looking like "an explosion at a bad thrift store." Our music was not treated so kindly, though the song *Gorilla* usually brought applause sustained for well over a second.

We planned to be stupid, even billing ourselves as the world's worst band. And the people accepted us as just that. Success at last.

Here was the line-up of The Rain Kings in 1965:
  Shave Haircut – lead vocals, guitar
  Little Stevie Screamer – bass guitar, vocals
  Retched Plankton – harmonica, vocals,
    screechophone
  Dig Doglegger – lead guitar, vocals
  Victilla The Hun – electric lead tambourine, electric
    klaghorn, vocals
  Phil "Rimshot" Korsakov – drums when he
    showed up

The Imposters

OK, that list of the band members is a fake, though they are the names we used on stage. The real names of the guilty parties are Steve Howard, Steve Lowry, Richard Parker, Doug Dossett (replaced by Dennis Keys), Vic Nuuttila and various drummers including Mike McIver, Johnny Smith, Randy Dossett and David Anderson. From the start we knew that we were at best, "raw" in the talent department and so we made a conscious decision to make that fact the focus of our act, what there was of it.

161

We had a guitarist and a bass player who could play. We ran through six different drummers in three years, all of whom could at least keep a beat. We had a lead singer who actually had a very nice voice. But once we decided on being a "comic rock band" we stuck with it. Often we intentionally sang and played much worse than we were capable of, just to keep the "world's worst" idea alive. We referred to this as "singing in the key of R".

We began as "The Imposters", but in 1965 we changed our name to "The Rain Kings" after a Saul Bellow novel called "Henderson The Rain King". Then came the period that made us so very, very like every other local band in every other locality. We played at school dances in the gym, school assemblies in the auditorium, parties at friends houses, local teen dances (including one called – no kidding "Broadway Skateland and Sock Hop A-Go-Go".)

We got paid, usually. It often came to three or four bucks per man, but still it was a paying gig.

Like most bands, there was always a better band down the street, and they were pulling in the big bucks. In our case, we attended a very large high school and as we said before, there were a dozen working bands just out of that one school!

The Rain Kings In Person! (No, of course not really!)

162

The stars in the school were the subjects of this book, Kenny and the Kasuals, who were good friends of ours. (When the Kasuals weren't playing and we had a gig, their organist Paul Roach would join us, including at our sold-out gig at The Studio Club.)

Other high school bands in the area in 1965 – 1966 included those referred to in a previous chapter (like Kenny and the Kasuals, The Chessmen, The Briks, The Novas, The Chaparrals plus the older, established, full-time groups like The Five Americans, Mouse and the Traps, The Floyd Dakil Combo and the number one Dallas band of the early 50s, still kicking hard in the mid-sixties, The Nightcaps.)

Just too much competition for the average local band, especially ours.

The Rain Kings: LtoR: Dennis Keys, David Anderson, Steve Lowry, Richard Parker and Steve Howard.

Lo-Fi Recordings

Knowing in our hearts that we were about to make musical history, we wanted to make sure that this legacy would live throughout the ages. The only way to do this of course was to make a record. So we booked one solid hour Seller's Recording Studio, an upstairs, downtown recording facility, which was famous for recording on *two* tracks! This was the big time.

The hour that we booked included the time it took us to unpack the cars, load our equipment up the stairs, set up and tune up (man, I wish we had recorded that tune-up, as it was one of our very best.) In the same hour we also had to tear down the equipment and get it the heck out of the studio to make way for a local gospel choir or somebody, who had booked the following fifteen minutes of studio time.

That left us with about seventeen minutes of actual recording time for our four songs. This turned out to be more than enough and we spent the last five minutes smoking cigarettes and planning our Grammy acceptance speeches. In the session, four lasting musical memories were perpetrated: *Lydia, Everybody Out of the Pool, Lewis Lewis* and the tune which would inevitably become our signature song, *I Know What You're Trying To Do But You Can't Get Away With It.*

We decided to go for broke and pressed one hundred copies of our record, and in six short months we had sold almost one-third of them for a clear profit of sixteen cents.

The Dog Head Move

For the band's entire professional career (about two years) people gave The Rain Kings "the dog head move".

For those of you who are lucky enough to never draw the dog head move from others, let me explain what it is.

Have you ever done something truly stupid in front of your dog without realizing that he was watching? Like singing some cartoon song in a falsetto, or admiring your muscles in the mirror or putting a towel on your head and pretending you are Yul Brynner in *The Ten Commandments?*

Then all of a sudden you realize that Rover is watching you. You glance at him and there it is. His head is cocked to one side, looking at you as if trying to figure out why God made this crazy species called humans. It's "the dreaded dog head move" and it's how you know you're doing something idiotic. Even your dog knows it.

In my life I have done stupid things. About sixteen times a day, if my calculations are correct. And inevitably there always seems to be some very straight person looking at me, someone with all the imagination of a dog. And this person will slowly cock his head to one side in the dreaded dog head move.

Personally, I would prefer that he just say "Hey, you're stupid." The dog head move is much worse because it says you are stupid and so much more. It also implies that you are certifiable and possibly not to be trusted with sharp objects. I hate the dog head move, although after all these years I am used to it.

The Rain Kings soldiered on until 1968, after another name change to "Gretta Spoone and Her Magic Moustache Band" which was shortened by the Pompeii record company to simply The Gretta Spoone Band. We released one record on Pompeii which made history as the "45rpm Disc Most Quickly Pulled From Store Shelves and Forgotten." Our story is living proof that every band can't be Kenny and the Kasuals.

On the left, the U.S. Pompeii release, and on the right, proof that we recorded for the same label as The Rolling Stones, the London label.

Chapter Nine
Nothin' Better To Do

Kenny Kontinues: In the mid-sixties one of my very best friends was Doyle Bramhall, now unfortunately deceased. Doyle had replaced Tommy Carrigan as drummer in The Chessmen, one of those great Dallas bands that gave us the most competition for gigs. Before that he had a band in Oak Cliff with his brother Dale called The Cobras. (Oddly enough years later he had *another* band called The Cobras which featured Denny Freeman and 17 year old Stevie Ray Vaughan. Try to match that guitar duo anywhere in America in the '60s and '70s.)

When he was in the original Cobras, I met him at a local dance and we hit it off immediately.

By the time he had joined The Chessmen, they were a hot band and he and I were close friends.

The Chessmen's story begins in Denton where the founding four members were all attending school at North Texas State University. The original line up was guitarist Robert Patton, Tommy Carter on bass, Tommy Carrigan and Ron Diulio on keyboards. Replacing Diulio was guitarist Jimmy Herbert, formerly with The Diminshuns at Bryan Adams High. It was this line-up that recorded the great garage punker *I Need you There* b/w *Sad*. Robert Patton screamed the vocals on *I Need You There* and Jimmy contributed the hot lead guitar work. After that Johnny Peebles replaced Jimmy and Doyle took over for Tommy Carrigan. This line up recorded the British-style song *You're Gonna Be Lonely* which got a lot of local radio play.

Robert Patton was a good-looking guy, a solid guitarist and sang many of the leads. Doyle however had an incredible bluesy voice and sang most of the bluesier, harder-edged songs. His signature song was the Ray Charles' version of the standard *Georgia*. Studio Club regulars swear that if you closed your eyes you would not have been able to tell that it was not Ray Charles singing. Years later Doyle and first wife Linda named their daughter Georgia, in honor of the song. (As a side note, I take a little credit in the above story since it was I who introduced Doyle and Linda, who had been a cheerleader at Bryan Adams.)

In 1966, Robert Patton died tragically, drowning in a fraternity prank at White Rock Lake. He was in a small boat and was knocked out by the mast. His body was not located for four days, when a trio of ex-Bryan Adams students found Robert in 15 feet of water.

Meanwhile over in Oak Cliff this young kid named Jimmie Vaughan had been leading a three piece combo called The Pendulums. After Patton's death The Chessmen asked Jimmie to join. Johnny Peebles left soon after, replaced by Billy Etheridge on keyboards and guitar.

The Chessmen photographed shortly before Robert Patton's death – 1966. On the left:Tommy Carter. Top: Johnny Peebles. Right: Robert Patton. Front: Doyle Bramhall

I remember going with Doyle several times to the Vaughan's house to pick up Jimmie, and seeing his little brother, Stevie who was just a kid at the time, probably junior high school age. Once we came in and Stevie was sitting Indian-style on the floor listening to the first Jimi Hendrix album. We left and came back several hours later and Stevie was still sitting in the same spot, still listening to that same album. Years later, Stevie would credit Hendrix as one of his major influences and I can verify that fact.

Though The Chessmen never achieved a lot of success outside of North Texas, just look at the talent that was in that last incarnation. Vaughan went on to co-found The Fabulous Thunderbirds. Etheridge played in several Austin-based bands including ZZ Top for a while. And Doyle went on to a Grammy nomination and a long career in blues often partnering with Stevie Ray Vaughan.

THE STUDIO CLUB

In July of 1965, Dallas entrepreneur Larry Lavine opened The Studio Club on Sherry Lane in Preston Center, a very fashionable part of Dallas. It was not the first "teen nightclub" in the city and certainly not the first regular teen dance location, but The Studio Club almost instantly became the favorite such venue in the city. The location had formerly been a "dance studio" (hence the name) run by local dancing instructor and dance recital promoter named Dick Chaplin. That's why the interior of the club was so fancy. Most teen clubs were converted stores or roller rinks, and looked like it. Those clubs usually had cement floors, painted construction block stone walls and regular retail store cheap dropped ceilings.

In contrast, The Studio Club had beautiful crushed velvet walls, luxurious curtains, an elaborate chandelier over the dance floor and an actual stage, not just a bunch of saw horses covered with planks. Guests could go up one of two wrought-iron staircases to sit in the fancy balconies and watch, or sit at tables downstairs which were on either side of the expensive hardwood dance floor. The acoustics were good too, making the place one of the best places to dance and listen to local bands.

The stage was on one end of the dance floor and at the other end was a walkway which led to the "bar". It was soft-drinks only of course, as the club catered to teens exclusively. (Some of the guys may have smuggled in a half-pint of peach brandy or cherry-sloe gin, if their fake ID was good enough to buy some in the wet areas of town. But boozing was not the draw – the best teen bands in Dallas played at The Studio Club.)

On stage at the Studio Club, fall 1965. L to R: Lee, Tommy, Bird, Kenny and Paul

The bands loved to play at the club. They sounded good and they also looked good on a stage draped with fancy curtains behind them. The crowd that showed up was truly appreciative of the music too, because they had paid more to get in than at almost any club that admitted teens. The dancers hadn't just showed up to loiter with their buddies at twenty-five cents a head. This was not a place you went to stag. It was not only a date-night destination, but a grade-A date night occasion. The boys wore coats and ties (although they usually shed the jacket to dance.) The girls wore what girls had to wear to a "dress up" date in those days. Dresses, hose and all of those "getting-to-third-base" preventative undergarments that went with it. (Safe sex back then meant no sex at all and that's what the birth-control outfits that the females wore would guarantee.)

This photo of the Dallas band The Gentlemen, was taken inside The Studio Club. Notice the elegant décor, a far cry from most teen venues. The band members: Tommy Turner, Tim Justice, Mike Kelley, Bruce Bland, Seab Meador.

The bands played from 8PM to Midnight on Fridays and Saturdays. Some weeknights during summertime also featured live entertainment. The place was packed every night it was open.

We became virtually the house band, playing one night almost every weekend. The Chessmen, Novas and Briks were the other most regular groups that played there.

This bumper sticker was seen on teen's cars all over Dallas in the mid-sixties.

"We were setting up early at the Studio Club one afternoon," Tommy Nichols recalls. "Nobody else was there except maybe Larry Lavine. After the set-up, Kenny was sitting on the stairs to the balcony strumming random chords. It started to sound pretty good and we realized that there was a real song in there somewhere. So he and I just started brain storming lyrics back and forth. I'm pretty sure I came up with most of the first verse that included the phrase "Nothin' Better To Do" then we just built on that. Anyway, Kenny put his guitar case across his lap with a sheet of paper on top of it and started writing the stuff down. Lyrics with chord notations over the words where the chords changed. It was written in less than an hour. Probably closer to thirty minutes. A funny thing is - and I never mentioned it at the time or since - was that after I read the lyrics I actually remember thinking.....oh oh ...the girls ain't gonna like *this* song at all."

Well, that was how we wrote our first recorded song *Nothin' Better To Do*. And Tommy is right – it was a very sexist song in its attitude. It was about a guy who was only dating this girl because he had...wait for it...nothin' better to do. But the girls didn't hate the song after all, it was a different era. And we sold quite a few copies mostly at dances and at a few local record stores. Lee Lightfoot remembers what we did with the rest of the records.

"I can remember going down to White Rock Lake with a full box of the records and skipping them across the water like stones," Lee says. "We had sold about all of them that we were going to so it seemed like a good idea at the time. Talk about nothin' better to do!"

In those days it was very common to record a throw-away instrumental to stick on the other side of any record. Well, we did better than that. On the b-side we recorded a really nice instrumental that Tommy had written called *Floatin'*. It was a classic slow-dance type song and was requested often at our dances.

"Ok, as long as I'm telling stories that I've never told before, I might as well finally give some credit to Jackie Ludwig for inspiring *Floatin'*", Tommy relates. "Jackie was a good friend of ours at BA and one day he was over at Kenny's house. He started fooling around with Kenny's guitar and showed us these chords....E, F#m and G#m. There was no song or tune,just these three beautiful, almost eerie chords. Right then I started thinking about those three chords and began working out the melody lead in my head. So when we recorded *Nothin' Better To Do* we had an original song ready to go."

Yes we did and I *still* think that it's a very pretty song. It features Tommy's lead guitar and Paul's nice stop-and-go organ styling. A couple of years earlier and it would have been a perfect song to dance the Low Life to.

176

Back then the radio stations were a lot more accessible. For example you could take a record to the KBOX radio station which was in a low-slung house-like building near our neighborhood, and just give it to them through the window. We did that exact thing and handed a copy to Frank Jolle, one of the top jocks on the station.

He listened to it and said "Hey this is pretty good. Be listening..." We went out to the parking lot and sat in the car, and after less than ten minutes here came *Nothin' Better To Do*. We thought it sounded pretty good, we were discussing the mix of the recording and the levels of the instruments, not even realizing that half the kids in Dallas were listening to it too.

Meanwhile the money actually started to come in. Not from record sales, we pretty much broke even there, but from gigs. We still played the Studio Club regularly, and for a bit more money, but the real paying gigs were upscale private parties and frat house dances.

The KBOX Studios looked like a modern house from the outside, but inside the broadcast booth itself was small and outdated.

Frank Jolle

The Dallas Club Scene in the 60s

Dallas had a thriving nightclub scene long before the rock era. My dad and uncle were musicians around town in the thirties and forties at various clubs including the high-toned Century Room in the Adolphus Hotel, and were the house band at The Sylvan Club on Greenville Avenue in the '40's. Other local pre-rock music venues included The It'll Do Club, The Mural Room, The Coconut Grove, Pappy's Showland, The Band Box and The Bagdad. Each featured live music from jump and jive combos to the biggest of the big bands.

In the early rock era Dallas clubs like The Vegas Club (owned by Jack Ruby), The Guthrey Club, The Chalet, The Dunes, Jack's Blue Room, The Red Jacket and The Hi Ho Ballroom gave what few local rock bands there were some steady employment. The Guthrey Club was located at Corinth and Industrial, where in the late fifties the house band was Tommy Brown and the Tom Toms. Trini Lopez was the star attraction for a time at The Vegas Club on Oak Lawn.

In the sixties when we were first active, the club and dance scene had expanded greatly. In addition to The Studio Club, there were dozens of places for teens and young adults to dance to live rock and roll.

LouAnn's

One of the clubs you always hear about when people discuss the rock venues of Dallas in the sixties was LouAnn's. It was a club that had been around for a quite a while and made the transition to rock and roll very successfully. LouAnn's was on the corner of Lovers Lane and Greenville Avenue. It was one of the oldest standing clubs in the city at the time. The club was not run by a person named LouAnn, but by Ann Bovis and her husband Lou (hence "LouAnn's"). LouAnn's was a giant barn of a place with fairly good acoustics and a huge wooden dance floor. It opened on June 8, 1940 and was originally a home to big bands and famous performers.

The first New Years Eve dance and show featured nationally known big band of Phil Baxter. Through the 1940's it was a very popular local dance hall, featuring a wide variety of different acts from crooner Vaughn Monroe to blues singer Alberta Hunter. Jimmy Dorsey, Stan Kenton, Woody Herman, Louis Jordan, Harry James, Ray McKinley, Les Brown and Gene Krupa filled the hall with jitterbuggers from opening night through the end of the fifties.

By 1960 though, LouAnn's was alternating big band singers with rock and blues bands. Bo Diddley, Chuck Berry and Jimmy Reed were booked regularly into the large venue, while the next attraction might have been Les Elgart and his Orchestra or crooner Mark Dinning. In the mid-sixties the place had become virtually an exclusive venue for local rockers. New Year's Eve 1966 found The Chessmen, The Reasons Why and Theze Few entertaining. A far cry from Phil Baxter's Orchestra. We played there several times.

Jamie Bassett of The Chaparrals recalls LouAnn's: "When we played LouAnn's, Ann Bovis used to have us play dinner music for her and her family before the club opened. They'd be on the patio at the club having pizza or whatever and here's this long haired rock band trying to ease through *Canadian Sunset*. She also was the first employer we ever had who told us that if a fight broke out, to stop whatever we were playing and just launch into the National Anthem. It never happened but I always kinda hoped a fight would start. It would've been interesting to hear us segue from *Baby Please Don't Go* to *The National Anthem.*"

Tim Cooper has a fun LouAnn's story too: "We (The Diminshuns) were at LouAnn's for an audition once when one of the cooks came out of the kitchen and wanted to talk to us.

He said his name was 'Gene Vincent' but we of course knew he wasn't THE Gene "Be Bop A Lula" Vincent. He said he had a record deal and wanted us to back him on four cuts at the old Top Ten Studio. I can only recall two of the songs we did with him – *Blue Tears* and *One Two Many*, the second one co-written by me, James Anderson and this 'Gene Vincent' guy. We didn't get paid, neither did the studio and we never heard from the guy again. I still wonder who he really was…"

The Three Thieves

This was the most fun club in which I've ever played. We jammed there every Sunday afternoon in late '66 and '67 with all our band friends. The bands that played most often those Sundays were Just Us Five, The Chaparrals, The Jackals, The Chessmen and us. Usually a few members of each band would show up on Sundays and there could be ten or more of us on the small stage at once. The club was located on Lovers Lane and where the Dallas North Toll way is now. I remember the wall behind the bandstand had a gigantic eyeball painted on it. So the bands were being watched from the front and the back.

A highlight for me of those days is the memory of Steve Davis of Just Us Five singing *I'm So Lonesome I Could Cry*. He did that song the best next to Hank Williams himself. Steve died in a car accident in Arkansas in the early 2000's.

The Pirate's Nook

Jamie recalls The Pirate's Nook as well: "We played a lot of clubs around town, but maybe most often at The Pirate's Nook. The crowd there was great. It was a club more for listening than dancing. If they had a dance floor at all it must
have been a small one. We were playing there one night and Michael Rabon of The Five Americans was there taking in our show. We were just going into our break song when smoke and then flames started coming out of my old Vox bass amp. I mean flames were *shooting* out of that amp. Then we took our break and Mike Rabon said to me, "Man that was great. How did you get your amp to do that?' He thought it was some cool type of pyrotechnic effects. I said 'Mike, I didn't do anything. My amp just caught fire and burned to the ground'."

After The Chaparrals moved on, The Chants became the house band, and released a record called *Hypnotized* on the "B. Ware" label (Bill Ware was the owner of the Pirate's Nook). Soon the place was booking different bands each weekend, like almost every club in town. It was a fun place despite all it had – or didn't have – going for it.

The thing about dumps was they were a lot of fun because they always had such a weird mixture of people there. You had your older hardcore alcoholics lining the bar, young rockers dancing to the bands, ladies of the evening, drug dealers and the rest of your average everyday sleaze balls hanging out there. It was not the type of place where a girl could leave her purse unattended when she went to the restroom. From the descriptions I've read of The Beatles' early days playing the Cavern Club in Liverpool or the dives in Hamburg, Germany, the Pirate's Nook seems to compare to those venues.

The Chaparrals at The Pirate's Nook

The story I remember the most about the Pirate's Nook was when my granddad (my father's dad, whom I called "Warren Daddy"), was in the hospital with throat cancer from smoking Picayune cigarettes for over fifty years. He was in terrible shape, and I remember that he had a feeding hose in his stomach. Well, one night my granddad just got bored with hospital routine and snuck out somehow. He was on the street in his hospital pajamas and hailed a cab to take him to the Pirate's Nook for a drink. (He liked his whiskey, and he was half Cherokee Indian and maybe half werewolf.)

My dad got a call from the police who ask him asked to come down to the police station to get Warren Daddy. He got drunk at The Pirate's Nook and was dancing with a barmaid on a table with his privates flying out of his pajamas half the time. I will never forget that night. It was in 1966. He was born in 1889, so he was 77 years old and still had a thing for the ladies. They didn't put my grandfather in jail, they just let Dad return him to his hospital bed. Bill Ware, the owner of the Pirate's Nook, still remembers that night, but he never knew it was my granddad until I recently told him the story.

Other rock music clubs and teen band venues in the Dallas included The Ali Baba, The In Crowd on Knox Street, Surfers A Go Go, The Hullabaloo, The Lantern Club at the Lamplighter, The In Crowd (which became The Phantasmagoria), The Box, and a regular dance called "Broadway Skateland and Sock Hop A-Go-Go" in the Broadway Skateland Roller Rink near Casa View Plaza. Plus there were dances at all the local high schools and junior highs, a dozen sock hops each week at various recreation centers, private parties at The Dreyfus Club and Winfrey Point at White Rock Lake, frat parties, house parties, apartment party-room dances and Saturday night roller rink dances all over town, like at The Twilight and The Stardust over in Oak Cliff. It was a hoppin' scene.

Stories From The Road

"There've been good times, there've been bad times.
I've had my share of hard times too..."
  - from "Good Times Bad Times" by The Rolling Stones

Yeah, there were good gigs and there were bad gigs.
Paul remembers two of them that were just...*weird*.

Paul Remembers...

"In forty–five years I have played a lot of gigs at
very different locations. Some ritzy (like the Zodiac
Room at Neiman-Marcus) to bizarre (a boxcar on a
train). Most of the gigs were fun, energetic events
while a few have been weird or just plain bad. Here
are two examples. As the popularity of Kenny and the
Kasuals grew in the '60's, it became necessary to
travel more and more. Soon the band was playing all
over Texas. We were booked into a club in Houston
but I don't remember the name. What I do remember
are the events leading up to the gig. I was in the
advance car with our manager, Mark Lee. We were
going down to check into the hotel and set up for the
pre-gig party. I loaded a dozen cases of malt liquor
into Mark's Mustang and we took off for Houston.

"On the ride down to Houston, Mark and I began
to drink the malt liquor stacked in the back seat.
Before we got halfway to Houston I was drunk and as
we pulled into the large driveway of the hotel, I was
about to pass out. I had no idea we were going to stay
in such a nice hotel. I also had no idea how I

was going to get up to the room, but I tried to sober up as the bellman greeted us with a strange look and welcomed us to the hotel. The bellman brought a cart over to Mark's car to get our luggage. Mark told him to be sure and get all of the malt liquor too. Mark and I headed inside to check-in. We walked inside a very elegant lobby. Behind the desk stood the hotel staff stared at us with a look of disbelief. I really needed to lie down but the hotel manager wanted each of us to register and then they asked Mark how he was going to pay for the rooms. Mark told them he would be paying by check. So they asked him to write them a check.

"By this time I was dying and just wanted to go lie down when a registration card was shoved in front of me. I picked up a pen and scrawled my name and finally we get to go to the room.

"I fell into one of the beds and passed out. I was awakened by a knocking on the door. I couldn't get up. Someone kept knocking and finally Mark got up and answered the door. The hotel's manager and assistant manager were standing at the door. The first thing they wanted to know was my name. It seemed that they couldn't read what I had written on the card. Mark told them that I was indisposed but that I would come down and sign the card in a while. Then they told him that they called his bank in Dallas and that there was not enough money in the account to cover the check. Mark left with them and called his mother to cover the check.

"I woke up and went in search of food. As I got off the elevator, I saw Kenny and Jerry our lead guitar player followed by two of our high school's prettiest girls. Both girls were in shorts and their beautiful legs were streaked with motor oil. It seems that Jerry's car had an oil leak and that the oil seeped on to the carpet of the interior and all over the girls' legs. They had yet to notice it, but I sure did. Now the hotel staff who were already on high alert from their earlier encounter with me and Mark, just stared at the girls covered in oil as they walked to the front desk. The hotel staff refused to let them check-in. So everyone came up to Mark's room to decide what we were going to do. Before any decision could be made there was a knock on the door and the hotel manager told us to leave.

"On the way out of the hotel the girls decided to take some pillows with them since I guess they thought we were going to have to sleep in the car. This turned out to be a very bad move because the hotel quickly inventoried the room and when they found something missing they called the police. The police came and were about to arrest everyone. Mark ended up paying the hotel $200 for the pillows.

"I had left with Bird to go on to the gig. We setup and played to a half-full house because we simply weren't known that well in Houston. Bird and I drove back to Dallas after the gig. The girls didn't even get to keep those pillows."

To The Above Story, Kenny Adds...

Taking girls on the road. This could pose a real problem sometimes. We all had girlfriends and they always wanted to go with us whenever the gig was a fancy, cool or an especially fun job. In the '60's not many local bands went on road trips all over the world like they do today. Remember this is the beginning of rock and roll and to have a gig in another city or town was an exciting adventure. The girlfriends insisted that they should go along and, hey we didn't complain.

187

This was the road trip to Houston that Paul described above. Paul couldn't recall the gig but it was a frat party for Mark Lee's fraternity. (Mark was attending The University of Texas at the time, which is in Austin, and the party was in Houston, and we drove down from Dallas…yeah I don't know how all that happened either.)

We had Jerry's 1962 Chevrolet Impala, Lee's 1966 Corvette and Mark's Mustang. So Lee and Cheryl, his future wife, went in the Corvette and Jerry and I and our dates went in Jerry's Impala. Mark and Paul went in Mark's Mustang.

When we arrived at the hotel, we noticed that Mark and Paul had already checked in. What we didn't know is that they were smashed beyond their usual mushiness from the malt liquor that they had graciously consented to carry down for us all. The hotel manager was staring at us as we were checking in. It seems that Mark and Paul had made quite an impression on the hotel staff.

Mark had written that hot check Paul referred to but the lack of funds to cover it had not been discovered yet. When management found out that the check would bounce higher than the hotel roof, the manager went to their room and knocked on the door. Mark and Paul were on the floor passed out, but Mark struggled to his feet and went to the door. There was a problem with Paul's sign in card and they wanted to speak with him.

"Mr. Roach has retired for the evening," Mark slurred. The fact that we had girls with us at the hotel and we were not married to any of them made this situation a problem for management. They insisted we have the girls in one room and the band in the other. Not a problem we thought, it was a more innocent time and the girls were along for the gig not for hanky-panky anyway. The hotel management demanded we put the girls in one room and the band in the other. We agreed and the three girls went in one room and all the guys crashed in the second room. Just in case we had any naughty plans, the hotel sent a guard to sit in a chair in the hall and make sure we did not go back and forth between the rooms. Well this just made us want to go visit the girls even more. If they hadn't insulted us with the dang guard we probably all would have just gone to sleep. But no, this was a challenge to our manhoods! (Or is that "menhood"? Whatever...)

We were ten stories up and there were balconies on the outside of the building so of course we decided to climb from one balcony to the next to visit the young ladies. OK, remember that we were teenage boys, filled with malt liquor and hormones and we had just been challenged by the evil hotel staff – so it never crossed our minds that we could all die. We couldn't see any problem with our plan, just as long as we didn't look down. The Lord must have a special place in His heart for idiotic drunken teenagers. We all lived through it.

The way I remember "The Great Pillow Heist" was that the hotel called the Texas Rangers and they caught up with us about forty miles out of town on our way home. Mark paid through the nose for a few one dollar pillows and we had to promise never to come back to Houston ever again.

Paul Continues...

"Another bad booze scene I remember came in the fall of 1966 at the Adolphus Hotel in downtown Dallas. We played at the Adolphus a lot in those days. The gig was a big one, in the main ballroom. What would be a first for the band, was that it was an open bar for the party. At that time most of the gigs we played were either for teens or didn't serve alcohol. Most of the drinking was under the table. So the boys in the band got to go to bar and order what they wanted. We took advantage of that, I'm afraid.

"As the evening wore on Bird had a lot to drink and he got into a war of words with Kenny. Bird and Kenny had never gotten along to begin with. Now add the booze factor to this mixture and by the end of the evening, Bird had become "overserved" and very mad. As we're starting to pack up our gear I see Bird coming across the stage, lurching toward Kenny, getting ready to hit him with his overhead cymbal. Mark Lee, our manager, stepped in front of Bird at the last second and pushed him. Bird was so drunk he fell over backward and passed out on stage.

"We continued loading our gear on the dollies and in a few minutes we realized that Bird was still passed out, so we loaded him on the dolly with the equipment. We started moving the equipment (and Bird) to the freight elevators. We had to go back and get another load, so we left Bird on the dolly next to the freight elevator. When we returned we found one of the hotel employees trying to steal Bird's watch, right off his wrist. Bird had come to just enough to realize that somebody was trying to steal his watch. All he could do was swat at the guy and yell, "cease that crap", before he fell off the dolly. The thief took off without Bird's watch and we loaded Bird back on the dolly.

"At that time we hauled all the band gear in an old black hearse. It was a total piece of junk but it looked cool and that was all that mattered for a '60's rock band. We loaded the gear into the hearse and put Bird in one of the jump seats.

It was cold that night, about 20 degrees and everybody was freezing except Bird since he was so drunk.

We started the drive back to Mark's house to unload. On the way there, Bird starts puking out the window. There is vomit all down the side of the hearse.

"We arrived at Mark's house and everyone is mad at Bird for getting out of control. Nobody knew what to do with him because he couldn't drive home. I suggested we leave him in the hearse to sober up but it was very cold and Lee thought he might freeze. So in the end we carried Bird into Mark's house where he spent the night and survived. I guess it was a good thing since Bird went on to become a well-respected member of society – a "double doctor" (M.D. and PhD) and still practices today at a large hospital in Dallas."

Local Teen Musicians To Help Raise Funds

Fast-rising professional and amateur stars on the local teen music scene will appear from 7-9 p.m. Monday at a roof-top hop at Sanger-Harris' Preston Center store.

A swinging evening of entertainment has been planned to help the Dallas County Youth Council raise funds for a trip to the Texas Youth Conference this month. Funds raised from admission, 50c per person, will be contributed to DCYC's travel fund.

Headlining the party will be Kenny and the Kasuals, the Floyd Dakil Four, the New Generation and Ron Chapman with the Little Group from WFAA-TV's "Sump'n Else." Several members of the Dallas Cowboys will be on hand to sign autographs.

Rounding out entertainment will be several of the top groups competing in the Starfinder '66 talent search conducted by American Airlines and Vox. The competition is statewide and involves young people from 12 to 22.

Sanger-Harris' Young Texan Board members will act as hostesses for the roof-top session.

All of our gigs weren't wild affairs. This one wasn't a hellraiser, it was a fundraiser for The Dallas County Youth Council.

A Goode Story From The Excels

Here's another Adolphus Hotel story, which James Goode of The Excels shared with us:

"The Excels played for a NTSU homecoming Party at the Adolphus Hotel in Downtown Dallas. We had never played in such a swanky place like this before. Four country bumpkins from McKinney in downtown Dallas, and we almost got ticketed twice before we even made it to the hotel, once for going the wrong way on a one way street, and once for jaywalking! Welcome to town...

"Anyway, there were four homecoming parties, we were told, all going on in the Adolphus, all at the same time as the one we were playing. We were also told that the other parties had some big name rock bands playing. We started at 8PM with a slow song until one of the guys in the fraternity yelled out that they didn't want to hear anything but fast and loud! Roger didn't say a word but just struck out on a long, loud and nasty lead lick that was an intro to Chuck Berry's *Johnny B. Goode*.

"The guys in the fraternity started yelling, they grabbed their dates and got on the dance floor. We were soon told to turn down our amps by an official of the Adolphus Hotel. He was tossed out of the room by the frat guys and was warned to stay out. It got really weird. We must have been drowning out the bands in the other parties because people from those parties began to come through the big doors of our party room. The party got so large and attracted such a crowd that the hotel staff had to take down the removable walls to accommodate the overflow. I was told that the other bands were paid off and told to take the rest of the night off. People from the restaurant and bar on the top floor of the hotel started coming down and joined in. Seen at the party among the crowd was the then mayor of Dallas, Earl Cabell. Also seen dancing was another party crasher, Jane Mansfield and her husband, Mickey Hargitay.

"After the party, we were paid 125 bucks apiece. My God, we thought were rich!"

The Excels included Danny Goode on bass, James Goode on rhythm guitar, Roger Bennett on lead guitar and Gibson Harris on drums.

Tommy's Girl Friend Goes National

Tommy Nichols remembers: "Kenny had a good friend whose Dad owned a local Chevy dealership, and one day the man loaned him a brand new white Corvette Stingray to drive around town. Kenny came by and picked me up and in turn we picked up my then current girlfriend who was this incredibly beautiful young lady named Bobbi Ertel. So, here we are driving around in this 'Vette with Bobbi between us and Kenny's guitar case sticking up behind us.

"We made a quick stop in a downtown building, and when we were walking back to the car a man approached us and said to me, 'Hello, my name is Stu (Somebody) and I'm a photographer for Playboy magazine. Would you mind if I asked your girlfriend if she'd be interested in appearing in the magazine?' Very polite and professional. He talked to Bobbi and gave us both a card. We all said something like "Wow, that was amazing," and drove on. Bobbi later called the guy and after she was assured that the photos would be tasteful, she agreed to pose.

And then, sure enough a few months later there was Bobbi in a photo spread called "The Girls of Texas" in the June 1966 issue. The pictures *were* tasteful, too, artistic rather than explicit. She and I were still dating at that timeand I'll never forget the day we opened the magazine and saw those photos. We thought we owned the world."

Kenny Recalls "Donnie the Roadie"

There was a friend of one of the band members and he wanted to be our roadie. Let's say his name was Donnie (it isn't really, but I can't bring myself to use the guy's real name in an embarrassing story like this). Donnie was not the sharpest knife in the drawer but, he worked hard and did it for free. One time he was taking our equipment to a gig in Denton, Texas where we were playing at the National Guard Armory Hall. This was in our early days and we had a small trailer to carry our equipment hooked up behind an old van. When Donnie showed up at the Armory, he did not have our equipment in the trailer.

I asked him "OK, Donnie where is all of our stuff?"

"Well, I ran out of gas and didn't have any money to buy any, so I left the equipment as collateral at the gas station," Donnie replied.

"How much gas did you get?" I asked him.

"I filled her up!" he said with a smile.

Apparently Donnie thought he had done something very smart. It never occurred to him that the equipment was more important to us at the gig than the trailer and him. And he never made the connection between the value of the gas and the collateral he had left behind with a bunch of strangers.

"Wait a minute, Donnie," I said, not believing that this was really happening. "You left my '62 Fender Stratocaster, my Fender Band Master amplifier, Lee's Fender Jazz Bass and his Fender Bassman amp, Jerry's Fender Jazz Master guitar, and his Vox Super Beatle amp, Paul's Vox Continental Keyboard and his Vox Foundation amp, plus Bird's Ludwig five piece drum set with four Zildjian cymbals, high hat, drum stool and all the hardware for his drums? Let's not forget four Electra Voice 664 vocal mics and all the mic cords and stands, an echoplex, and two reverbs. You left all that behind for a tank of gas?!"

"Yep!" he replied, in a tone of voice that let me know that he was proud of the smart deal that he had made. OK – let's review. In 1965 gas was about 26 cents a gallon and we had a twenty gallon tank on the van. That means Donnie left at least $5000 dollars worth of the best gear our parents could afford as collateral for $5.20 worth of gas! We hotfooted it back to the gas station, paid our $5.20 ransom and retrieved our gear. That night after the gig, Donnie was let go.

The Kasuals Meet The White Tornado

Paul remembers: "Mark Lee, the Kasuals' manager was always trying to make things happen. He "encouraged" the DJ's at KLIF to play his label's records. Sometimes he took the money from a gig we played and went out and bought our records at the record stores that were surveyed by the radio stations for their charts. Hype and promotion – all an essential part of the music business. Mark decided to put Kenny and the Kasuals together with the Blues Bag and play concerts around Texas."

(Editor's rude interruption: The Blues Bag was a soul-based white combo led by Marc Benno, who later went on to fame as a part of Asylum Choir and as a songwriter. The Bag had evolved from The Outcasts, a popular North Dallas band that was a regular attraction at The Studio Club. See the lists at the end of the book for more info on this band.)

Paul continues: "Kenny and Kasuals musical style was garage punk and The Blues Bag style was like James Brown. In fact, Marc Benno did a part of the show all dressed in white as "Bennie Darvon, The White Tornado". Musically the show was solid and Marc's considerable talents were well showcased but the two musical styles really didn't work well together. The music appealed to two totally different crowds so attendance was low. When you combine the odd mix of bands with the fact that many of the venues were awful, made the thing a big flop.

"The photo below was from one of the shows, the second drum set was Bird's drum kit. Everything was setup so that bands could play back-to-back without a set change.

In the end Marc Benno went on to become a successful and accomplished singer and songwriter. So I guess his time in Texas as Bennie Darvon can be viewed as part of the natural evolution of his musical career."

Marc Benno as Bennie Darvon

Straight Talk About Hair Straightener

In 1966 we would practice at my parent's house on Lake Highlands Drive near White Rock Lake. It's a great big two story house with five bedrooms and four bathrooms. My bedroom was upstairs. Paul, Lee and I were in my room talking about The Beatles and how cool their hair was. Paul and I had long brown, very curly, thick hair. There was nothing wrong with that of course, but we wanted to have straight hair like The Beatles. So Paul and I hatched a plan that would give us the rock star hair we wanted.

I went to the beauty store and bought the best hair straightener that money could buy. Paul and I tore into the box and began to apply the product to our heads. Now I want to make this clear – there was nothing wrong with the product. The problem was "pilot error" plain and simple. We didn't bother to read the instructions fully and just started putting the stuff on. Big mistake. We did read far enough to see that we should leave it on our head for ten minutes. We didn't read the rest of the instructions that said to NOT leave it on your scalp for *longer* than ten minutes.

We assumed if we left it on for twenty minutes it would work twice as effectively. After about fifteen minutes Paul asked me if my scalp was burning like crazy. I said yeah, I guess that means the stuff is working. Then I noticed a small trickle of blood running down Paul's forehead. I looked in the mirror and noticed that I too had blood running down my forehead. Paul and I screamed and jumped in the shower together and washed it out. Our hair was burnt so bad it was like dried straw. I took another look at the instructions and noticed a warning sign. It read: "Do not leave on scalp for more than the prescribed ten minutes. Be sure to saturate the scalp with Vaseline before using this product. Caution: Ingredients Contain Lye".

Our beautiful hair was ruined. We managed to control the damaged hair for years with hair tonics and moisturizers. In 1968 when I was drafted, they were shaving my head for boot camp, the guy shaving my head said I would be losing my hair one day as the hair follicles were totally burned. He was right. By 1980 I was losing my hair very fast and today Paul and I have the same pattern baldness. We have the Phil Silvers look. Bald down the middle with hair on the sides. Oh well it could have been worse I suppose... anyway we have something to blame our hair loss on other than fickle genetics.

Hair straightener is the reason I wear a hat today.
That's me on the left, Jerry in the middle and Lee on the right in a
recent photo.

We Played With The Yardbirds (Sort of)

One night in the mid-to-late '60's we were playing at The Studio Club. Larry Lavine, the owner of the club (and the man who later started the Chili's restaurant chain) liked for the bands to hide inside the kitchen of the club during breaks, so as not to mingle with the peasants. He thought it made the club classier and the bands more star-like. So, we were all sitting around in the kitchen during our first break when Mark Lee our manager came in and told us that The Yardbirds had just dropped in to check out the local club scene and wanted to get onstage and play a couple of songs.

Well, we knew that it couldn't be the *real* Yardbirds, they would never come to a local teen club and play for free. So we said "sure, let 'em play." A few minutes later the music started. It was *I'm A Man*. And it was indeed The Yardbirds. The audience went crazy. Keith Relf was blowing into his harp, Jeff Beck was on guitar, Jimmy Page had just joined them and was playing bass that night. McCarty on drums. Dreja on rhythm.

After *I'm A Man*, the audience wouldn't let them leave the stage, so they launched into one of their greatest tracks *The Nazz Are Blue*, a song that we had also performed in our earlier set. Jeff Beck blew the place away with his guitar lead, and all we could do was peek through the kitchen door. After the second song, The Yardbirds waved to the crowd and disappeared.

"And now folks, here they are again, Kenny and the Kasuals!" Yeah, well I think not. It took them thirty minutes to coax us out of the kitchen and onto the stage. We avoided playing any Yardbirds' songs the rest of the evening and stuck to Stones, Kinks and Zombies material.

Above is the Yardbirds line-up that blew us off the stage at the Studio Club. L to R: Jeff Beck, Jim McCarty, Chris Dreja, Jimmy Page and Keith Relf.

How Four Unknown Guys From Dallas Became a Famous British Rock Band

They were unknown at the time, at least. Two of them went on to fame in ZZ Top. L to R: Seab Meador, Dusty Hill, Frank Beard and Mark Ramsey.

This is such a great story, I've just got to relate it even though it has nothing to do with Kenny and the Kasuals or related bands. In the late sixties, the great English group The Zombies had been broken up for a couple of years. And then – surprise – a song they had recorded much earlier became a big hit in America. It was called *Time of the Season* and was a truly cool song that went to Number One in 1969. Not bad for a group that didn't even exist any more.

And that was the problem. There was a huge national hit, but no band to tour and promote it (and make money for some promoter.) So, some promoter got a brilliant idea.

"No one in the states has a clue what these guys look like, so I could just get any four guys and take 'em out on the road. Right?" He thought to himself.

And as nutty as this sounds, that's exactly what

happened. The phony Zombies were all from Dallas: Seab Meador formerly of The Gentlemen was the lead guitarist. Dusty Hill and Frank Beard (from The Warlocks and the American Blues and later two-thirds of ZZ Top) were on bass and drums respectively. And a friend of Frank's, Mark Ramsey was on rhythm guitar. The promoter (who will remain nameless) somehow convinced these four young men that he had obtained the right to use the name of the band The Zombies, and hired them to tour under that name. Never mind that The Zombies had hits with jazzy, light rock and these four Texas lads were bluesy-hard-edged rockers. And forget about the fact that The Zombies sound was built around the organ playing of Rod Argent and the light, breathy vocals of Colin Blunstone. These Texas Zombies had no organist and sang hard and heavy. And finally, ignore the fact that these four guys didn't even know any of The Zombies songs and had no intention of learning them.

Just try and imagine what the audiences must have thought when five jazzy lads from England magically turned into four hard rockers with Texas drawls. I wonder what it was like to be in the band, hear requests for *She's Not There* and *Tell Her No*, and instead have to launch into some swampy, Texas blues-rocker. It's a wonder they were never arrested for fraud.

As The Zombies they toured all across The U.S. and Canada. No one who came to see them would ever want their money back now, of course, because they were able to experience something even cooler than seeing the actual band. They saw ZZ Top, before they were ZZ Top, being The Zombies without playing any Zombies' songs. Now *that's* something to tell the grandkids about.

I Stole Mick Jagger's Pants

Sometimes we all have to face up to some of the misdeeds we may have committed as young people. I have more of those than I'd care to admit. With most of those misdeeds that I committed I was hurting no one but myself. But confession is good for the soul, and so I feel I must come clean on one bit of criminal mischief that cost someone else. In fact it cost Mick Jagger a pair of pants.

In November of 1965, my favorite band of the time, The Rolling Stones, came to Dallas to play at the huge Memorial Auditorium. I certainly wasn't a star, but had some pretty good connections with the local promoters and so I was able to get backstage during the concert. Although I didn't get to meet the Stones in person, I did get to invade their privacy.

When Mick and the boys took the stage for their set, I was still hanging around backstage and noticed that the door to their dressing room was open just a crack, so I wandered in to look at how the upper class lived.

Once inside the dressing room I nibbled from their sumptuous snack tray (promoters didn't even send chewing gum to *our* dressing rooms when we played around town), and boldly went through the Stones' stuff that was laying around. I was snooping through Mick Jagger's suitcase and I came upon a treasure.

Gorgeous, gray wool slacks, interwoven with lavender stripes, expertly tailored with just a hint of bell-bottom flare at the cuffs. My guess was that those pants cost more than my car did at the time. I decided that I had to try them on for size. So, there I was, trespassing, breaking and entering, illegally snooping, stripped to my underwear, putting on Mick's trousers. And they fit! No, they more than fit...they hugged me, they were painted on me, they were made for me!

And so I just took them. Changed back into my pants, folded the stolen slacks under my arm and high-tailed it outa there with my loot. I wore those pants every chance I got, but in my secret guilt I never told anyone that I had swiped them from Mick Jagger.

Those pants were magical. When I wore them I believed I sang and played better. The girls looked at me with increased interest. I was taller, braver, smarter and looked like Tony Curtis. OK, maybe all that was just in my mind, but that was *some* pair of pants!

I was still living at home at the time, and one day I couldn't find my magic Mick pants. "Hey, Mom," I yelled. "Have you seen my gray wool pants with the lavender stripes?"

"Oh those old things? I sold them at the garage sale," she answered.

My mom sold Mick Jagger's magic pants for three bucks. The very thought of it made me crazy, but I guess it was my payback for a momentary lapse into a life of crime.

If I had found the sweater Mick is wearing above,
I probably would've stolen it too.

Chapter Ten
"Let's Give It To 'Em, Right Now!"

"Louie Louie brings down the house every time."
Frank Zappa

I know we've already talked about the song *Louie Louie*, but damn it, you just can't say enough about how important this song was in the formation of sixties rock music.

Berry to Holden to Roberts to Ely

Written and originally recorded in the late fifties by r&b semi-star Richard Berry, the song *Louie Louie* did not become a hit. Instead it received a good bit of airplay along the West Coast and became a staple of Berry's stage act. As recorded and performed by Berry, the song was a choppy, medium tempo, faux-west-indies tearjerker about a Jamaican sailor who missed his girlfriend.

Enter another late fifties and early sixties West Coast road band – Ron Holden and the Thunderbirds. Although Holden had a huge hit in 1960 with *Love You So* (which went all the way to the Top 10 nationally), the band was unable to create a follow-up hit, and went back to performing at the clubs and frat blasts of the northwest.

Louie Louie became a showstopper in Holden's act, requested as much as his only hit song. In the evolution of the song, the tempo was increased and the driving power of the "dum dum dum" rhythm became more pronounced. Garage bands along the West Coast adopted and adapted the song for their teen-and-frat audiences and soon the song was much more of a rocker than a pseudo-calypso chant, and almost every working northwest band included it in its repertoire.

Rockin' Robin Roberts, a northwest teen solo singer, often sat in with area bands including the stars of the northwest, The Wailers. Roberts' specialty was a high-pitched rock rendering of *Louie Louie*. In the early sixties, he went into a local studio, and with backing by The Wailers, recorded the song. Once again the song went nowhere nationally, but was well received locally.

Then, The Kingsmen and Paul Revere and the Raiders each recorded a version of the song, in the same small northwest studio, within a week of each other. The Raiders' version was closer to the calypso rock of the original Richard Berry version, and went nowhere. But when the vocalist for The Kingsmen (at that time Jack Ely) half-learned and sorta-taught the Roberts' version to The Kingsmen, their wild, rugged recording of it became one of the biggest rock hits of the sixties.

Even though The Kingsmen did their best to faithfully record the Rockin' Robin Roberts arrangement of *Louie Louie* (right down to the shouting of "Ok, let's give it to 'em right now"), the song in their hands took on a harder edge, a grungier feeling and much more of a rainy-day-in-the-northwest tonality to it. The crude one-take recording with all the mistakes intact, and the unrehearsed, take-it-or-leave-it attitude caught on immediately with American teens. Had it been a smoothly performed, well-rehearsed recording, like the Raiders version, it might have gone into obscurity along with the earlier versions of the song.

But it was none of those nice things. It was a raw, mean-sounding and very give-a-damn performance.

It was and still is the only real version of *Louie Louie* among the 2000 versions reportedly recorded since.

The song was a hit twice in 1963 and 1965, and the only artists that kept it from being the number one song in America in 1963 were The Singing Nun and Bobby Vinton (with *Dominique* and *There I've Said it Again* respectively.) Fittingly two of the most non-punk songs ever kept the most punked song ever from the top slot. It was one of the last times pure happy-pop was able to sabotage the grungers.

Every '60s rock band played *Louie Louie*, even if they won't admit it now. The song opened the doors to a sixties flood of garage bands and entrepreneurs of the era. If an unknown, half-baked band from Portland, Oregon could make sixty-eleven-bazillion bucks by recording an unintelligible song for a few dollars using one microphone, then that god-awful band The Rain Kings from down the street could too. Couldn't they?

Well…actually…yes and no. Some local bands (like Kenny and the Kasuals) could record a bunch of songs, experience local hits and national exposure. The vast majority of local combos couldn't, but tried anyway.

THE KINGSMEN

*The original recording lineup of The Kingsmen including the
actual "Louie Louie" singer Jack Ely, second from left*

The lineup that toured and made all the dough.

Louie Louie By The Numbers

1 – One take on the hit recording by The Kingsmen
1 – One microphone used in the recording.
1 – *Louie Louie* never hit the number one position on the US charts.
2 – Top twenty hits of the song – by The Kingsmen and by The Sandpipers.
2 – Times The Kingsmen version became a hit ('63 and '65)
5 – Members of The Kingsmen who recorded the big hit   version
30 – Minutes it took to record The Kingsmen version and the b-side.
50 – Dollars to record the song and b-side.
2000 – Recorded versions of the song (probably more)
100,000 – Dollars spent by the FBI investigating the song's "dirty" lyrics.
8,000,0000 copies reportedly sold by The Kingsmen.

Richard Berry, the original "Louie Louie" man.

The Actual Lyrics To *Louie Louie* As Recorded By The Kingsmen

Are you ready for some really filthy lyrics? Well, then you're in for a major disappointment. The words to *Louie Louie* are downright wholesome. A lonely sailor sings about missing his girlfriend back home. That's it. Sorry to burst the bubble in the gutter of your mind.

According to Richard Berry (the songwriter and original recording artist of the song) *Louie Louie* is being sung in a pseudo-Jamaican dialect to a bartender named Louie, who is listening (as all good bartenders will) to the lonesome woes of his customer, who misses the girl he left behind.

The only song I can think of that is cleaner than this one is perhaps *Jesus Loves Me*. If you don't believe me, listen to The Kingsmen's version of the song while reading the lyrics below. Here are the words:

Louie Louie

Louie Louie, oh no, I said we gotta go
Ai ai ai ai I said,
Louie Louie, oh baby, I said we gotta go.

A fine little girl she waits for me
Me catch a ship across the sea.
Me sail the ship, ah, all alone
Me never think how I'll make it home.

(Chorus)

Louie Louie, nah nah nah nah, I said we gotta go
Oh no, said-a
Louie Louie oh baby, I said
We gotta go.

Three nights and days, I sail the sea
Think of that girl, ah, constantly.
On that ship I dream she there,
I smelled the rose, ah, in her hair.

Louie Louie, oh no, I said we gotta go
Ai ai ai ai I said
Louie Louie oh baby, I said
We gotta go.

(Spoken:) Ok, let's give it to 'em right now!

See...see Jamaica the moon above
It won't be long hey baby 'til I'll
Take her in my arms again
And tell her I'll never leave again.

Louie Louie, oh no, I said we gotta go
Ai ai ai ai I said -
Louie Louie oh baby, said
We gotta go. We gotta go now.

(Spoken:) Let's get this one on outa here. Let's go!

(Words and music by Richard Berry.)

Kasual Knuggets of Knowledge:

(From the "Your Tax Dollars At Work Department".) In the sixties, the FBI spent the equivalent of a million bucks in today's money investigating the song *Louie Louie*. They wanted to discover if the song actually contained dirty lyrics. After a while they gave up, stating that the lyrics were indecipherable at any speed. Ok! Let's give it to 'em right now!

$1,000,000

Chapter Eleven

Kasuals Face The Truth

By early 1966 we were going strong. We were without a doubt the most successful working band in the North Texas area. We were booked for big money (at the time) at the biggest events. We opened for Sonny and Cher, Herman's Hermits, The Yardbirds, The Beach Boys (three times!) and played on the same bill with so many well-known bands and performers it still makes my head spin. (See the Appendix Lists for a complete listing.)

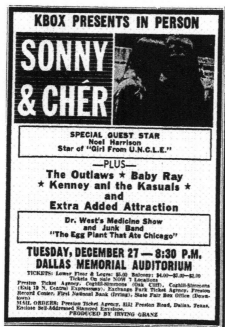

There's that spelling again: "Kenney" just like on the cover of "IMPACT". Well at least they spelled "Kasuals" right.

Half the time the newspapers printed it as "Casuals".

Paul remembers: "We had already performed as an opening act for Sonny and Cher and we were asked to open for the Beach Boys. The concert was at Dallas Memorial Auditorium on April 1, 1966. Everyone in the band had on new clothes. I remember walking out on stage and thinking I had forgotten something. The set went really well. At that moment the band was at it's zenith in terms of popularity and proficiency. A review of the show would say we were better than the Beach Boys. Looking back it was one of those peak experiences. As I walked offstage everyone was laughing and joking, we had performed well. Then I looked down and realized I had forgotten to zip up my pants! I had played in front of 10,000 people with my fly open."

Big spending fraternities kept us busy too, as did the biggest of the local clubs. We played gigs in gigantic halls where there were so many people dancing, that we couldn't see the end of the crowd from on stage.

We naturally wanted to take advantage of this regional fame by making more records. The year before, at the urging of our manager Mark Lee, we decided to cut two more 45 singles. First we released *Don't Let Your Baby Go* and *The Best Thing Around*, in 1965 on the Mark label (the label name of course was from "Mark" Lee). Tommy was still our lead guitarist, and he co-wrote the a-side with Paul and I, and Tommy and I co-wrote the b-side.

On September 7, 1965 the local Dallas teenage TV dance show, "Sump'n Else", featuring local personality Ron Chapman, debuted on WFAA-Channel 8. The show was broadcast from a studio at NorthPark shopping mall, right in the center of town.

The show was a local version of American Bandstand and not only featured local teens dancing to records, but occasional live acts. Big names like Sonny and Cher and the Sir Douglas Quintet played the show as did a few selected local bands.

We were one of those bands, who along with The Novas, appeared on "Sump'n Else" more than any others. Ron Chapman was also a radio DJ on KLIF under the name Irving Harrigan. He and Dan McCurdy were the local stars on their "Charlie and Harrigan" show, which was as much a comedy act as a music program. As a DJ he had a chance to hear the records of local bands and when his TV show

launched, he began featuring us on the program. This radio and TV exposure pushed us and The Novas one more notch up on the pay and popularity scale of local bands. This of course just made us want to make even more records.

So, in the fall of '65 we recorded another single which came out on the Mark label in the spring of 1966. Both sides of this record were British rock hits and staples of our live act. Our versions of *It's All Right* by the Kinks and *You Make Me Feel So Good* by The Zombies received a lot of local airplay but could hardly be considered local smashes.

Then we decided to make a record that we fully expected would not be played on the radio. It was to be our first LP – a full length album just like our idols! It was not uncommon in those days (or these days for that matter) for bands to record an album which was then sold at their live performances. Ours was called "The IMPACT Sound of Kenney and the Kasuals Live at the Studio Club". Maybe we could have crammed a few more words into that monster-long title, but I guess we ran out of room on the cover. The part about the album title that really bugged me the most was that they misspelled my name. Kenney??!

During the recording process for the LP, Tommy left the band and was replaced by Jerry Smith. We had previously recorded *It's All Right, Money, You Make Me Feel So Good* and *Farmer John* with Tommy and had those in the can. So we needed eight more cuts to fill the album and we went into the studio with Jerry and knocked out the rest of the tunes. They were all from our regular stage repertoire of Kinks, Stones,

Zombies and garage standards, and in fact the original plan was to record the eight tracks live at the Studio Club. As it turned out the facilities at the club, as good as they were for listening and dancing, were not suitable for recording, so we ended up at Robin Hood Bryans' studio in nearby Tyler, Texas to lay down the tracks.

Photo of Kenny and the Kasuals shortly after Jerry Smith's arrival. Left to Right: David "Bird" Blachley, Lee Lightfoot, Kenny Daniel, Paul Roach and Jerry Smith.

Even though the cover says it was recorded "live at the Studio Club" the only thing live or Studio Club related is the very first opening part - a spoken word bit from the receptionist at The Studio Club. As the album starts, we hear a phone ring. A male voice answers it and as the song *Chicago 60616* starts up in the background he lets the female caller know that the band playing that night is Kenny and the Kasuals. Full disclosure – that song *Chicago 60616* is actually just a rip-off of *2120 South Michigan Avenue*, a Stones instrumental cut and our regular "break song".

The album was meant to be just for fun and to make us a few bucks selling them at our gigs. If I had known that decades later people would still be listening to the doggone thing, I guarantee we would've spent more than a few hours recording it. But then again, I've been told that one reason people like the LP so much is that it captures that live, impromptu let's-have-a-party sound and attitude that we had when we really were "live at the Studio Club".

Maybe if we had taken more time and care with the recording, original copies wouldn't sell for over $2000 like one did at an auction in April of 2010.

To show just how seriously we took the recording session, the first time you hear my voice on the record it's in the background of the intro to *Money*, yelling "What key? What key?" In case you don't know, that was a sixties in-joke among musicians after we heard one of Little Stevie Wonder's back-up musicians shout it in earnest during the recording of *Fingertips*.

Copies of the "Impact" album were sold mostly at the front desk of the Studio Club. Some others we sold out of the trunk of our cars at gigs. And quite a few more were warped and ruined by the Texas summer heat while in the back seat of Mark Lee's car. We had only pressed 500 to begin with so it wasn't long before the whole stock was gone.

We never even considered pressing more copies at the time, because we were suddenly off in a different direction. We began experimenting with the heavier sounds that were just starting to appear on the music scene. Even though our live shows continued to feature the garage classics of the Stones, Animals and Them, our recording ambitions were growing.

Raindrops to Teardrops and *Strings of Time* were the two songs on our next single release. They were each more reflective, thoughtful and serious in tone than anything we had ever done before. Jerry and I co-wrote both sides and we were - and still are - proud of those songs. We recorded them in Tyler again, in the spring of 1966. *Raindrops to Teardrops* sold very well in the North Texas area, thanks to good airplay on local KLIF radio. It was our best selling record and best-received recording up to that time.

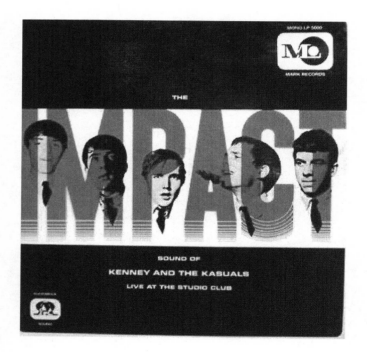

It gave us the courage to take a few more chances in recording. In the late spring of 1966, we went into The Sumet Studio to record a rocker entitled *Things Gettin' Better*, and ended up recording what people think of as our most famous song. We had finished *Things Gettin' Better* and one other track and still had a couple of hours of pre-paid studio time left over. So Mark and Jerry went off into a corner and wrote some lyrics in about twenty minutes. Jerry had a guitar riff he had lifted from The Kinks and we built the tune around that. Lee was anxious to try out the fuzz tone box we had just acquired and so he plugged into that just to see how it would sound. We ran through the last-minute concoction a few times and then recorded it. It was called *Journey To Tyme*.

For decades some folks have referred to the song as "Journey Into Time" which is not at all what the song is about. The title came from a magazine article Mark had read about a city In England named Tyme, where experiments were being conducted on some new drug they called "LSD". The concept of psychedelic sounds was brand new and the lyrics just sort of hint at what we thought the new sound was all about. I more spoke the lyrics than sang them, a choice I made on the spot.

The song was released in the summer with *I'm Gonna Make It* as the b-side. It was a different sound for us, that's for sure, and we hoped that our fans would at least give it a fair listen. Mark took the record down to Jimmy Rabbit, the program director and top DJ on KLIF. Rabbit loved the song and put it on the air that same day. The reaction from the Dallas area was immediate.

Everybody just seemed to dig it. It made the KLIF Top Ten quickly and garnered some serious interest from national record labels. One national company that contacted Mark very early on about the record was United Artists.

Now *this* was the big time as far as we were concerned. United Artists had had huge national hits with known and previously unknown artists. *Tell Him* by the Exciters, *Cry Baby* by Garnet Mims, giant hits with Jay and the Americans and Little Anthony and the Imperials. Records by Gene Pitney...the hit theme to "Goldfinger", for cryin' out loud. So should we sign with UA? Yes! Yes! Oh, hell yes!!!

And so we did and we didn't. We signed with UA for that one record, but Mark was hesitant to give up any real decision making to the record company. And he certainly made it clear that he wasn't going to sign over the band itself to the label. I think that maybe he had an idea that he was the next Brian Epstein and that we were the next Beatles. And so in September of 1966, the master of the song was *leased* to United Artists.

The song took off in various parts of the country. Many people had never heard the likes of it. In Buffalo and Pittsburgh the record went to Number One. In other cities it was receiving excellent airplay and sales were starting to take off.

Then UA pressed Mark again to try and gain control of the band and Mark again refused, flatly.

At that moment the record stopped receiving promotion from the record company and began to slide from the charts and disappear from the radio.

Without promotion, no radio play. Without radio play, no sales. But we had already gotten noticed in New York City and we decided that now was the time to hit the biggest big city, while our names were at least fresh on the minds of New Yorkers.

I had a close friend and sometime-roommate — let's call him Louie — who...well, let's just say he was well connected in The Big Apple. He made a couple of phone calls and we suddenly had gigs in New York including at the prestigious Rolling Stone Club. So, we were on our way north. (I found out just how connected Louie was when we were cruising the streets of New York and he drove off the road and completely took out a fire hydrant. The police arrived, took one look at Louie's name on his license and sent us on our way without even a frown.) Anyway, there we were in the big city...

We were excited of course. New York! Well, most of us were excited. Paul wasn't convinced that rock music was going to be his career and since he had just graduated from Bryan Adams High in June, he decided that he would stay in Texas and go to college. The rest of us decided to go north and go crazy, which we did.

We added Richard Borgens of The Briks to the band, and even though we missed Paul and the sound of the organ, Borgen's hot guitar playing made up for it.

Paul remembers it a bit differently: "Musicians for the most part just want to play their music. This leaves a lot of opportunities for hangers-on to move in, take over and in some cases ruin the band. Such was the case for Kenny and the Kasuals. When we recorded *Journey to Tyme* and it started to climb the local charts it eventually landed the band a record deal with United Artists. I remember signing the recording contract in the basement of the Studio Club in Dallas. The Studio Club was where we had cut our teeth, perfected our sound and built our following, so it was an appropriate location for the signing.

"What happened next was classic young, egotistical, I-know-everything behavior that hurt the band. After a very short time Mark Lee decided that the record label was not doing enough to promote the band. The new plan was to take the band to New York, play some gigs and try to find a new label. What Mark didn't realize was that the record industry is a very small world (especially in the 1960's) and all the record people knew each other. I remember telling the guys in the band that Mark's plan would torpedo the band. Since I was the 'baby' in the band, no one believed me. They all wanted to head off to New York, play gigs and get a better record deal. That was it for me, I quit the band, not that I didn't want to go to New York but I knew it was not going to work out well. Anyway, my plans included college."

Kenny Kontinues: We loved playing at the Rolling Stone Club. The Young Rascals were there just before us, and Leslie West (who later formed the band Mountain) followed us with his hot garage band The Vagrants.

We were all really excited because we had been booked into the famous Albert Hotel in Greenwich Village. We were told that The Lovin' Spoonful would be living downstairs from us and The Seeds were living upstairs.

This was the sixties rock lifestyle and we were ready for it. Well, reality bit us bad. And so did the bedbugs in the
beds in the Albert Hotel. Rock and roll royalty stayed here?

I wouldn't have booked the royal stable boys in thatplace. When we went to the closet to get our clothes for the day, we had to shake them vigorously to get all the roaches out of them. The hotel was right at 100 years old when we stayed there, and it looked as if it hadn't been cleaned in all that time. We never saw The Seeds or The Spoonful in the place and my bet is that they wouldn't have been caught dead in the hotel.

Every once in a while our manager Mark would drop by to remind us what a wonderful time we were having and how we were poised at the edge of
greatness. Mark was staying at the high rise apartment of a friend, and not, I assume, sharing his accommodations with bedbugs.

Without much money in our pockets we had nothing to do all day but walk around or stay in the room. Sometimes we climbed up and down the fire escape outside the hotel, just to relieve the boredom. Most of the time we simply sat in the room, drinking and staring out the window at Washington Square and the fountain. One day Richard Borgens was sitting in the open window, playing an amazing classical piece on his acoustic guitar when he lost his balance somehow and fell out. Luckily we were only on the second floor, as Richard wasn't hurt at all. He came back into the room, went back to the window, sat down and finished playing the piece. Amazing days indeed.

If the Seeds or the Lovin' Spoonful were there,
we never saw them...

We Become Famous By Opening For The Beatles Even Though It Never Actually Happened

There we were in New York, still experiencing a little heat from our recent record *Journey To Tyme*. We had played clubs and had a small following. We were starting to get some serious street credibility. But we were really, really not ready for the offer that came to us next.

"So how would you guys like to open for The Beatles in Shea Stadium?"

Well...I dunno. Let us think about it for about one one-millionth of a second. OKAY! How much do we have to pay you to let us open for The Beatles?

As it turns out, they were actually going to pay us! To open for The Beatles! The Ronettes (*Be My Baby*) Bobby Hebb (*Sunny*) The Cyrcle (*Red Rubber Ball*), this English group called The Beatles and us! I would have done it even if they had told me that they were going to shoot me dead right after the concert.

But it was not to be. The word we got later was that it was probably retribution for Mark Lee's refusal to sign us over to United Artists. Another hot young garage band – The Remains – took over our spot and opened for The Beatles, and then went on to The Ed Sullivan Show. But for years there was a continuing rumor that we had opened for the Fab Four, and I never bothered to deny it for over two decades. Finally I told someone "No...it's a rumor. We almost opened for them, and then it got all screwed up."

However, now and then someone will still come up to me and say they saw us open for The Beatles in 1966 at Shea Stadium. I usually just nod and say "how nice". I wonder if anyone ever tells Barry Tashian of The Remains that they saw his band at The Studio Club in Dallas?

So, we came home. Played more gigs. Had tons of fun. For our first gig at The Studio Club after getting back, the lines were around the block and applause almost drowned out Lee's opening bass run to *Journey To Tyme*. It was good to be home, but damn it...we had just almost made it big. Really big. And now here we were back in The Studio Club. Don't take that wrong – I ain't bitchin'. I'm just sayin'...

"In the end the band would go to New York, play a couple of clubs and come back home," Paul says. "Once they returned home, United Artists informed them that they were no longer interested in the band. UA held all the publishing rights on the band's material and the name for the next ten years. The guys would form another band under a different name – Truth – but at that point it was all over."

Anyway, we all felt we were blessed just to be living the life we were. Let's face it, in high school none of us were football heroes or valedictorians. We were just five guys out of 4,000 students in a giant school. Then we discovered what it meant to be in a rock and roll band. Just to be a member of a hot band during that time was great, even though it was not much more than a little talent and a lot of good luck and good timing. We were the closest thing to stars that existed around there, even in a big city like Dallas. We were actually chased down streets by girls and hounded for autographs all the time.

The guys we went to high school with who had been big time studs in our school days, were now just a bunch of unknowns scrambling for good grades in college or a raise from their boss at the gas station. They had peaked during their senior year and we – the former junior high nerds – were just hitting our stride as local rock stars. Now that was justice!

Back in Dallas, the band was about to be pulled apart by military service and college. During the Vietnam buildup, the draft was cutting into band line-ups around the country. It was 1968 and with me looking at an almost certain draft call-up, it was just a matter of time for Kenny and the Kasuals. So, when I received my draft notice, I gave the Kasuals notice. "Kenny and the Kasuals" without Kenny? No, that wouldn't work. So the band drafted Dale Bramhall (brother of Doyle) to take over the lead vocals. The combination didn't come together and so Dale exited and Richard Borgens stepped into the vocalist role. The group was renamed Truth and they began preparing for their first record. It was called *Chimes on 42nd Street* with *As I Knew* on the b-side.

The recording had already been made with me singing lead, but now it was re-dubbed with Richard Borgen's voice for the actual release.

It was a good song and received some decent airplay but it didn't sell well for whatever reason.

The Flower Fair

At this time in 1968, Mark Lee put together one of the first music festivals, calling it The Flower Fair. It was held at the cavernous Market Hall in Dallas on April 11th through the 13th. There several stages were packed with local and national bands for a multi-day indoor festival. In addition to the final performance of Kenny and the Kasuals, such stars and soon-to-be-stars as The Doors, The Box Tops, The Spencer Davis Group, Neil Diamond, blues legend Jimmy Reed and Mitch Ryder and the Detroit Wheels packed fans into hall.

45,000 fans attended the three day rockathon, which sounds small compared to Woodstock a year later, but was an incredibly large number for a local indoor rock show at the time. (The Rolling Stones drew 6,200 fans for their November 1965 concert at Dallas' Memorial Auditorium.) Mark suggested that I reunite with the Kasuals for what we all assumed would be our last performance together ever. It was a memorable weekend, which I faced with mixed emotions.

Entertainment Schedule For 1968 Flower Fair

Here's the entertainment schedule for Flower Fair '68. All attractions will be featured on the center stage at Market Hall.

THURSDAY

2:00—(The return of) Kenny and the Kasuals.

4:30—Spencer Davis, Jimmy Reed.

6:45—Kenny O'Dell and the Beautiful People, Jimmy Reed.

10:00—Kenny O'Dell, Spencer Davis.

FRIDAY

2:00—ATNT.

4:00—Jimmy Reed, LeCirque.

7:00—Mitch Ryder and an all new revue, plus Jimmy Reed.

10:15—Mitch Ryder, LeCirque.

SATURDAY

2:00—Kenny and the Kasuals.

4:00—The Lemon Pipers, Jimmy Reed.

7:00—Neil Diamond, Rain.

9:45—Jimmy Reed, the Lemon Pipers, Neil Diamond.

Additional acts at the Flower Fair included The Box Tops, The Doors as well as several local bands.

Chapter Twelve
Armed and Dangerous (for me!)

Two days after The Flower Fair in April of 1968, I was in the Army. It was a Monday. Two days before that I was rock star wearing a multi-colored outfit and sharing the stage with some of the biggest stars in the music business. And now I was a guy with a burr haircut dressed all in green, sharing lunch in the mess hall with a bunch of guys I'd never met.

I left for Fork Polk Louisiana that Monday afternoon of April 6th, and did my basic training. After nine weeks of grueling, intense training and gaining twenty pounds of muscle, I went to Fort Knox Kentucky for nine more weeks of A.I.T. (Advanced Infantry Training). I learned how to be a tank gunner. I was actually in the same barracks where Elvis Presley did his time in the Army.

The M-60-A-1 tank was the best full size tank the U.S. Army had to offer at the time. 56 tons of steel. 105 millimeter main gun. 1-50 caliber machine gun and 1- 30 caliber 7.62 machine gun. Made for one thing, and that was to kill and destroy.

"Hey wait a minute..." I thought to myself... "what the hell am I doing here?" After five years of love, peace and rock and roll, I was suddenly a trained "Government Killer". (Although I never even shot at anybody, much less did any killing.) I suppose I could have avoided the draft, but I was proud to serve my country and felt that I did owe America for the privilege of living in the best country in the world. No regrets whatsoever.

I did find it suspicious however that the father of the girl I was dating at the time was on the draft board and he didn't like me. "Surprise, Kenny, you're in the army now!"

She was a good-looking wealthy girl from Highland Park (a very la-de-da section of town) and her father did not like the fact that her daughter was dating some rock and roller from East Dallas, who went to Bryan Adams High School and who had been married before and had a child already. Too many strikes against me with Mr. Draft Board, although my draft notice could have been just a coincidence.

After A.I.T. I was sent to Bamberg, Germany for a year. I was assigned to the 2nd Armored Calvary Tank Squadron and was on border patrol at the East German border. This was during the cold war and in 1968 the Russians were threatening to invade Germany from Czechoslovakia. If they had decided to do that, our squadrons job was to hold them at bay until the armored division could get there from Berlin. It would have been a suicide mission for sure. The proof that the Russians never followed through with the threat is that I'm here to tell you about it.

I was then levied to Vietnam and attached to the 101st airborne division for a very short time. Tanks were not very effective on such soft ground, so we were not needed as much there. About all I did in Vietnam was to fire a lot of artillery and smoke for troop cover. Although once I did actually get wounded, though it was an unintentional self-inflicted wound.

We spent inordinate amounts of time stuck in that tank of ours. It was extremely cramped quarters as you can imagine. Once we were on some type of maneuver and we knew we'd be in the tank for hours before we'd even be called upon to do anything, so I decided to catch a quick nap. The only place to stretch out inside a tank was up front, right under the main gun, a 105mm cannon. There was just enough space to slide my head under the gun, with maybe an inch and a half to spare. So I squeezed in and settled down for the nap.

One thing was worrying me, though. They had the internal heater going in the tank and it was hot as blazes. I was laying down right next to a box of white phosphorus rounds, and I knew that they were highly volatile. I was afraid if those rounds got too hot they would explode. (Those white phosphorus jobs were dangerous as heck, too. They could just eat right through metal, so imagine what they would do to a human body.) Anyway amid the worry and the heat and the live ammo I managed to drift off.

Then suddenly I was awakened by the sound of pop-pop-popping. White foam-like stuff was all over me and I tried to get out of there as fast as possible. Forgetting where I was, and thinking only of white phosphorous eating through me, I bolted straight up, whacking my head on the cannon. But I didn't stop there. I tried twice more to get up, both times crashing head first into the gun.

Finally I woke up enough to realize that the explosion had not been the live ammo, but was from the fire extinguisher next to me which had gone off due to the heat. I was covered with fire extinguisher foam and blood from my self-inflicted head wounds. No Purple Star for Kenny.

Not too long after this big event I was shipped back to Germany to finish my tour of duty.

Chapter Thirteen
How Huckleberry Hound Came To Hate The Chaparrals
(Another damn interruption by Richard)

Here's a story I just have to tell you about a friend of mine. His name is Jamie Bassett. Way back in the 60's, Jamie was in a band in Dallas. They were called The Chaparrals, and they were up there in local popularity with Kenny and the Kasuals and The Chessmen.

Unlike my band, The Rain Kings, Jamie's band played well, with actual musical sounds coming from their instruments and singing emanating from their vocalists. His band was paid in American money for playing music at professional clubs and dances where people would dance rather than throw objects at the bandstand. They rarely if ever received the dreaded dog head move from their audiences. They did not feel it necessary to change the band's name after each performance. They recorded songs that sounded like actual songs you might hear on the radio. In other words, they were nothing at all like The Rain Kings.

But this band's path crossed with our band's rocky road in a way which would have made record industry history if anybody cared to remember the event, which of course, they don't.

Here's how The Rain Kings torpedoed the career of Jamie's band.

As I said, The Chaparrals were good. They recorded a demo tape of some of their original songs (perversely at the same little studio where The Rain

Kings had pled guilty to various musical misdemeanors), and had an appointment to play the tape for an executive of an honest-to-goodness national record company in Hollywood, which was then located in California.

Now, this successful record company was owned by the same group that made cartoons featuring Huckleberry Hound, Fred Flintstone and Snagglepuss, so their musical taste was unquestioned. If they liked The Chaparrals' recordings, a national record contract would follow, which would logically lead to international fame, appearances on The Ed Sullivan Show and unbridled orgies with groupies with names like Rainbow, Moonbeam and Starshine.

The day for the meeting came and there was one small problem. Except for Jamie, the band was nowhere to be found. To this day, Jamie believes that they were either in jail in Mexico or at the library. Either way, they had the only copy of the recordings with them.

The band's manager went to Jamie (who wasn't in jail in Mexico because he had slept late the day before and missed the bus heading south, and wasn't in the library, ever) and demanded a recording of something – anything – to play for the record company's Vice President In Charge of Subverting Taste To Make Money.

But the only original non-released recording of anything that Jamie had with him that day was a worn copy of The Rain King's legendary semi-released one hundred record pressing of *I Know What You're Trying To Do But You Can't Get Away With It, Lydia, Lewis Lewis* and *Everybody Out Of The Pool*. It was decided that these songs were better than nothing, which of course couldn't have been further from the truth.

They took two of the songs into the music czar's office – *I Know What You're Trying To Do But You Can't Get Away With It* and *Everybody Out Of The Pool*.

The Chaparrals on stage at the Pirate's Nook.
Jamie Bassett on the right.

Why these two songs? Well, it was decided that *Lewis Lewis*, being a lisping, limp-wristed version of *Louie Louie*, was just too light in the loafers for presentation. *Lydia* on the other hand had lyrics that were so bad that even The Rain Kings were embarrassed by them (including the immortal line "If you should leave, my name is Steve.")

That only left the other two atrocities to let loose on the unsuspecting music executive. *I Know What You're Trying To Do But You Can't Get Away With It* was about seven minutes long (it seemed even longer), and consisted almost entirely of the repeated lyrics: "No baby no, not no more, never again". And *Everybody Out Of The Pool* had no real lyrics at all, because during the recording of the song, each of the four simultaneous lead singers just sang whatever came into his head. So the words pretty much sounded like "Raza fazza rebo fenolomena" as sung in four different languages at once and then run through a blender.

So, it came to pass that for Jamie's band's big once-in-a-career chance, they were forced to present the worst songs of the world's worst band to the top dog at a big time Hollywood record company.

The executive told The Chaparrals manager "we'll get back to you on this." But of course, they didn't. The next week, some other group performed on The Ed Sullivan Show and sold a million copies of their record.

When last heard from, Jamie's band members were parking cars at a Lithuanian music hall in Pratt Falls, Montana for tips only and all the hubcaps they could steal. (No, not really.)

The Rain Kings were never heard from again, and thank God for that. And now back to our story...

"A lot of rock bands are truly legends in their own minds."
David Lee Roth

Chapter Fourteen
Country Punk

<u>Kenny Kontinues</u>: When I got out of the Army in April 1970, Kenny and the Kasuals (or Truth as they had become known after I left) were no longer a band. Jerry Smith had joined the Air Force to keep from being drafted and the others had gone on to school and various careers. I came back to Dallas and drifted for a while from job to job, before I realized that music was the only thing I really wanted to do with my life.

I had come home to a different kind of music that was going on. They called it progressive country music The early '70's were a time when "outlaw country" sometimes called "progressive country" was really taking hold. Willie Nelson, Poco, Pure Prairie League, Jerry Jeff Walker. I listened to what was going on and found out that I liked it. A lot. So I gathered up a few musician friends and started an all new band called "The Summerfield Band", which in short time became known as simply "Summerfield".

Ted Brumm had gone to the same high school as I way back when, but graduated a few years behind my class. I didn't know Ted was a singer until much later – I knew him originally as a show-off fancy diver at our local recreation center pool. It was at Harry Stone, the same rec center that held weekend dances including DreamAires. It was there that so many local teens would go during the hot summer months to swim and meet girls. It cost a quarter to get in and an ice cream sandwich and Cokes were only a dime each.

On those wonderful, lazy summer days, I would watch Ted dive off the high board and do these crazy fancy dives, twists and flips that I certainly could not do. Ted, even then, admitted that he was as much showing off for the girls as he was practicing dives. He had one dive where he would roll into a ball and come out of the ball just an instant too late and land on his back or stomach. This would make a huge smack on the surface of the water. Ted would practice this dive over and over always with the same outcome. *Smack*, onto the water. I would pay him a quarter to keep doing it as the crazy dive was very entertaining (and he certainly *did* need the practice). It looked and sounded like it must have really hurt when he hit the water like that. He told me years later that it didn't hurt at all, and he was just doing it for the money I was giving him. That was just the first time Ted conned me.

I got to know Ted better in the mid-seventies and then as a folky-country crooner and guitarist. When we first sang together it was a natural fit. Our voices just blended together in effortless harmony like they had been poured from the same syrup bottle. At that time Ted was doing a duet act with a multi-talented musician named Tony Vinsey who was yet another graduate of Bryan Adams High School. Ted was (and is) an excellent singer and guitar player and Tony sang as well as playing fiddle, mandolin, flute, guitar and harmonica. He was very talented on all those instruments. I walked into a place, I think was the old Texas Tea House, or it could have been the Ritz Pub, to see their act. They were the best duo I had ever heard live, bar none. I started sitting in with them after a year or so. Then we added Grant Gerondale on bass, Mike Lovas on drums and "Wild Bill" Ingram on sax, clarinet and several other instruments. We nicknamed Mike "Lazlo", and he soon proved to be funny, smart and a great drummer. We didn't have a permanent name until Lazlo suggested "Summerfield", a town in far west Texas south of Amarillo. He had seen the town sign on the highway and the name stuck with him.

Kenny singing with Summerfield, 1975.
"Wild Bill" Ingram in the background on saxophone.

Bill Ingram on the left. Kenny on the right.

Summerfield (the band, not the town) was very well received and in no time we were writing our own songs and playing at big and nice clubs. We were to be found pickin' and grinnin' at The Willie Nelson Fourth of July Picnics, playing with the likes of Leon Russell, Waylon Jennings, John Sebastian, Asleep at the Wheel, Leon Russell, Jerry Jeff Walker, Ray Wylie Hubbard and others. In Dallas we were the house band at a nice club on upper Greenville Avenue called Fannie Ann's from 1974 to 1976. Other musicians came to hear us there, which is always a great compliment. One night when a band I didn't know came in to hear us I asked them their name and they said "Little Feat". I thought they meant "Little *Feet*" and I told them that it was a very funny name. (Actually "Little Feat" is a funny name too, now that I think about it.) We also made the regular club circuit in Dallas playing gigs at Sneaky Pete's, The Abbey Inn, and other top venues.

We opened for The Nitty Gritty Dirt Band one night in the summer of 1974 at the Lone Star Jamboree, and Ted, Tony and I closed our set with a special bit. We sang John Prine's *Diamonds In The Rough* with just three part harmony vocals and no instruments. The audience loved that and we received a fantastic applause. Then The Dirt Band took the stage and it took about ten minutes for them to get the audience into their set. We were well liked that night by all *except* The Nitty Gritty Dirt Band.

Summerfield may have been the most talented, well-rounded and professional band that I ever had. Unfortunately, I really blew it when my ego took charge. I started listening to advice from all the wrong people and I fired basically the whole band in the summer of 1975. The band members all drifted off in different directions, and I'm not sure where all of them are today.

The super-talented Tony Vinsey died of a heart attack in October of 2007. Other members of Summerfield who came and went included Dennis Cavalier, Bubba Jacoby and Bill Ingram, each one a spectacularly talented musician.

Bill Ingram. Few rock or country bands had a clarinet player! Just one of the unique qualities of Summerfield.

Summerfield

Fannie Ann's is featuring the Summerfield Band through Saturday and on Sunday and Monday, Pore, Cooke and Neal. At Crossroads Junction, Slowpoke will be playing through Sunday.

Meanwhile, the "new" Summerfield band that I replaced them all with just never had the group charisma and straight-up talent of the original line-up. After a bitter break up of this second edition of Summerfield in 1976, I began looking to form yet another band in the progressive country field and this time to focus on getting a recording contract and becoming a true national act.

With that goal in mind in 1977, I formed "The Next Band From Texas". This was a very talented bunch of experienced rock and progressive country players – with Ted Brumm from the original Summerfield on guitar, Rollie Anderson from the rock bands Texas Rose and Daniel on guitar, John Davis from Pecos Star on bass and Philip Laughlin from Broken Spoke on drums. All of the players had known each other during their previous bands' incarnations.

Rollie remembers it this way: "In 1976, I had just wrapped up my final gig with Texas Rose and was ready to take off in a new direction. Kenny and I realized that we shared an interest in putting together a group where the main focus would be centered on vocal harmonies, with the instrumentation being secondary. We were tired of the loud rock sound that had characterized the bands we had been involved with before and we wanted something more controlled and personal.

The first jam session that Kenny and I participated in was with Dan Green and Danny Smith but the spark just didn't happen for any of us."

Rollie and I kept looking around, and always in the back of my mind was Ted Brumm. Like Rollie says, we wanted a vocal-based band with the focus on harmony and of course, Ted fit that perfectly. So Rollie and I got together with Ted, and then later with John, whose band Pecos Star had recently broken up. Once all four of us got together in the same room, we instantly hit it off and discovered that the blending of our four voices was ideal. We had a band, except for a drummer...

The Next Band From Texas. Left to Right: Ted Brumm, Kenny. John Davis and Rollie Anderson

"We also discovered that we shared a love of the same style of Country/Folk-Rock music that was being written and recorded by groups like The Eagles and The Band and individual artists like John Prine and Randy Newman," Rollie recalls. "At first we also agreed to further emphasize the vocals by not adding a drummer to the group. Instead, we used tambourines, maracas and congas to provide the necessary rhythms."

Pecos Star, John's previous band, was the primary house band at The Abbey Inn. That's John on the far right. The late, great pedal steel specialist, Danny Porter, is second from the left

Kenny Kontinues: There were several clubs in the Dallas / Fort Worth area that at least occasionally booked progressive country or light country rock bands at that time like Whiskey River, Faces, Sneaky Pete's, The Abbey Inn, The Texas Tea House, Fannie Ann's, Pub Royal, Mother Blues, Showdown and others. There was also a popular upper Greenville Avenue restaurant and bar called The Randy Tar, and even though it had an old-time nautical motif, the place featured nuevo-wavo country bands like ours. We became the regular band there as we honed our act and became accustomed to each other's playing. Once we felt we were ready, we headed to Los Angeles to try and make it big.

The Randy Tar in the '70's

Left: Texas Rose. Right: Next Band From Texas, in California

"Three chords and the truth — that's what a country song is."
Willie Nelson

The Next Band From Texas

Rollie remembers it this way...

"Sometime in early July Kenny made a fateful and shocking announcement. He was going to move (along with as much of the band as was willing to accompany him) to Los Angeles to pursue a record deal. He had just turned 31 years old and it was now or never as far as he was concerned. He truly felt that the band had enough good songs and talent to make a realistic run at a record contract if they had the guts to move to where the real music business was happening. We could stay in Dallas and play in the same bar for years to come or risk everything and reach for the brass ring in California. Kenny was choosing the latter option. His strong conviction was enough to convince the rest of the band to pull up roots and relocate to the West Coast. It was a huge decision for all of us, especially John and Ted who were married. And the fact is, none of us were sure whether or not Kenny was bluffing about the gigs awaiting us in California.

"We had by then given in to the demands of our fans who wanted to dance and added a drummer, Phillip Laughlin, to fill out the sound. For two days in mid-July 1977 the band took a private hiatus (without wives or girlfriends) to an estate on Lake Travis just outside of Austin that was owned by a friend of Kenny and Phillip's. The stated purpose was to hunker down and write new material to take to California but it turned out to be yet another drunken party and all we got out of it was a massive hangover."

Kenny Kontinues....

Just as New York City was to become the draw for punkish bands on the rise, L.A. had become Mecca for progressive country types. The California sound had changed over the years from The Beach Boys to The Eagles.

We lived in Hermosa Beach about two blocks from the ocean and got a regular job the first day we arrived playing at a club called Shenanigans. We thought "well that was easy...we're gonna take this town by storm." Well...we might have, too except for one thing – the incredibly easy access to drugs that we had.

But before we succumbed we actually took a shot at stardom. With our regular gig drawing more and more fans each night, we were able to attract a manager named Scott Goldman who began to get us more bookings and start to snoop around for a recording deal. During this time we played at many of the better clubs in the L.A. area including the famous Troubadour, The Roxy and Sweetwater. We also met a rich guy, a successful Beverly Hills plastic surgeon who helped us financially to record. We had written several new and good songs and booked time at the Village Recording Studios on Hollywood Boulevard in Santa Monica. While we were recording in the mid-level studio, in the upstairs studio there was the Doobie Brothers recording their *Living on the Fault Line* album. Meanwhile, in the downstairs studio Fleetwood Mac was also recording, and our lead guitarist Rollie became good friends with Lindsey Buckingham. We met and hung out with Rick Danko of The Band and went to his rehearsals for a solo album he was working on. Then we began to hang out with too many big stars to name out in Topanga Canyon, the home of the cowboy-hippie musicians of the day.

More Rollie Remembrances...

"Word gets around fast in Los Angeles when a talented group starts up a stir and soon potential managers and agents were showing up to get a listen. Our manager Scott wanted to get us into the studio as soon as possible. On Halloween as Kenny says, we went into the studio and recorded three

The Next Band from Texas with drummer Phillip Laughlin on the far right.

original songs with a seasoned producer who had worked with Sergio Mendez. *A Teardrop's Worth of Difference*, and Kenny's *So Sharp* and *Money* were taped over a three-session timeframe.

"Of course, all this went straight to the band members' heads and we became convinced beyond a doubt that we on the verge of landing a lucrative recording deal.

"One of the obvious advantages to living in the bay area was our proximity to the fabulous beach. It was literally just yards away from our houses and we took advantage of it almost daily. The smog and congestion that typified the city were practically non-existent in Hermosa, Manhattan, and Redondo Beach and it made living there a beautiful and totally new experience for us. The volleyball and touch football games, boogie-board and body surfing and invigorating jogs along the strand were exciting recreations for them all and gave us a fast escape from the pressures that surrounded the group.

"Although we each had a $200 per week allowance from our management, we still needed to perform for pay and to keep our sound sharp. We played regularly at the Scotch and Sirloin club and restaurant and The Topanga Corral. Meanwhile, Scott stayed busy getting the demo tape in front of as many record people as he could. On the night of January 14th, 1978 we played a successful showcase at "The White House" theater in Los Angeles for the many record executives and big shots that Scott had invited. The place was packed. Kenny personally prepared a giant pot of his spicy Texas chili for the guests and a great time was had by all. We unveiled several new songs written by Kenny that night. *You Tell Me*, *Piano Man* and *You'd Better Move* had been added in rehearsals for the show. The response was overwhelmingly positive.

"In one eventful year the band had come from playing in a noisy burger joint (where uncouth patrons would sometimes hurl cheesy nachos at the stage) to recording in one of the most prestigious studios in the world, backed by a wealthy Hollywood entrepreneur, and having a real, connected, L.A. agent / manager. To a man, we thought we were in the big leagues.

"But reality has a way of bringing you back down to earth in a hurry and the very next night we played an embarrassing and humbling audition at a disco complete with the obligatory lighted circular dance floor and gaudy mirror ball hung from the ceiling. We still had to make a living, it seemed, and Scott was trying to find us employment wherever he could.

"On January 30th we went into 'Sunswept Studios' to record another batch of demos. The studio was literally dug into the side of a small mountain. To enter the control room one had to climb through a trap door in the adjoining house and go down a ladder. After five days of work we came away with strong tapes of John's *I Get High*, Kenny's *You Can Have It* and *Green Eyes*, and *Wait a Minute, Baby* by Kenny and me. Veteran rocker Bill Champlin (soon to join 'Chicago') contributed his keyboard expertise to three of the songs and producer Don Markese added saxophone and flute. The result was a bigger, funkier sound that was a slight departure from the guitar-dominated recordings we had produced before.

"But we had an unrealistic expectation in thinking things should continue to happen at an unbelievably fast pace. The response from the record executives was positive but no deals were being offered. In general Scott and the band were hearing 'We don't deny that the song material and the ability of the band is of the highest quality but they're just not what we're looking for at this time.'

"Trends were changing in Hollywood. The country-rock movement that had been successful for so many years was starting to wane in 1977-78. Disco had invaded the airwaves and made its mind-numbing mark but it, too, was starting to fade. What was "happening" was punk rock and new wave music. But The Next Band from Texas bore no resemblance whatsoever to that rebellious, noisy revolution that was rising up in the business. It was obvious that it would likely take years of networking rather than months to get the band on a label. And that kind of time was something that Kenny Daniel didn't feel like he had.

"By the middle of February Kenny had fired Ted and Phillip and the band started to drift downhill. In the meantime, using a stand-in on drums, we competed in the Monday night talent contest at 'The Palomino Club' and lost to a *one-handed* blues guitarist. The signs of doom were all around. On March 6th, Kenny Daniel quit 'The Next Band.' He eventually moved back to Dallas where, ironically, he would reform Kenny and the Kasuals as a popular punk-oriented band and record a new album of material.

"Ted rejoined the band and he and John and I added some players and the band went on. We recorded, played some great gigs, and even appeared on national TV on 'ABC Presents Tomorrows Stars', the prototype show that became 'Star Search'. But progressive country music was slowly sinking in the west and we had missed that window of opportunity."

John and Rollie at The Troubadour in L.A.

The Next Band on national television.

*Rollie at the Sunswept Recording Studio with
The Next Band From Texas.*

Kenny on The Final Days of
The Next Band...

We had a great start. Club gigs, recording sessions, really good connections and close friends in the top ranks of the business. But we had one other thing — a next door neighbor who was a big-time drug smuggler. He worked for an airline and was somehow able to bring into America all kinds of verboten stuff. He was way too good of a friend and in no time we were worthless drugged-out idiots. This was the downfall of The Next Band from Texas. Bad drugs lead to bad decisions and I made a few of those. Who knows, we could have met with fame and fortune on the left coast if it weren't for the constant distractions and the self-inflicted brain woozies.

After that whirlwind first few months, things for us went from good to bad to terrible in a very short time. My car — a cool 1977 El Camino — was repossessed and I was dead broke. I called my cousin Gregg in Northern California to come and save me from further degradation. This he did, picking up me and my cat and taking us home to live with him. Eventually I dried out and went back to Texas when my mom was kind enough to send me the airfare to get home.

Punked Out

In the late spring of 1978 Mark Lee called me and said he wanted to put Kenny and the Kasuals back together. I had no idea what he what talking about or why we would want to reform a band that hadn't existed for a decade.

"Kenny, we've got a hit record in France," Mark told me.

Of course I didn't believe him. We hadn't recorded anything in so long that it simply was not believable. But it was indeed true.

Someone in France had pulled the song *Gloria* off the 'Impact' album and bootlegged it. Radio stations picked up on it and began playing it. By the time Mark heard about it, the illegally reproduced record was selling like crazy in Europe. Of course we never got a dime from those sales, but we did eventually profit from the rediscovery of Kenny and the Kasuals.

"And Elvis Costello has been telling everyone in England about the Impact album and there's a ton of curiosity about the band. It's time to tour over there." Mark added.

Well, I thought, why not? Nothing I like better than playing music. And if they want to see and hear us, then I'd love to play. So, the first person I called was Dan Green.

"I heard from Kenny in the summer of 1978 and immediately wanted to get involved," Dan recalled recently. "The plan was to record a completely new album and tour Europe. We got a few players together and began rehearsing at the Firehouse Studio. By the time we started to record, the final line-up was Kenny on vocals and guitar, me on bass, Jerry and Jack Morgan on guitar, Rosebud on drums, and Karl on keyboards."

We recorded the album at Goodnight Sound in Dallas, in the studio they called the "Old Church". It was called that because it really had been a church sanctuary sometime in the distant past. You could still see remnants of the original structure and artifacts, and the place had great acoustics with a hard to find natural "presence" in the sound. The full musician credit for the album is as follows:

Kenny Daniel - Vocals, Rhythm Guitar, Harmonica, Fuzz Bass, Percussion
Dan Green – Bass
Rosebud – Drums
Jerry Smith – Acoustic slide guitar
Jack Morgan – Electric slide guitar
Karl Tomorrow – Keyboards
Wally Wilson - Keyboards
Ron Mason – Keyboards, congas, vibraphone
Max Ball – Saxophone
Tony Vinson – Electric violin
The Cain Sisters – Backing vocals
Prioduced by Kenny Daniel and Mark Lee
The engineers were Jerry Hudson and Tom Gondolf

"We recorded *Garage Kings* basically live, running through each number as a group until we liked the sound," Dan recalls. "We did only minimal overdubs on the recording."

With the album in the can and ready for release, we put an actual traveling band together and began to play gigs. This version of the band toured for only about seven months between Oct 31, 1978 and May of 1979. My cousin Gregg joined the band, along with Dan, Karl and Rosebud.

"Mark wanted the band to tour so we needed to dedicate ourselves to practice", Dan recalls. "We all quit our regular jobs and by that fall we were in a practice facility which was really just a converted storage garage. We really were 'garage kings'. We called the place 'the Temple' although it was anything but. We practiced everyday but spent an equal amount of time playing nerf football out in the parking lot."

Our first official gig was on Halloween Night, Oct 31, 1978 at the Palladium Ballroom in Dallas opening for Norton Buffalo. We weren't exactly the Kenny and the Kasuals of old, as we were embracing the new punk style – musically and visually. No more white saddle oxfords or the greatest hits of The Animals. We punked out and we were good at it. That first night we blew everyone away and received very good press for the show. We continued to practice and we really wanted to play more gigs, if for no other reason than to get the feel of a live audience. We didn't care if we were on stage at the Palladium or at some little dive on Greenville Avenue. We felt that we needed to bounce our stuff off of real, live people. Mark didn't want us to play around, especially in small clubs because it thought it "cheapened the act". We all felt that it would have "sharpened the act", but Mark was doing the booking.

Finally by mid-December, Mark felt we were ready for public performances and on Christmas night we played at a cool medium-sized club off upper Greenville Avenue called Popsicle Toes.

Our next gig was New Years Eve, and after our Halloween and Christmas performances, we were beginning to wonder if Mark was only going to book us on holidays. That New Years Eve we played at Faces, a trendy Dallas club. With that night came the worst ice storm in the history of Dallas. If you're not familiar with North Texas ice storms, it's not like a snowstorm elsewhere. It's a complete deal-breaker and stops the city cold, so to speak. Despite the cold weather and the incredibly dangerous driving conditions, quite a few folks came to see the new Kenny and the Kasuals, and the gig went well. At least until Dan tried to drive home in the wee hours of January 1st and had a wreck.

A pin-on button made for our fans during the punk years

After this we began to play on a regular basis and we started to feel really good about the music we were making. We opened for the hottest punk band of the era, The Ramones at the Palladium and the local ABC affiliate TV show "PM Magazine" did a feature story on us which, when it aired gave us some great exposure.

We then traveled to Austin to play at Armadillo World Headquarters with Bugs Henderson, and in March took off on an extended tour through the Midwest and East Coast. We first traveled and played our way north through Oklahoma, Kansas, Minnesota and Wisconsin. In Minneapolis we ran into a snowstorm and while stuck in our eighth floor room at the Andrews hotel, we amused ourselves by tossing slices of bologna out the window to some homeless guys down on the street.

We skipped out on the hotel bill there (dang, we were a bunch of worthless young jerks) and headed to Chicago, Detroit and on to Washington D.C. where we played at the famous PsycheDeli – home of The Nighthawks – and heard our music played on the radio. On an off night in DC we went to Peter Tosh concert, got in for free because we such big local stud stars, and met Keith Richards backstage.

From there it was on to New York City – The Kasuals' second chomp at the Big Apple. Then to Boston, Atlanta and all points in between. It was a lot of fun and totally hell all at the same time. Touring can be a real drag. As Ringo said in the movie *A Hard Days Night* "...so far I've been in a train and a room, and a car and a room and a room and a room..."

There were fun times, too, but I have decided not to go into too much detail about what went on during this road trip. I will only say "far out, man" and leave the rest to your imagination. (I *will* say that we all swear to this day that we saw Bigfoot during a blinding snowstorm on our way to Pittsburgh.)

Iggy Pop was a trip. We opened for him around 1978. We were sitting in the car out in the club's parking lot before the gig, snacking on chips and having a beer, when the car door opened up and Iggy squeezed in.

"Hi I'm Iggy. Got a beer?" That was our introduction to the ultimate icon of punk music. We had a beer and so we gave it to him. And a second and a third. And the chips. And soon all of our beer and all of our snacks were devoured. And Iggy said "OK, then, see you inside."

I still don't know if Iggy knew that we were the opening act and not just some early arriving club goers, because we did see him inside later and he introduced himself to us as if we had never met. By the way, he was amazing that night, and I'd open for him again tomorrow if he asked.

Iggy

In April of 1979 we went on short tour with The Boomtown Rats (Austin, Dallas, Houston and finally Tulsa) and they lived up to their name. (My mom used to tell me "If you can't say something nice about someone, don't say anything at all." So I'm not gonna say much at all about The Boomtown Rats.)

We opened for them at Cain's Ballroom in Tulsa, Oklahoma. Cain's has been around since the 1930s and was the original home of Bob Wills and the Texas Playboys. (And yes, the irony of The *Texas* Playboys headquartered in Oklahoma is not lost on me.) Almost every well-known country performer from Hank Williams Sr. to George Jones played this club. By the late 70's the ballroom was booking a wide variety of acts from country and jazz to The Sex Pistols. It's a splendid venue - all wood floors and air conditioned, it was a magical place to be. The spirits of all those great performers just made it fantastic. It has a great stage, great dressing rooms, great everything except for people we had to perform with that night. (Oops, sorry Mom. I said something bad about someone.)

We got to Tulsa early and began our usual pre-show warm up by throwing a football around the huge, empty ballroom for hours. We had one of those smaller foam footballs with which you could throw a perfect spiral for thirty yards. The Boomtown Rats were setting up as we passed the ball around the ballroom. They did not get what we were doing. We told them it was called football, and they said "no it isn't." (I now know that Britishers call soccer "football". What do they know? They call an elevator a lift and a truck a lorrie.) I suppose if we had a soccer ball or a cricket ball and bat, they would have understood. "This is America", I shouted as I threw the football to Dan Green the guitar player, who caught it and spiked it. The Rats already didn't like us and now they liked us even less.

We had done shows with them in Austin, Houston and Dallas for a few nights before this. They resented us big-time because the local Texas audiences were fans of ours and many of them actually came to hear Kenny and the Kasuals. As The Boomtown Rats performed in Dallas, some audience members were waving their Kenny and the Kasuals "Impact" album covers in the air to the beat of the music, and yelling for us to come back on.

Let me make it clear — the audiences liked The Rats, but were already fans of ours. They weren't trying to insult those guys or anything. But The Rats thought the audience was really putting them down and it ticked them right off.

The Boomtown Rats let us know that they simply hated us. We thought it was hilarious. So, we went around Tulsa and put up Kenny and the Kasuals fliers all over the city. We covered the telephone poles all over town, with posters announcing that we were playing at Cain's. (Gee whiz, I guess we forgot to mention The Boomtown Rats in the posters.) Then in retaliation, The Rats went around town and drew moustaches on my picture on the posters and wrote some pretty awful stuff on them.

It was war! We would repel the attack of the British just as we had in the Revolutionary Days! But without guns or violence or anything. Instead as The Boomtown Rats took the stage, we noticed that their management company had sent a sumptuous buffet into their dressing room for The Rats to enjoy after the show. They had a table that must have been close to thirty feet long filled with everything from lobster and steak to fresh veggies, multiple desserts and all the trimmings. It was a feast. Or at least it should have been. After we got through feasting at their expense, we had a food fight that ended with us dancing and prancing along the length of their banquet table. Then we split. Fast.

After that tour we played quite a few more gigs – a college concert in Nacogdoches, opening for The Guess Who in San Antonio while drunk as skunks from our all day booze-a-thon on The Riverwalk. We played in Lubbock where we ended up owing more for beer than we made. We also performed in Fort Worth in front of 20,000 fansand then recorded a hot, live concert at a Sound Warehouse store – that recording has recently been released as our "Battlezone" CD.

"Shortly after that we had all had enough of no money and Mark Lee," Dan says. "This short-lived '78-'79 version of Kenny and the Kasuals disbanded in May."

With an almost entirely new line-up I reformed the Kasuals and went on the road again. This group consisted of Alan McDaniel on guitar, Jerry Smith on bass, Danny Duncan on drums and me on rhythm guitar and harmonica. We went on a tour of the country and played with some exceptional performers of the era including Iggy Pop, Patti Smith and The Runaways.

The lure of the highway was really starting to lose its luster, and soon we were back in Dallas. Mark Lee had opened a punk-club on Maple Avenue that is still legendary in Dallas. He called it The Hot Klub and Kenny and the Kasuals (the punked out version) became the virtual house band. The Klub closed in 1983.

Again, there were good times, there were bad times. Most of those times I can't remember and some of the ones I can remember, I can't repeat among mixed company. Eventually the punk years just faded away and I went back to making music the way I began – with good old sixties style rhythm and blues and rock.

"Punk rock is a word used by dilettantes...about music that takes up the energies, the bodies, the hearts, the souls, the time and the minds of young men who give everything they have to it."
Iggy Pop

Alan, Jerry, Kenny and Danny – The second punk version of the band.

Kenny, Jerry and Lee, 2010

Chapter Fifteen
Still Stompin' After All These Years

Lee, drummer Dennis "Boom" Howard, Kenny and Dan Green

After forming once in the sixties, once again in the seventies, Kenny and the Kasuals re-formed one more time in the late 1980s and have been going strong ever since. As the kids who danced to the music of the Kasuals at The Studio Club in the mid-sixties grew into successful adults, their tendency to look back with nostalgia took hold. But now they had the discretionary income to pay to relive those glory days. The band began to reappear, first at club gigs and private parties, then at high school reunions all over North Texas.

In the twenty-first century Kenny and the Kasuals have played at several festivals and rock-revival concerts such as The Ponderosa Stomp in New Orleans, The Hippiefest, South by Southwest and the "Rocking Into Summer" concert at the Lakewood Theater in Dallas.

Class reunions are a big part of The Kasuals schedule now. As of this writing (the year 2015) anyone who wants to book the Kasuals would be well advised to call six months in advance for any weekend night in the summer – the season of high school reunions. Club dates fill up the rest of the year with appearances at The Balcony Club, The Lakewood Bar and Grill and The Lone Star Café as the most regular gigs.

Kenny the Country Gentleman

Kenny, Lee and Paul are still the mainstays of the performing band and they still sound as good as ever. The original five-piece band is now usually six or more at reunions and large events. Other local musicians of the sixties era like Dan Green and Dennis Howard make up the "new" members. For years Rollie Anderson was often featured with the band at the larger gigs.

"I've played rock n roll music for over forty-five years!" Paul mused recently. "When I started playing I never dreamed it would last this long. However, one gig we played recently was a real wake-up call – a grand opening for a retirement community! The best comment of the day was from Lee Lightfoot who said 'this is surreal...' Actually I found it more like being in a Fellini movie – just freaking weird. One thing I have learned about aging is that you are only as old as you think you are and since my mental age is about 19, I'm in real trouble there. But I've decided to try a different mental approach to performing. I'm still going to do all the gigs with Kenny and The Kasuals, but I think we should add 'retirement communities' onto the list of venues that we play. This seems like a logical progression for an aging musician doesn't it? From 'sex, drugs and rock n roll' to 'early bird specials, prescribed medication and rock n roll'."

Kenny and the Kasuals

1965   *1985*

Above: At the House of Blues in New Orleans, 2007
Lower: On stage, 2008

Kenny and the Kasuals - 2010

Above: The Kasuals played at "Hippiefest" at the Nokia Theater in 2010.
Below: Some of the Hippiefest performers backstage, including Flo and Eddie (The Turtles), Mitch Ryder (in the sunglasses), Rod Argent and Colin Blunstone (The Zombies).
Kenny is second from left, front row.

Kenny, Ted and John with Rollie at the top,
sometime in the mid 1980s

Rollie and Kenny, 2010

Kenny and the Kasuals and Related Discography and Lists

Singles

Nothin' Better to Do / Floatin' – Mark Records #911-1

Don't Let Your Baby Go / The Best Thing Around – Mark #1002

It's All Right / You Make Me Feel So Good – Mark #1003

Raindrops to Teardrops / Strings of Time – Mark #1004

Journey To Tyme / I'm Gonna Make It – Mark Ltd. M-1006

Journey To Tyme / I'm Gonna Make It – United Artists 50085

See Saw Ride / As I Knew – Mark Ltd. M-1008

Chimes on 42nd Street / As I Knew (Truth) – #1009

LPs:

IMPACT

1. Chicago 60616
2. Money
3. All Day All of The Night
4. You Make Me Feel So Good
5. I'm Not Talking
6. Empty Heart
7. Its All Right
8. Gloria
9. You Better Move On
10. Baby Please Don't Do
11. Got a Good Thing Going
12. Farmer John

TEEN DREAMS
1. See Saw Ride
2. Strings of Time
3. Things Gettin' Better
4. As I Knew
5. Everything Seems Fine
6. Come Tomorrow
7. Revelations
8. Raindrops to Teardrops
9. I'm Gonna Make It
10. And There You Were
11. Come On Kid
12. Can't Keep From Crying
13. Who Stole My House
14. Journey to Tyme

KENNY AND THE KASUALS ARE BACK
(7 INCH, 331/3 EP)
I Love To Go Flying / Early Warning
C'mon Shake It / Live At Casa Chaos

GARAGE KINGS

1. Shake It
2. Out of Control
3. Makes no Difference
4. Everybody's Making It
5. Discogoer
6. Candy Little Girl
7. I love to go Flying
8. Why Did We Ever Call It Love
9. Lost Women (live)
10. Jesus (Arms of Love)

NO EXIT

1. Oh Sharon
2. Candy Girl
3. Everything Seems Fine
4. Shake it
5. You Better Move On
6. Hot Rod Holly
7. Have Your Hand Stamped at the Door
8. Next Saturday Night
9. Kids Stuff
10. Never See My Name

SUMMERFIELD – **LOST TAPES**
1973-1976

1. Too Bad
2. Like It Used To Be
3. Greeneyes
4. That's You
5. Oh Nelly
6. Jealousy
7. What Is and What Should Never Be
8. Easy Rolling
9. Texas Man
10. I'd Like To Get To You Know You
11. Piano Man
12. CIF
13. Austin
14. Country Tune
15. Sweet Lady

BATTLEZONE (LIVE)

1. Lost Women Blues
2. I'm So Excited
3. Outta Control
4. Klassified Lover
5. Disco Goer
6. Break The Rules
7. Early Warning
8. (Don't) Crack Your Whip On Me
9. Live at Casa Chaos
10. Journey to Tyme

Performers With Whom Kenny and the Kasuals Have Played

Steppenwolf
The Guess Who
Sonny and Cher
The Beach Boys (three times!)
Herman Hermits
The Casinos
The Buckinghams
Iggy Pop
Joe Perry
The Cars
Leon Russell
Chicago
The Ramones
Crosby and Nash
Little Feat
The Selectors
Tommy Tutone
The Yardbirds
Mitch Ryder
Jimmy Reed
Spanky and our Gang
The Spencer Davis Group
The Moody Blues
Rod Stewart
Jimmy Vaughn
Stevie Ray Vaughn
Doyle Bramhall
Willie Nelson
The Nitty Gritty Dirt Band
The Lovin' Spoonful
The Go Go's
Joan Jett
Patty Smith

Boom Town Rats
Elvis Costello
Little Richard
The Young Rascals
George Thorogood
Pure Prairie League
Creedence Clearwater Revival
Gary Myrick
Bugs Henderson
Johnny Nitzinger
Chuck Berry
The Romantics
The Police
Eddie Money
Neil Diamond
Marc Benno
Iron Butterfly
The Zombies
Badfinger
Mitch Ryder
The Turtles (Flo and Eddie)
Lesley West and Mountain
Country Joe and the Fish
The Freddy Steady 5
Ace Cannon
Scotty Moore
Dale Hawkins
James Burton
Mouse and the Traps
The 13th Floor Elevators
ZZ Top
The Dixie Chicks
Corky Lang
Pantera
The Chessmen
The Five Americans

Roy Head
Bo Diddley
Archie Bell
Little Freddy King
Fever Tree
Denny Freeman

PART TWO
THE GARAGE BAND REVOLUTION
OF THE SIXTIES

What follows is a compilation of lists,
facts, figures, memories and more, all
pertaining to the "Garage Band Era"
we've covered in this book.

Think of it all as an "extended appendix",
wherein you can find something about
almost every garage band that ever was.

The Seeds of Time

(Rock Opinions, Appendix and Highly Biased Lists)

Subjects:
1. Dallas Music
2. North Texas Discography
3. Texas Music
5. Sounds Like The Sixties To Me
6. Garage Bands – More Than You Ever Wanted to Know

The Jokers

"I don't care much about music. What I like is sounds."
Dizzy Gillespie

DALLAS MUSIC

The Dallas Top 20

The hottest local hits by D-FW artists of the 50s and 60s, in alphabetical order. Each artist is given one mention, though some had several local hits.

Big Blue Diamonds — Gene Summers
Several hits in Dallas, but he never cracked the national charts.

Can You See Me — The Briks
Leader Richard Borgens later joined the Kasuals.

Dance Franny Dance — The Floyd Dakil Combo
They planned to record on the stage of The Pit Club, but ended up recording in the ladies room because the acoustics were so cool there.

Didn't We Have A Good Time — The Mystics

Do It Again — Jon and Robin and the In Crowd
Jon was Jon Abnor whose father owned the record label.

I See The Light — The Five Americans
Their national hit was *Western Union*.

If You Really Want Me To I'll Go — The RonDels
Hot band from Fort Worth featured Delbert McClinton. They began as The Straightjackets.

Journey To Tyme – Kenny and the Kasuals
It seems to me that I've heard of this band, but I can't remember exactly where.

Midnight Hour – Kit and the Outlaws
Kit Massingill led this North Dallas band.

A Public Execution – Mouse and the Traps
Ronnie "Mouse" Weiss was the Dylanesque lead singer.

The Right To Rock – Trini Lopez
The superstar is from Dallas and began his recording career locally.

Rollin' Dynamite – Scotty McKay
With just average vocal pipes, he was blessed with great looks and unstoppable ambition. Kenny and the Kasuals recorded this song in the seventies.

Sen-Sa-Shun – The Sensors
Bugs Henderson was the lead guitarist. 'Nuff said.

She Said Yeah - The Tracers (aka The Trycerz)
They had a local hit with this Stones album cut (which was co-written by Sonny Bono using the name Sonny Christy – a little songwriter trivia for ya.)

Slippery When Wet – The Diminshuns
From Bryan Adams High School

The Smell Of Incense – The Southwest FOB
England Dan and John Ford Coley came out of this band.

Summer's Comin' – Kirby St. Romain
Big hit in Dallas, made it to the national charts in
1963.

Wine Wine Wine – The Nightcaps
THE rock 'n' blues band in Dallas in the late 50s and
early '60s. Billy Joe Shine (vocals), Jack Allday
(drums),
Mario Daboub (bass), Gene Haufler (rhythm guitar)
and
Dave Swartz (lead guitar). Other regional hits
included
24 Hours and *Thunderbird.*

You're Gonna Be Lonely – The Chessmen
Jimmie Vaughan and Doyle Bramhall were the leaders
of this band.

(You're Mine) We Belong Together – Jimmy Velvit
This song came on the radio and thousands of Texas
teenagers said "listen, they're playing our song."

Spotlight On T-Bone Walker (1910 – 1975)

What symbolized rock and roll more than the electric guitar? It is the ultimate weapon of the rock revolution.

Although he was not the very first to use an electric guitar (Les Paul, Charlie Christian and others beat him to it), Aaron Thibeaux "T-Bone" Walker was the first to adapt its use to rockin' blues. A consummate showman, T-Bone not only was all over the guitar, but the guitar was all over him – behind his head, between his legs and anywhere else he could put it and still play. Chuck Berry credits Walker with his inspiration for playing the instrument and playing *with* the instrument.

In fact, every blues guitarist or rocker who followed him owes the rock and roll guitar sound to T-Bone Walker. Born in Linden, Texas he moved to the Oak Cliff section of Dallas early on. Recording first in Dallas as a teenager, he was originally billed as "Oak Cliff T-Bone".

Twenty-Five Essential Bones

Wichita Falls Blues - 1929 (first recording)
T-Bone Blues - 1940
Mean Old World - 1942
I'm Still In Love With You - 1945
Bobby Sox Baby - 1946
Call It Stormy Monday 1948
Long Skirt Baby Blues 1948
I'm Waiting For Your Call 1948
West Side Baby 1948
T-Bone Shuffle - 1949
T-Bone Boogie - 1945
I'm In An Awful Mood - 1946
T-Bone Jumps Again - 1947
I Want A Little Girl - 1949

Strollin' With Bone - 1950
Travelin' Blues - 1950
I Got The Blues Again - 1951
Street Walkin' Woman - 1952
Blue Mood - 1952
Bye Bye Baby - 1954
Strugglin' Blues - 1954
Papa Ain't Salty - 1955
T-Bone Blues (remake) -1955
Evenin' - 1957
Two Bones And A Pick – 1959

T-Bone Walker

Hot Shots of the '50s, '60s and '70s Who Are From The Dallas Area

Michael Nesmith
Michael Martin Murphey
B.W. Stevenson
Ray Wyle Hubbard
Denny Freeman
England Dan and John Ford Coley
Rocky and Dusty Hill
Rocky Erickson
Boz Scaggs
Steve Miller
Trini Lopez
Jimmie Vaughan
Stevie Ray Vaughan

Jimmie Vaughan and Stevie Ray Vaughan

A Recording History of North Texas Rock Bands and Performers of the Sixties

(Unless otherwise noted, the performers are from Dallas)

The American Blues
If Were A Carpenter / All I Saw Was You (Karma 101) (1969)
Shakin' All Over - Unreleased (1967)
One Too Many Mornings - Unreleased (1967)
Psychotic Reaction - Unreleased (1967)
LP: *American Blues Is Here* - Karma 1001 LP (1968)

The Antons
Larry's Tune / Green Eyes – Ty-Tex 104

The Bards (Ft. Worth)
Alibis / Thanks A Lot Baby (Emcee 013) (1966)

The Barking Spyders
I Want Your Love / Hard World - Audio Precision 4201

The Barons (Ft. Worth)
You're Gonna Get Hurt / I'll Never Be Happy – Torch 102
Live And Die / Don't Look Back - Torch 103 45 - (1965)
Don't Burn It / I Hope I Please You - Brownfield 1035 (1966)
Without Her - Torch 101 45 - (1966)
Don't Blame Me – Unreleased - (1966)
You're On My Mind

The Bear Fax
Love Is A Beautiful Thing / *I Wanna Do It* - Fuzz 0901
(1966)
Out Of Our Tree / *Turn Over* - Fuzz 4141

The Beefeaters
Don't Hurt Me - Unreleased - (1967)

The Benders
Sharpest Little Girl / *Lost It Again* - Jamaka 640J-1927
(1965)

Berry Street Station with Carole Sullivan
I Don't Care No More / *King Bee* – LeCam 630
Chest Fever / *One* – LeCam
Chest Fever / *Maybe I'm Amazed* – Charay 306

The Big Sounds
Go Ahead & Cry - San Dun 003/4 – (1965)

The Boards
You're A Better Man Than I / *Please Tell Me Why* –
Yardly 400 (1966)

The Boys (Fort Worth)
You Deceived Me / *When I Think* - (Emcee 015/016)
(1966)

The Briks
Can You See Me? / *Foolish Baby* - Bismarck 1013 (1966)
Can You See Me? / *Foolish Baby* - Dot 16876   (1966)
NSU / *From A Small Room* Bismarck 1020 (1967)
Keep Down - Unreleased (1967), *It's Your Choice* –
    Unreleased (1967)
I'm Losing - Unreleased

Debbie Brimer (Linden)
I Turned To The Bottle / *Hotel Happiness* - Danrite 103
(1963)

The Brimstones
It's All Over Now But The Cryin' / *What Is This Life* -
MGM 13653 45 (1966)

The British Colonels
Come Back - Unreleased

Bruce & Patty
Thanks – Charay 102

Brym-Stones Ltd. (Tyler)
Times Gone By / *You'll Be Mine* – Custom 143

The Buccaneers
You Got What I Want / *Standing in the Shadow Of Your
Love* – Sevens Int. 1007 (1966)

The By Fives
I Saw You Walking / *That's How Strong My Love Is* –
Tomi 106 (1966)

The Canadian Rogues (recorded in Ft. Worth)
Oop-Poop-A-Doop / *Keep In Touch* – Charay 5017 (1966)
Do You Love Me? / *Mickey's Monkey* – Rogue (1967)

Casper and the Ghosts
Rockin' Around the Tombstone

The Cast of Thousands
(featuring Stevie Ray Vaughan)
Have It Your Way / *Power Vested In Me* (Soft 1002)
(1967)

My Jenny Wears A Mini / Girl What You Gonna Do –
Soft 1002 (1966)
My Jenny Wears A Mini / Girl What You Gonna Do –
Tower 276 (1966)
Long Way To Go / Carter's Grove – Amy 11-040
Country Garden s / The Cast's Blue – Amy 11-056

The Cavaliers
Turntable / Wow – Soft 1025
It's Up To You Girl / Wow – Soft 1025

Cellar Dwellers (Ft. Worth)
Bad Day / Call - Steffek 1921 - (1968)

Changing Times
*She Don't Know About Me And You, Near You Babe,
Life's A Game* (all Unreleased, (1966)

The Chants
Elaina / Hypnotized - B.Ware 869-1 (1966)

The Chaparrals
So Good, Blues From and Airplane (unreleased at the
time.)

The Chaps
Jemima Surrender / Ozark Smokehouse - Soft 1032
Maybe I'm Amazed / Wait A Minute – Soft 1032 -
(1969)
Golden Slumbers / Carry That Weight - Soft 1033
Get Me Off This Plane In Time / Little Red Wagon - Soft
1043
To Kingdom Come / Wait A Minute - Soft 1032 (1969)

The Chessmen
Save The Last Dance For Me / *Dreams And Wishes* (Bismarck 1010) (1966)
I Need You There / *Sad* - (Bismarck 1012) (1966)
You're Gonna Be Lonely / *No More* – Bismarck 1014 (1966)
No More / *When You Lost Someone You Loved* - Bismarck 1015 (1966)

Charles Christy and the Crystals (Fort Worth)
Will I Find Her / *Cherry Pie* – HBR 45 (1965)
In The Arms Of A Girl / *Young and Beautiful* – HBR 473 (1966)
Also recorded: *I'm Down, For Your Love*
As Charles Christy and the Martians:
Come On Baby – Mammal 200

Chocolate Moose
Chocolate Moose Theme / *Take a Ride* – Spotlight 1012 (1966)
Half Peeled Banana – Spotlight 1015 (1966)

The Coachmen (Dallas?)
Mr. Moon / *Nothing At All* - Bear 1974 – (1966)
Linda Lou / *I'm A King Bee* - Bear 1976 – (1966)

The Counts
Surfer's Paradise / *Chug-A-Lug* – Manco 1060 (1964)

Court Jesters
Drive Me Crazy / *I'll Play Your Silly Game* – Jester 2034

Crowd Plus One (Fort Worth)
Mary Ann Regrets / *Whatcha Trying to Do To Me?* – Box 6604

The Cynics (Ft. Worth)
You're A Better Man Than I / Train Kept A Rollin' –
Bear 001 (1967)
I'll Go - Hue 375 (1967)

Floyd Dakil (The Floyd Dakil Combo, The Floyd
Dakil Five, and the Pitmen)
Dance Franny Dance / Look What You've Gone and Done -
    Jetstar 103 (1964)
*Dance, Franny, Dance / Look What You've Gone And
Done* – Guyden 2111 (1964)
*Dance, Franny, Dance / Look What You've Gone And
Done* – Earth 402 (1965)
Bad Boy / Stoppin' Traffic - Earth 403 (1965)
Kitty Kitty / It Takes A Lot To Hurt - Earth 404 (1965)
Stronger Than Dirt / You're The Kind Of Girl – (1965)
Merry Christmas Baby I'm Coming Home / One Girl –
    Pompeii 66687

The Floyd Dakil Five

The Diminshuns (Jimmy Herbert, Tim Cooper, Mike Davis, James Anderson)
Firewater / *Slippery When Wet* – Division 101 (1961)

The Dirte Four (Fort Worth)
Hang Up / *On the Move* - Charay-34
On the Move / *I Want to Give You All* - Charay

Dust
Vicious Delusion / *Signed DC* (unreleased at the time)

Electric Love (Ft. Worth)
This Seat Is Saved / *Gotta Get Back To My Baby* - Charay 40

The Elite (Fort Worth)
One Potato / *Two Potato* - Charay 17 (1966)
My Confusion / *I'll Come To You* (Charay 31) (1967)
Bye Bye Baby / *All I Want Is You* (Charay 56) (1967)

The Esquires (Irving)
Come On Come On / *Loneliness is Mine* –
    Glenvalley 103 (1966)

Come On Come On / Loneliness Is Mine – Texan 103
(1966)
Time Don't Mean So Much / Summertime –
  Glenvalley 104 (1966)
Judgement Day / These Are The Tender Years – Glenvalley
105 (1966)

The Excels (McKinney)
Walking The Dog / Let's Dance - Gibson 210 (1965)
Merchant of Love / The First Kiss – Gibson (1965)

The Exotics
Morning Sun / Fire Engine Red - Monument 984 (1966)
Come With Me / Hymn To Her TAD 2410 (1967)
Queen Of Shadows / I Was Alone TAD 6701 (1967)

The Fabs
That's The Bag I'm In / Dinah Wants Religion –
Cottonball 1005 (1967)

The Fabulous Five (Tyler)
Girl Of My Dreams / We're In Love - Custom 157-1

The Felicity (Denton) (featuring Don Henley)
Hurtin' / I'll Try It - Regency 974 (1967)
Hurtin' / I'll Try It - Wilson 101 – (1967)
*Jennifer / Simple Little Down-Home Rock 'n' Roll Love
Song For Rosie* – (1968)

Jerry Fisher & The Nightbeats
I've Got to Find Somebody To Love
I've Got To Be A Singing Star – Three Speed 714

The Five

I Don't Care If It Rains All Night / *She Doesn't Love Me Anymore* - Britian 100 (1966)

The Five Americans

It's You Girl / *I'm Gonna Leave Ya* – Jetstar 104 (1965)
I'm Feeling O.K ./ *Slippin' and Slidin'* – Jetstar 105 (1966)
Show Me/*Love Love Love* – ABC-Paramount 10686 (1965)
Abnak AB-106 - Five Americans - *Say That You Love Me*/*Without You*
I See the Light / *The Outcast* – Abnak AB-109
I See The Light / *The Outcasts* HBR 454
EVOL Not Love / *Don't Blame Me* (HBR 468) (1966)
Good Times / *The Losing Game* (HBR 483) (1966)
Reality / *Sympathy* (Abnak 114) (1967)
If I Could / *Now That It's Over* (Abnak 116) (1967)
Western Union / *Now That It's Over* (Abnak 118) (1967)
Sound Of Love / *Sympathy* (Abnak 120) (1967)
Zip Code / *Sweet Bird Of Youth* (Abnak 123) (1967)
Stop Light / *Tell Ann I Love Her* (Abnak 125) (1967)
7.30 Guided Tour / *See-Saw Man* (Abnak 126) (1968)
No Communication / *Rainmaker* (Abnak 128) (1968)
Lovin' Is Livin' / *Con Man* (Abnak 131) (1968)
Generation Gap / *The Source* (Abnak 132) (1968)
Virginia Girl / *Call On Me* (Abnak 134) (1969)
Ignert Woman / *Scrooge* (Abnak 137) (1969)
I See The Light '69 / *Red Cape* (Abnak 139) (1969)
She's Too Good To Me / *Molly Black* (Abnak 142) (1969)

The Five of a Kind

Never Again / *I Don't Want To Find Another Girl* – Vandan 3668 (1966)

The Five of a Kind from Bryan Adams High School

The Four Speeds (Linden)
(Don Henley, Richard Bowden, Jerry Surratt, Fred Neese)
Variety / *El Santa* - Crabbe Records (1964),
Why Did You Leave me / *Bedrock* - Crabbe Records (1964)

Front Page News (Ft. Worth)
You Better Behave / *Thoughts* - Dial 4052 (1967)

The G's (Denton)
There's A Time / *Cause She's My Girl* - Young Generation 108 (1966)

The Galaxies (Garland)
(Bubba Tomlinson, Bobby Lake, Robert Foster, Ken Pugh & Ray Windt)

Beg Me, Makin' Money, Someone to Love You, Surfin' Back to School, Roll over Beethoven, Night Train, Think About the Good Times, Lucille, Beg Me, Tell Me I'm the Most, Little Girl Make up Your Mind, You Better Don't, Back in the U.S.A,. The Door Is Open, Whole Lotta Shakin' Going On, Only Child, It's All Wrong, Stuck on Lovin' You, Let Me In, She Blows My Mind, Round and Round, Gitchy Gitchy Goo, The Late

Gator Shades Blues Band (Kenny and the Kasuals & Scotty McKay)
Down in Mexico – Mark Ltd. 2000

Johnny Gee and the G-Men
You Got The Nerve / *If You'll Be Mine* – Nu-Child 101
Boys Don't Cry / *Yes I'm Loving You* – Emit E303

The Gentlemen
It's A Cry'n Shame / *You Can't Be True* - Vandan 8303

The Gnats (Fort Worth)
That's Alright / *The Girl* - Emcee 014 (1966)

The Gretta Spoone Band
I Do Believe You're Dreaming / *Close Your Eyes* –
   Pompeii 66694 (1968)

The Guys Five
Talking About Freedom / *I'm Gonna Find It* - Ara 1916
(1966)

The Guys Five (yeah I know there's only four of them!)

Bob Haydon
Hey Suzanne / Gonna Go – Knight 1046
[Bob Haydon was an original member of The Marksmen, the Dallas high school band which featured Steve Miller and Boz Scaggs.]

The Hear and Now
The Hear and Now (LP) – Pompeii

The Heard (Longview – recorded in Tyler)
Exit 9 / You're Gonna Miss Me – One Way

The Heartbreakers
Hold On I'm Comin' / Going Out Of My Head – Tomi 119
I'll Show You How To Love Me / Mustang Sally – Tomi 121

The Highlifes
Choose Me Over Him / *No One To Tell Her* – Pit 403 (1966)

The Images (Ft. Worth)
My Kinda Woman / *A Swingin' Summer* - Music Mill 404

Jack & The Rippers (Fort Worth)
Jack The Ripper - Jade 8420

The Jackals
Love Times Eight – (1966) (unreleased at the time)

The Jades (Fort Worth)
I'm Alright / *Till I Do* - Ector 101 (1965)
Sha-La-La-Lee / *I'm Coming Home* - Strawberry 10 (1966)
Little Girl / *Mercy, Mercy* - Emcee 012/13 (1966)
Also recorded: *Run and Hide, Don't Bring Me Down, Sometimes Good Guys Don't Wear White, 96 Tears, Time Won't Let Me , Midnight Hour, Don't Let Me Be Misunderstood, Good Lovin'.*

The Jades

Jimmy C and the Chelsea Five
(Jimmy Holbert, Scotty Celsur, Randy Ridell, Mike Farr, Sammy Simmons)
Play With Fire / *Leave Me Alone* – Zero Z-1003 (1965)

The Jinx
Mister You're A Better Man Than I
I Can't Go On Loving You
Come On Up (all Unreleased 1966)

Jon & Robin & The In-Crowd
Lonely One / How Come - Abnak AB-111
If I Need Someone—It's You / I Can't Make It With You –
    Abnak AB-113
Hey Girl / If I Need Someone—It's You –
    Abnak AB-115
Do It Again A Little Bit Slower / If I Need Someone—It's
You - Abnak AB-119
(as The In Crowd) - *Big Cities / Inside Out* - Abnak AB-121
Drums / You Don't Care - Abnak AB-122

I Want Some More / *Love Me Baby* (1968) - Abnak AB-124

Dr. Jon (The Medicine Man) / *Love Me Baby* - Abnak AB-127

(As The In Crowd)- *Hangin' From Your Lovin' Tree* / *Let's Take A Walk* - Abnak AB-129

You Got Style / *Thursday Morning* - Abnak AB-130

Save Me, Save Me/*Thursday Morning* - Abnak AB-133

Gift of Love/ *Gift Of Love* - Abnak AB-135

(As Robin) - *Dirty Old Man* / *Honey Bee* — Abnak AB-136

Give Me Your Love/*Lonely One* - Abnak AB-138

There's An American Flag On The Moon, Part 1 / *There's An American Flag On The Moon, Part 2* — Abnak AB-140

If You've Got it Flaunt It / *I'll Come Running to You* — Abnak AB-141

Jim Jones & the Chaunteys (Ft. Worth)

Baby (Better Get On Home) / *Together* - Keye 10 - (1966)

She's a Doll / *Kiwi Boogie* — Manco 1068

Playboy / *The Rains Came* — Pacemaker 242

Turn On Your Love Light / *If You Knew How To Start* — Capri 516

Sweet Dreams of You / *Baby May I Love You* - Sunglow
    Next Exit / *One Fine Mice* — Sunglow SG-131

Jim Jones and the Chaunteys

Just Us Five
Tennessee Stud / I'm So Lonesome I Could Cry —
WA Records 111

Ronnie Kelly
Tough / This Boy – Charay 101

Kempy and the Guardians
Love For a Price / Never - Lucky Sound 13 (1966)
Love For a Price / Never - Romunda 1 (1966)

Kenny and the Kasuals
(See the Full Kenny and the Kasuals Discography above)

Kit and the Outlaws
Midnight Hour / Don't Tread On Me - BlacKnight 902
(1966)

Midnight Hour / *Don't Tread On Me* – Philips 40420
(1966)
Worlds Apart / *Fun, Fame And Fortune* – In 102 (1966)
No Doubt About It / *Mama's Gone* – Empire 1 (1967)

Kit and the Outlaws

The Knights
Stay / *I Know It Now* - Knight 1050

The Kommotions (Garland)
Little Black Egg (unreleased at the time?)

Lady Wilde (see The Warlocks)

Larry & The Blue Notes (Fort Worth)
She'll Love Me / *Everybody Needs Somebody* - Charay 20
(1966)
She'll Love Me / *The Phantom* – Charay C 20
There's No Other / *You Cheated, You Lied* - Charay
In And Out / *Love Is A Beautiful Thing* - Charay

In And Out / I'll Be True To You - Charay 44 (1965)
Love Is a Beautiful Thing / I'll Be True to You –
    Charay 44 (1966)
In And Out / No Milk Today - Charay 44 (1966)
Love Is A Beautiful Thing / In And Out - Charay 44
(1966)
Night Of The Phantom - 20th Century Fox 573 (1965)
Night Of The Sadist (Unreleased) (1965)
Everybody Needs Somebody / Talk About Love –
    Charay 20 45 (1966)
Everybody Needs Somebody - Epic 9871 45 (1966)
Train Kept A Rolling - Unreleased (1966)
What Made Me Lose My Head - Unreleased (1965)

The Living End (Fort Worth)
Gotta Get Back To My Baby / I Got To Have It Girl –
    Soft 1012
You Make Me Free / Your Kind Of Love – Soft 1031
Today / You Don't Want Me – Soft 1033
I Got To Have It Girl / Society - Soft
Society / The World's Goin' Round – Soft
Foolish People / Life Is A Search – Shalimar 303

The London Fog
The London Fog (LP) - Pompeii

Loose Ends (Ft. Worth)
A Free Soul / He's A Nobody - Mala 538 (1966)
Free Soul / He's A Nobody - Decade 6601 (1966)

Jesse Lopez (brother of Trini)
My Way – Hoda 8888
It's Gone / Do I Love You - Hoda 8891
Lookin' So Much Better / Little Bitty Pretty One –
    Dot 17065 (1968)

Trini Lopez

The Right To Rock / Just Once More - Volk V-101 (1958)
Yes, You Do/My Runaway Heart – King 5173 (1959)
Since I Don't Have You / Rock On - King 5187 (1959)
Here Comes Sally / Love Me Tonight - King 5198 (1959)
I'm Grateful /Don't Let Your Sweet Love Die –
     King 5234 (1959)
The Club for Broken Hearts/Nobody Loves Me –
     King 5824 (1959)
(Won't You Be) My Queen for a Day/Yes You Do –
     King 5849 (1959)
Nobody Loves Me/Nobody Listens to Our Teenage Problems
– King 5284 (1960)
Sweet Thing/Chain of Love - King 5304 (1960)
Jeanie Marie/Schemer - King 5324 (1960)
The Search Goes On /It Hurts To Be in Love – King 5344
(1960)
Then You Know/Don't Treat Me That Way – King 5418
(1960)
You Broke The Only Heart/One Heart One Life One Love
– King 5487 (1961)
Rosita / Only In My Dreams - DRA 7008 (1961)
Jeanie Marie /Love Me Tonight - King 5801 (1963)
Don't Go/It Seems - King 5820 (1963)
Nobody Loves Me/The Club For Broken Hearts –
     King 5824 (1963)
Yes You Do/Won't You Be My Queen For A Day –
     King 5849 (1964)

LPs:

King 863 "Teenage Love Songs" (1963)

The Lynx (Tyler)

You Lie / She's My Woman - Thunderball 135 (1966)

Scotty McKay (AKA Max Lipscomb, 1937 – 1991)

Rollin' Dynamite / Evenin' Time - Event E-4295
    Parkway 806 (1959)

Rollin' Dynamite / Evenin' Time (1959)

Midnight Cryin' Time / Little Lump Of Sugar (1960)
    Swan S-4049

I've Been Thinkin' / It's A Funny Thing - (1960) Lawn L
102

Little Liza Jane / Let The Good Times Roll - (1960) Ace
603

Brown Eyed Handsome Man / Cry Me A River - (1960)
    Ace 608

Ole King Cole / Pull Down The Sky – Ace 623 (1961)

I've Got My Eyes On You / Shattered Dreams - Ace 636
(1961)

You're So Square/The Girl Next Door – Squire 101
(1961)

You're So Square/The girl Next Door Went A Walkin'
    Dot-16324- (1962)

Olive Learned To Popeye/ Shame – Ace 652 (1962)

Little Miss Blue / Half A Heartache – Ace 8003 (1962)

Mess Around / Sittin' Down And Crying – Claridge-309

Mess Around / Sittin' Down And Cryin' – Philips 40109
(1963)

Dixie Doodle Dandy / Love Is Magic – Capri 508 (1964)

Mess Around / Sittin' Down and Crying - Desk 1001

You Can Dance / Let's Do It - Savannah Sound SSS 35

You Can Dance / Let's Do It - DESK 1001

Waikiki Beach / I'm Gonna Love You – Falcon 101
(1966)

Waikiki Beach / I'm Gonna Love You - HBR 495 (1966)

High on Life / If You Really Want Me To I'll Go –
    Charay 1001 (and 1004)

High on Life / If You Really Want Me To I'll Go – UNI
55205

The Train Kept A'Rollin / The Theme From The Black Cat
— Falcon FIC-101
All around the world / Here Comes Batman —
    Savannah Sound - 501
Four on the Floor — (as "The Shutdowns") - Dimension
Waikiki Beach / I'm Gonna Love You — SP HBR 495
(1966)
Truly True / Salty Water Man — Pompeii 66692
LP:
"Tonight In Person" - Ace LP-1017 - (1961)
*Sea Cruise, Roberta, Lonely Lonely Nights, I Got My Eyes
On You, Shattered Dreams, Olive Learned To Pop-Eye, Cry
Me A River, Little Liza Jane, Let The Good Times Roll,
Brown Eyed Handsome Man, You're So Square, Shame*

Billy McKnight & The Plus 4 (Tyler)
You're Doing Me Wrong / Time Wasted - Custom 127
(1966)

The Menerals (Denton)
My Flash On You - Unreleased

The Minute Men
Disillusion - TMM (no number) (1968)

The Misfits (Fort Worth)
Work Song / Turn On Your Love Light — Charay 27

The Misfits
Route 66 / No One Else - Repent 520

The Mistakes (Fort Worth)
Time Is All / Hey Baby - Spotlite 1013 (1966)

The Mistics
Memories / Without Love — Capri 531

Mitch and the Mistys
Patsy / She's So Fine - Charay
Gonna Leave / Hey Baby - Charay
I Lost My Head / Let It Be Me - Charay

The Mods
It's For You / Days Mind The Time - Cee Three 1000-01
(1966)

Mouse and the Traps
A Public Execution / All For You (Fraternity 956)
(1966)
Would You Believe? / Like I Know You Do
    (Fraternity 971) (1966)
Do The Best You Can / Promises, Promises
    (Fraternity 973) (1966)
Maid Of Sugar, Maid Of Spice / I Am The One
    (Fraternity 966) (1966)
Cryin' Inside / Ya Ya (Fraternity 989) (1967)
L.O.V.E. Love / Lie, Beg, Borrow And Steal
    (Fraternity 1000) (1967)
Sometimes You Just Can't Win / Cryin' Inside
    (Fraternity 1005) (1968)

I Satisfy / Good Times (Fraternity 1011) (1968)
Requiem For Sarah / Look At The Sun
    (Fraternity 1015) (1968)
Wicker Vine / And I Believe Her (Bell 850) (1969)
Knock On My Door / Where's The Little Girl? (Bell 870)
(1969)

The Mystics
Didn't We Have a Good Time / Now And For Always –
Spectra S-7071
Didn't We Have a Good Time / Now And For Always –
Dot 16862

The Mystics

The New Breed
Sunny / P.M. Or Later - In Crowd 001 (1967)
Big Time / Summer's Comin' – In Crowd 1234 (1967)
Little Bit Of Soul / Someone - In Crowd 1235
High Society Girl / I'd Like To See Her Again –
    Fraternity 1003 (1968)

The Noblemen
Stop Your Running Around / Bend It - CJL 1001 (1966)

My Flash On You / *Here's Where You Belong* - Kaleidoscope 001

Nobody's Children
Good Times / *Somebody Help Me* - GPC 1944

The Nomads (Fort Worth)
I Saw You Go / *I Really Do* - Soft 958
Be Nice / *Empty Heart* - Spotlight 5020 (1966)

The Novas
Coronado's Puzzles / *Lakeside Lot* – GPC 1946 (1967)
William Junior / *And It's Time* - STAR 001
Also recorded: *One Too Many Mornings, I'll Feel A Whole Lot Better, Don't Let The Sun Catch You Crying, Shake!, Bus Stop, Mr. Weatherman, Taxman, Let Me Take You To The Rainbow, Help!, I'm A Man*

The Orphans
Leader of My Mind - Fashion (1966)
(The Orphans were also managed by Mark Lee)

The Outcasts
I Gotta Find Cupid / *Mexican Maiden* - Dot 16828 - (1966)
Hava Nagilla / *I'll Keep Coming Back* - Dot 16897 - (1966)

The Outlaws
Fun, Fame & Fortune - In 102
Worlds Apart

The Passions (Sherman)
Lively One / *You've Got Me Hurtin'* - Pic 1 117

Bobby Patterson & the Mustangs

If I Didn't Have You/What's Your Problem, Baby? –
    Jetstar 107 (1967)
You Just Got To Understand/Till You Give In – Abnak
AB-112
You've Just Got To Understand/? – *Abnak* AB-117
Long Ago/Till You Give In – Jetstar 108
Let Them Talk/Soul Is Our Music – Jetstar 109 *(1968)*
I'm Leroy, I'll Take Her/Sock Some Lovin' At Me –
Jetstar 110
Broadway Ain't Funky No More/I Met My Match –
Jetstar 111
The Good Old Days/Don't Be So Mean – Jetstar 112
Busy, Busy Bee/Sweet Taste Of Love – Jetstar 113
*T.C.B. Or T.Y.A. (Take Care of Business or Turn Yourself
    Around) / What A Wonderful Night For Love* –
Jetstar 114
My Thing Is Your Thing/Keeping It In The Family – Jetstar
115
*What A Wonderful Night For Love/My Baby's Coming
Back To*
    Me – Jetstar 116
Guess Who/My Baby's Coming Back To Me – Jetstar 117
*You Taught Me How To Love / If a Man Ever Loved a
Woman* – Jetstar 119

Ricky Pearson and the Royals
Stand By Me / And Now Nothing – IRI 1309

The Penthouse Five
Bad Girl / In His Shadow - Solar 7665-4211 (1966)
*You're Gonna Make Me / Don't Mess Around With My
Dream* –
    Hawk (1967)

Pierce Arreau
Let Me Take A Ride / *Chandelier Ball* (Mark Ltd 1010)
(1967)

The Pitmen
Summertime Blues / *Susie Q* – Earth
Surf Bored / *Cruisin' Along The Highway* - Pit 402

Positively 13 O'clock (Dallas/Tyler)
Psychotic Reaction / *13 O'Clock Theme For Psychotics* –
    HBR 500 (1966)

Prophet
Oh Pretty Woman – LeCam 722

Jimmy Rabbit
Pushover / *Wait and See* – Southern Sound SS-200
(1965)
Pushover / *Wait and See* - Knight 1049 (1965)
Wishy Washy Woman / *My Girl* - Knight 1052 (1965)
Wishy Washy Woman / *My Girl* – Josie 947 (1965)

The Rain Kings
Lewis, Lewis / *Everybody Out of the Pool* / *Lydia* / *I Know
What You're Trying to Do*
    (45rpm EP on Rain Kings label) (1965)

Joe Ramirez and the Jumping Jacks
The Push / *Hey* – Diane 1005

The Reasons Why (Fort Worth)
Don't Be That Way / *Melinda* - Sound Track ST-2000

The Reveliers (Avery)
Gonna Make It By Myself / *Take It Easy* – Julie 101

The Revolvers (Tyler)
When You Were Mine / Like Me - Ty Tex 127
Good Lovin' Woman – Ty Tex

The Riels (Fort Worth)
There'll Be An Angel / Tuxedo Junction – Charay

Paul Rios and The Rivieras
You Don't Know, Like I Know / She's My Woman, She's My Girl – Ivan IV 103

The Ripples
Don't You Just Know It / Walk Don't Talk - Abnak AB-105

The Rising Suns (Fort Worth)
I'm Blue / Little Latin Lupe Lu - Unreleased (1966)

Ray Roberts & The Sonics
Together Till the End of Time / Alpine Winter – Charay 79

The Rogues
Memory of Yesterday / Something Beautiful Is Dying – Mirage 601

The Roks
Transparent Day / Hey Joe - Mark VII 1012 (1967)

The Rondels (Fort Worth)
If You Really Want Me To I'll Go/ Walk About – Brownfield -18
If You Really Want Me To I'll Go / Walk About – Smash 1986
Matilda – Tina Shalimar 104

Matilda / Tina – LeCam 130
Matilda / All My Lovin' – LeCam 307
Picture Of You / Lose Your Money – Smash 2014
100 Pounds Of Honey / Hey! Baby - Charay
Diddley Daddy – Brownfield 13
Just When You Think You're Somebody / Lover In Demand – Brownfield 16
I Lost My Love / Crying Over You – Brownfield 33

The Roots (Fort Worth)
It's Been A Long Journey / Lost One - Brownfield 22 (1966)

Roy & the Romans
Mr. Pitiful / Security – Tomi 114

The Royal Khans (Fort Worth)
Blue Mist / Spirit Of '61 – LeCam 705

The Royal Knights (Arlington)
I Wanna Know / Matilda - Nite 1005 (1965)

The Royal Lancers
Is This The Place / Donna Jean - Rize 58-101/2R

Chris St. John (Mouse and the Traps)
I've Got her Love / As Far as the Sea – Fraternity 983

Kirby St. Romain
Summer's Coming / Miss You So – Inette 103
Baby Doll / Summertime Fun - Imco 2103 (1964)
Oh Baby Doll / Summertime Fun - Tear Drop 3036

Salt and Pepper
The Real McCoy / On The Road to Love – Pompeii 6671
I'll Spend Forever Loving You / In The Morning –
    Pompeii 66693

The Sensors (Tyler)
Sen-sa-shun / Side Tracked - Ty Tex 112
Rumble / Caravan - Ty Tex 115
Bat Man / Light Blues – Ty Tex 117
Honest I Do / Honest I Do - Ty Tex 120

The Shade
All Is Gone / Big Boy Pete – Twilight 2101

Shades Of Night
Fluctuation - Alamo Audio 111 (1966)

The Shape Of Things (Waco)
Psychedelic / Shape of Things - Mark VII 1022 (1967)

The Shutdowns (see Scotty McKay)
Four on the Floor / Straightaway – Karsong 101

The Sirs (Fort Worth)
Kiss and Run / Cool – Soft 1029

Six Feet Under
Chocolate Sugar / Hot Foxy Woman – LeCam 313

The Slocum Brothers
Sugar Plum – NuSound 7319 (1966)

Smoke (Avery)
All I'm Trying To Say / She's The Taker - SMS 42673

The Snowmen (Ft. Worth)
Tubb A Tina / Garbage Man - Campa 19 (1965)

The Soul Society
Get Out My Life Woman / Knock on Wood – Showco 001

The Souncations
Respect / Exit - Head 1001 (1966)

Sounds Unlimited
Keep Your Hands Off Of It / About You - Solar 101 (1965)

Southwest FOB
The Smell Of Incense / Green Skies GPC 1945 (1968)
The Smell Of Incense / Green Skies (Hip 8002) (1968)
Nadine / All One Big Game (Hip 8009) (1968)
As I Look At You / Independent Me (Hip 8015) (1969)
Feelin' Groovy / Beggar Man (Hip 8022) (1969)
LP1968: "Smell of Incense" Hip 7001

327

Smell of Incense, Tomorrow, Rock N' Roll Woman, Downtown Woman Nadine, All One Big Game, On My Mind, Bells Of Baytown, And Another Thing.

Bobby Spears
Patience Of A Fool / Two Hearts – Manco 1042 (1963)

The Speeds (Texarkana)
I'll Go Crazy / Hurtin' - Felicity 101 (1966)

The Starfires
Everywhere I Go / Somethin' Else – Romco 104 (1963)

The Startones (Fort Worth)
Lovin' You Baby / One Rose - Billie Fran 201 (1965)

Steps Beyond (Waco)
Go On Your Way Girl / Don't Let The Sun Catch You Crying (Mark VII 1021)

Tommy Strange (Fort Worth)
Purple Desert – Shamarie S90-1 (1964)

Theze Few (see: Southwest FOB)
I Want Your Love / Dynamite - Blacknight 901 (1966)
Also recorded: *Be Kind*

Robert Thomas (Fort Worth)
Salvation / Soul of a Man - Charay 87

Those Guys (Fort Worth)
Three Days / Gone - Black Sheep 103 (1967)
Stereopsis Of a Floret / Looking At You Behind –
    Black Sheep 104 (1967)
I Want To Hold Your Hand / Teresa - Charay
You Bet It Is / Teresa – Charay

Three Guitars
I've Seen Nothin' At All / *Who Could It Be* – Manco
1066
Gee Baby / *Friendship Ring* – Ty Tex TT107

The Tortians
Red Cadillac / *Vibrations* - Karry Way 106

The Tracers
(aka The Trycerz)
She Said Yeah / *Watch Me* – Sully 928 (1966)

The Tricks (Hamilton)
Party Crasher / *Fess Up* – TSM 8321 (1966)

Truth (see: Kenny and the Kasuals)
Chimes on 42nd Street / *When Was Then* – Mark Ltd MR
1009

The Trycerz (Fort Worth)
Almost There / *Taxman* - Jan-Gi 91 (1967)

It's Gonna Change (unreleased)

The Upper Class (Fort Worth)
Can't Wait / Help Me Find A Way – Charay 68
Renee / Wow – Charay

The Uptowners (recorded in Fort Worth)
Search Is Over / If'n – Le Cam 123 (1964)
She's Mine / Down The Pike – Charay 86
Vicki / You're A Habit - LeCam 126
Cry / You're A Habit – LeCam

The US Britons
Jambalaya – Polly 201
Come On - Unreleased (1966)

The Velveteens (Fort Worth)
Ching Bam Bah / I Feel Sorry For You Baby - Golden
Artist 614.

The Visions (Mineral Wells)
Take Her / She's The Girl For Me (Vimco 20) (1966)
Take Her / Route 66 – Vimco 20
Humpty Dumpty / You Won't See Me - Vimco 21 (1967)

The Warlocks
Splash Day / Life's A Mystery (Paradise 1021)
If You Really Want Me To Stay / Good Time Trippin' Ara
1017
(As **Lady Wilde and the Warlocks** - *Another Year /
Poor Kid* (Ara 1915)

Les Watson and the Panthers
Oh Yeah / A Love Like Yours – Pompeii 6669
Soul man Blues / No peace No Rest – Pompeii 66689

Wayne & The Wise Men
Take My Advice / *Cinda* – Charay

We Few (Fort Worth)
Baby Please Don't Go, Surprise Surprise (Unreleased at the time?)

Ron Williams
Let's Stop Wasting Time / *So Fine* – TyTex (1963)
Poor Little Lamb / *Hey! Little Pearl* – Pastel P-404 (1964)
Big Boy Pete / *Runaway* - Austin A-321 (1964)

The Wilshire Express
Lose Your Money / *Carla* - Austin 322

The Wind
Don't Take Your Love Away / *Midnight in Mexico* - BlacKnight 900 (1966)

The WordD (featuring Genie Geer)
You're Gonna Make Me / *You're Always Around* – Caprice 4983 (1966)
I Saw You Walking - Unreleased (1966)
Keep On Walking - Unreleased

The Wyld (Fort Worth)
Fly By Nighter / *If I Had It* – Charay 38 (1966)
Fly By Nighter / *Lost One* – Charay 38
Lost One / *Know A Lot About Love* – Charay
Lost One / *Alley Oop* – Charay 38-1 (1967)
Know A Lot About Love / *If I Had It* - Charay 38-2) (1967)

The Zeroes
Flossie Mae / *Twistin' With Crazee Baby* – Ty-Tex 104

Top: Jimmy C and the Chelsea Five
Below: The Briks

20 Band Names That Were Actually Used
By The Rain Kings - 1964 - 1968

The Imposters
The Roaches
The Rain Kings
The Moisture Monarchs
Monkey Circus
The Rugburns
Andy Bednigo and the Dippy-Dippy Strolls
Little Patty Ann Montgomery and Her Fat
Friends
Burvis and the Wonder Guppies
The Mockingbergs
The Panama Wheatcakes
Truth Decay
Gorilla Jockeys
The Fried Shoes
Gretchen and the Japanese Luggage
The Slithy Toves
The Prairie Spiders
Solid Jackson and the Catfish
Greta Spoon & Her Magic Moustache Band
The Gretta Spoone Band

(Please don't use any of the above names for
your band. They are cursed.)

MEET THE RAIN KINGS
The First Album by Casa Linda's Phenomenal Pop Combo

Capital
Low Fidelity

Includes the Hit
"I Know What You're Trying To
Do But You Can't Get Away With It"

*Yes, the above album cover is a fake. I'm
deeply ashamed of even putting it in the book.
But not enough to actually take it out.*

TEXAS

The Top Texas Tunes

These are all Texas natives or Texas-based rock artists who enjoyed big local or national hits in the 50s & 60s. Only <u>one song</u> per performer is listed. Most of these songs were also recorded in Texas. There are no repeats in this list from the "Dallas Top 20" above.

Action Packed – Ronnie Dawson
"The Blond Bomber" sounds like he's about nine years old here. (Other rockabilly songs included *Rockin' Bones*)

Chantilly Lace – The Big Bopper
He also wrote *Running Bear* prior to his death with Buddy Holly and Ritchie Valens.

D.O.A. – Bloodrock
From Fort Worth, originally known as The Crowd + 1

Everybody Clap Your Hands – The Levee Singers (featuring Ed Bernet, Ronnie Dawson and Smokey Montgomery)

Four on the Floor – The Shutdowns
A very "California" sound for this local studio band which included (and was produced by) Scotty McKay and Kirby St. Romain.

Hey Baby – Bruce Channel
Recorded in Fort Worth

Hey Paula – Paul and Paula
Originally known as Jill and Ray.

Hide Away – Freddy King
The Texas guitar wizard also recorded songs like
San-Ho-Zay.

Hot Rock – Johnny Carroll
Rockabilly rebel who led the house band at the
notorious Ft. Worth club The Cellar. (Other records
include *Wild Wild Women* a rockabilly version of Ruth
Brown's r&b classic.)

Hot Smoke and Sassafras – Bubble Puppy
From Corpus Christi

I Fought The Law – Bobby Fuller Four
West Texas rock written by Sonny Curtis.

I'm In Pittsburgh and It's Raining – The Outcasts
From San Antonio

If I Had A Hammer – Trini Lopez
The Dallas native recorded in Los Angeles, his other
hits included *Lemon Tree*.

Last Kiss – J. Frank Wilson and the Cavaliers

Linda Lu – Ray Sharpe
Fort Worth rocker, recorded in Arizona, produced by
Lee Hazelwood.

Look at Me Girl -- The Playboys of Edinburg
From Edinburg, Texas

Ooby Dooby – Roy Orbison
The original was recorded in Texas, by Wink, Texas native Orbison. Roy went on to superstar status with a series of timeless songs.

Party Doll – Buddy Knox and the Rhythm Orchids
West Texas pop-rockabilly.

San Francisco Girls – Fever Tree
From Houston

Shake This Shack – Sid King and the Five Strings
Rockabilly from Dallas.

She's About a Mover – The Sir Douglas Quintet.
Other records from this San Antonio based group included *Mendocino.*

Ronnie Dawson – The Blonde Bomber

Buddy Knox – From Happy, Texas

Hey Paula

Bobby is the one

Paul and Paula

PHILIPS

So Tough – The Casuals
Fifties teen-rock vocal group scored a semi-national hit. Lead singer and guitarist Gary Mears later joined The Nightcaps.

Somethin' I Said – Lew Williams
He also wrote and recorded *Cat Talk* and other early rockabilly songs.

Stormy Monday Blues – T-Bone Walker
One of the greatest recorded blues songs ever.

Treat Her Right – Roy Head and the Traits
Blue-eyed soul.

Ten Long Fingers – "Groovey" Joe Poovey
Rockabilly riot.

That'll Be The Day – Buddy Holly and the Crickets
The King of Lubbock's first biggie. (He also did *Peggy Sue, Oh Boy, Rave On*, etc. etc.)

Tighten Up – Archie Bell and the Drells
From Houston.

Tonight Could Be The Night – The Velvets
Cool doo-wop harmony from Lubbock, featuring lead
vocals by Virgil Johnson.

Wasted Days and Wasted Nights – Freddy Fender
Originally recorded in 1960 in Texas, by the ultimate
Tex-Mex rocker.

Wooly Bully – Sam the Sham and the Pharaohs (other
hits from this Dallas band included *Little Red Riding
Hood*, *Haunted House* based on Brother Dave
Gardner's classic haunted house comedy routine, and
*I Woulda Wrote You A Letter But I Couldn't Spell
%*#*%!*)

You Cheated – The Slades
This song was covered by a California group called
The Shields, who made off with the national hit.

You're Gonna Miss Me – The Thirteenth Floor
Elevators
Austin's wild psychedelic pioneers.

Lew Williams

341

Doug Sahm on the left and The Sir Douglas Quintet

Sam the Sham and the Pharaohs

SOUNDS LIKE THE SIXTIES TO ME

Forgotten, But Not Gone
This Ain't Horseshoes or Hand Grenades

Therefore, close doesn't count. At least not on the charts. But the following close calls really do count to those of us who appreciate good rock and roll, even if it never cracked the Top 40.

These great non-hits were all single releases. The performers and the record companies hoped they had a hit on their hands. 45rpm copies were sent to radio stations, a few of which actually may have played them a few times. Some of these songs bubbled-under or just inside the national hit parade but none of them were national Top 40 hits, at least on the *pop* charts. Why? Some of these songs became hits in England, even as they stayed on the ignore-list in the States. *River Deep Mountain High*, produced by Phil Spector for Ike and Tina Turner (well, just Tina in reality) went to very near the top of the British charts, even as it died a quick death in America. Ditto for *The Wind Cries Mary* by Jimi Hendrix. Some others became regional hits in the U.S., usually near their cities of origination, but were overlooked nationally.

Many – most – of these songs are a lot better than a huge portion of the list of mega-hits of the sixties. What was the answer? What caused these cool songs to limp to the finish line in last place? Who knows? But they aren't completely forgotten.

To make this list these songs placed no better than number 60 on the US pop charts:
Anna – Arthur Alexander
Any Day Now – Chuck Jackson

Baby Please Don't Go – Them
Bad Boy – The Floyd Dakil Four
Bad Boy – Larry Williams
Big Blue Diamonds – Gene Summers
Can Can – Peter Jay & The Jaywalkers
A Certain Girl – Ernie K-Doe
Close Your Eyes – The Bobbettes
Come Tomorrow – Manfred Mann
The Crying Game – Brenda Lee
Cryin' Waitin' Hopin' – Buddy Holly
Dance Franny Dance – The Floyd Dakil Four
Diane From Manchester Square – Tommy Roe
Expecting to Fly – Buffalo Springfield
Full Measure – The Lovin' Spoonful
Gloria – Them
Goodbye So Long – Ike and Tina Turner
Havin' A Wild Weekend – The Dave Clark Five
I See The Light – The Five Americans
I Still Love You – The Vejtables
It Will Stand – The Showmen
I Woulda Wrote You A Letter But I Couldn't Spell
    %*#*%! – Sam the Sham
If You Really Want Me To I'll Go – The Rondels
I'm A Man – Bo Diddley
Journey to Tyme – Kenny and the Kasuals
Just One Look – The Hollies
Let Her Dance – The Bobby Fuller Four
Miserlou – Dick Dale and the Del Tones
Out of Time – Chris Farlowe and the Thunderbirds
The Rains Came – Big Sambo
River Deep, Mountain High – Ike and Tina Turner
Rollin' Dynamite – Scotty McKay
Shakin' All Over – Johnny Kidd and the Pirates
Shot of Rhythm and Blues – Arthur Alexander
Soldier of Love – Arthur Alexander
Some Other Guy – Richie Barrett

Stop! Get A Ticket – The Clefs of Lavender Hill
These Arms of Mine – Otis Redding
Thunderbird – The Nightcaps
True Love Ways – Buddy Holly
24 Hours – The Nightcaps
We Belong Together – Jimmy Velvit
The Wind Cries Mary – The Jimi Hendrix Experience
Wine Wine Wine – The Nightcaps
You'll Never Leave Him – The Isley Brothers
You Make Me Feel So Good – The Zombies

Killer Filler – The Great Album Cuts

In the fifties and sixties, when long-playing albums became popular, the record companies believed they had good reason not to make the albums too darn good. If they filled the LP with hits or even songs that were good enough to be hits, the public wouldn't need to purchase as many albums. So the companies would usually put one or two hits, along with the b-sides of those hits, on each album. The rest of the LP was usually "filler".

Filler was provided in several ways. If the performers were also instrumentalists, they could record a few non-vocal recordings, usually invented on the spot. Sometimes they would just peel the vocals off of a recording and pass the instrumental version off as a separate cut. Even the superstars would do this. In one well-remembered case on a Chuck Berry album, the instrumental filler cut *Deep Feeling* was simply slowed down to half-speed and put on the same album as *Low Feeling*. The term "low feeling" must have also represented what the record companies felt about their punk-teen buying public.

All this changed in the mid-sixties with The Beatles, Bob Dylan and others. From their first LP releases, The Beatles filled their albums with songs that could not be described as filler. Even if the albums still only contained one or two hits, the other songs were of a quality that surpassed any filler that could have been added. Suddenly the LPs were filled with good songs, and listening to an album all the way through became more commonplace. In fact, many of the non-hit cuts on albums became favorite songs for many teens of the era.

I'm sure you have favorite album cuts that would qualify, and that many of the following songs would never appear on your list. But this is my list, so learn to live with it.

The Top 20 Killer Filler of The Sixties

Ain't Got You – The Yardbirds
Darlin' Companion – The Lovin' Spoonful
Do I Have To Come Right Out and Say It – Buffalo Springfield
Don't Be Taken In – The Dave Clark Five
Don't Look Back – Them
I Call Your Name – The Beatles
I'll Feel A Whole Lot Better – The Byrds
I Take What I Want – Aretha Franklin
Little Wing – Jimi Hendrix
Love Minus Zero/No Limit – Bob Dylan
My Flash On You – Love
The Nazz Are Blue – The Yardbirds
Play With Fire – The Rolling Stones
She Belongs To Me – Bob Dylan
She Said Yeah – The Rolling Stones
Sit Down I Think I Love You – Buffalo Springfield
So Mystifying – The Kinks
Something You Got – Wilson Pickett
Sportin' Life – The Lovin' Spoonful
Turn Around – The Beau Brummels

The Garage Bands
More Than You Ever
Wanted to Know

Garage Band Royalty
Part A: One Shot Hotshots

After The Kingsmen kicked the door open, dozens of Garage bands ran through to score medium sized hits. Although several of these garage bands hit the big time with big hits, more often than not they couldn't survive the sophomore slump. After one medium-to-huge record they each slipped off the charts forever. Mostly forgotten now, these groups set the standards for garage band repertoire.

Here are some of the most notable of the one-hit garage kings.

The Amboy Dukes
Led by Ted Nugent, they hit with *Journey To The Center of the Mind*.

The Balloon Farm
Question of Temperature was their only hit. From New Jersey

The Barbarians
A non-rhyming self-parody entitled *Are You A Boy Or Are You A Girl*, gave this Massachusetts band their only big hit in 1965. The next year, a follow-up, *Moulty* (about their one-handed drummer Victor Moulton) was a minor hit.

The Blues Magoos
From the Bronx in New York, their big hit was *We Ain't Got Nothin' Yet*.

The Castaways
The University of Minnesota produced this group whose big hit was *Liar Liar* in 1965. (Members included Denny Craswell, Jim Donna, Bob Folchow, Roy Hensley and Dick Roby.)

The Chartbusters
From Kansas, their only hit was *She's The One* in 1964, but it was somethin' else! A high-speed almost hillbilly song reminiscent of The Beatles had the lads from Liverpool been really juiced up and not so veddy, veddy British. (Members included Mitch Corday, John Dubas, Vince Gideon and Vernon Sandusky.) The group formed out of Bobby Poe and the Poe Kats.

The Count 5
Psychotic Reaction is the most familiar song from this San Jose, California group.

The Cryan' Shames
From Chicago. They recorded a remake of the British hit for The Searchers – *Sugar and Spice* – in 1966 and enjoyed a sizable national hit.

The Dartels
Their frat-fest chant was *Hot Pastrami*. This song may hold the record for the most times using the word "yeah" in the lyrics.

Bill Deal and the Rhondells
A great southern-fried frat band that hit with *I've Been Hurt*, a Carolina beach music anthem.

The Five Americans
Originally from Oklahoma, this band is associated with their home-base, Dallas. Their solid regional hit, a frat-madness rocker entitled *I See The Light*, was followed by a much more accessible pop song called *Western Union*, which became a big hit in 1967.

The Bobby Fuller Four
West Texas produced a lot of big time talent in the form of rockabilly and country performers. Bobby Fuller and his group were more of a fun-rock band than rockabilly, which they are sometimes labeled. *Let Her Dance* and *I Fought The Law* (the latter written by sometime-Cricket Sonny Curtis) were two of their best.

The Gants
Johnny Freeman, lead singer/guitarist Sid Herring, Vince Montgomery, Johnny Sanders and Don Wood from Mississippi. Their moment on the national charts came with *Roadrunner*.

The Gestures
This Minnesota band hit big with *Run Run Run* in 1964.

The Gentrys
Led by Larry Raspberry, this Memphis band hit with *Keep On Dancing*. One member, Jimmy Hart, became the famous wrestling promoter known as "the mouth of the south."

The Human Beinz   From Youngstown Ohio, they rocked up the Isley Brothers r&b song *Nobody But Me* in 1967. This song is familiar to new generations as it is still used regularly on TV commercials, but the band is all but forgotten. Like The Dartels above, The Human Beinz may hold a lyric record by using the word "no" the most times in a rock song.

The Knickerbockers
This New York band was incorrectly thought by many to be The Beatles incognito because of the similarities of style in their hit *Lies*.

The Leaves
Hey Joe. Who knows who recorded this essential garage band song first, but this band popularized it and placed it on the must-play garage band list.

Love
Arthur Lee (vocals) and Bryan MacLean (guitar) were the mainstays of this California band (*7+ 7 Is*).

The MC5
"MC" stands for Motor City. Although they began recording in the mid-sixties, this Detroit band didn't hit until 1969 with *Kick Out The Jams*.

The Mojo Men
From San Francisco, they played the garage circuit until hitting the big-time with a pop song, *Sit Down I Think I Love You*, written by Stephen Stills. The band: Jim Alaimo, Paul Curcio, Dennis DeCarr, Don Metchick. They also scored a local hit with *Dance With Me*.

The Music Explosion
1967's *A Little Bit of Soul* was a whole lot of garage rock. The band came from Ohio and included Don Atkins, Bob Avery, Jamie Lyons, Richard Nesta and Burton Sahl.

The Music Machine
From Los Angeles, they hit with *Talk Talk* in 1966. Members included Sean Bonniwell, Ron Edgar, Mark Lander, Keith Olsen and Doug Rhodes.

? And The Mysterians
96 Tears. In 1966 this song reached number one in the nation, one of the last true garage band grunge tunes to hit the top of the charts. The Mysterians (like The Premiers just below) were a Latino garage band, although originally from Texas. Their follow-up song *I Need Somebody*, was a minor hit, and then the garage era was over.

The Premiers
A Latino garage band from Los Angeles, they recorded the rawest garage band song of all time, *Farmer John*. This song sounds like it was recorded during a riot at a frat house, using tin cans for microphones and recycled tire rubber instead of recording tape. Wild screaming in the background often drowns out the song and the vocals can be generously described as rugged. The very unrehearsed, raw and semi-professional nature of this song only added to its appeal to the alienated teens of the sixties. This song was a staple for us and was included on our Impact album.

The Rivieras
Like a lot of bands associated with the California music scene, this band came from nowhere near the west coast. In fact the hitmakers of the 1963-1964 garage classic *California Sun* (one of the all time great frat-house rock party songs) came from South Bend, Indiana, about as far as you can get from an ocean and still be in the states. The band included Paul Dennart, Doug Gean, Otto Nuss, Marty Fortson and Joe Pennell. They also released three frat-party style albums in two years, *California Sun*, *Let's Have A Party* and *Campus Party*.

The Seeds
Featuring Sky Saxon, Rick Andridge, Daryl Hooper and Jan Savage, they hit with *Pushin' Too Hard* and followed it up with a minor chartmaker, *Can't Seem To Make You Mine*. Raw energy with the accent on the word "raw".

The Shadows of Knight
Chicago's Shadows of Knight recorded Them's *Gloria* in 1966 and hit mostly in areas where the original had not received a lot of exposure in its initial release. *Oh Yeah* was their follow up song.

The Standells
An L.A. group which featured a former mousekateer and the brother of a movie star. They had one huge hit in *Dirty Water* and a couple of lesser hits including the garage standard Sometimes *Good Guys Don't Wear White*.

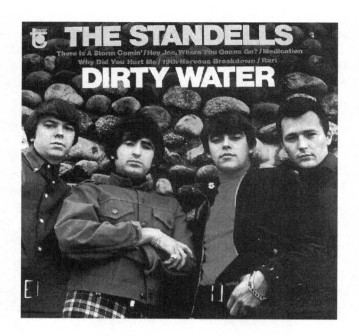

The Swingin' Medallions
The frat house royalty of the south, they hit big with
Double Shot of My Baby's Love in 1966. Like a lot of
garage classics, the poor recording, haphazard playing
and almost mindless simplicity of it all made it all the
more appealing. The song and the band are still
revered along the Carolina shores. The band's lineup:
John McElrath, Jim Doares, Carroll Bledsoe, Charles
Webber, Brent Forston, Steve Caldwell, James
Perkins and Joe Morris.

The Syndicate of Sound
With *Hey Little Girl*, this San Jose, California band
scored a three-chord masterpiece.

The Thirteenth Floor Elevators
Roky Erickson led this Texas based group which had a sizable hit with the early-psychedelic rocker *You're Gonna Miss Me*. One very unique sound on this and other songs by the band was the sound of a jug being hooted into in a weird, eerie manner by Tommy Hall. Hey, whatever makes the sound sound good, sounds good to me.

The Trashmen
The hitmakers of *Surfin' Bird*. Surfing in Minnesota? Well, why not? The lead singer on the song was drummer / screamer Steve Wahrer. Tony Andreason was on lead guitar, Dan Winslow on vocals and rhythm guitar and Bob Reed was the group's bassist.

The Uniques
Led by future country star Joe Stampley, this Louisiana band recorded a garage-ballad version of Art Neville's classic *All These Things*, and went to the national charts. Other minor hits included *You Ain't Tough Baby* and *Run And Hide*.

The Vejtables
From San Francisco, they had a mildly pop-garage minor hit with *I Still Love You* in 1965. The band featured Jan Errico on lead vocals.

J. Frank Wilson and the Cavaliers
Their big hit *Last Kiss*, was written and originally recorded by the amazing Wayne Cochran.

The Wailers

This group had a minor national hit with *Tall Cool One* but are more legendary for a hit they didn't have. The legends of the Northwest, this is the band from whom The Kingsmen learned *Louie Louie*. Although *Tall Cool One* was a rock instrumental, The Wailers were a full-service frat band (which sometimes included vocalist Rockin' Robin Roberts). The mainstays of the band were Ron Gardner, Kent Merrill, Rick Dangel, Mike Burk, Dave Roland, Mark Marush and Buck Ormsby. They learned *Louie Louie* from West Coast road band Ron Holden and the Thunderbirds (*Love You So*, 1960), who had learned it from the original version by Richard Berry. By the time The Wailers had wailed the song a thousand times, it had moved far away from its pseudo-calypso origins and had been frat-partied into a raw rock song. Rockin' Robin Roberts and The Wailers recorded the song back in 1961, before either The Kingsmen or Paul Revere and the Raiders, and were not only responsible for the most familiar "official" arrangement but for the scream of "Ok let's give it to 'em right now", going into the guitar break.

The Woolies

From Detroit, their only hit was a rockin' version of Bo Diddley's *Who Do You Love*. Stormy Rice (vocals) Bob Baldori (keyboards) Jeff Baldori (guitar) Ron English (bass) and Bee Metros (drums).

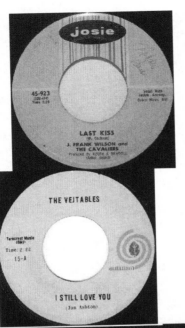

One shot wonderfulness from garage greats across the country.

Garage Band Royalty Part B: The Stars

Although it may seem like a contradiction to call international rock and roll stars "garage bands" since they obviously rose well above most of us, these bands began as local wannabes and set the sound standards in place for all future garage bands.

The biggest name on the list – The Beatles – had humble roots as a band that couldn't even keep a drummer on staff, wouldn't behave on stage and would play almost anywhere, anytime, for jam-and-toast or no fee at all, just for the sake of playing. A classic garage beginning.

The members of The Rolling Stones struggled mightily in dives and living rooms until breaking through on the international charts. Their vocal and instrumental style, as well as their rebellious bad-boy stance, made them the most influential band on future garage rockers.

Them began as a hard working r&b road band and finally cracked stardom with two of the grungiest garage anthems ever, *Gloria* and *Baby Please Don't Go*.

The other multiple-hit-makers on the list also began with similar stories, and went on to international fame, although in most cases, short-lived.

The very early Rolling Stones

A Few Big Name Garage Band Alumni

Name	Band
Alice Cooper	The Spiders
Bob Dylan	The Golden Chords
John Fogerty	The Golliwogs
Glenn Frey	The Mushrooms
Don Henley	The Four Speeds
Billy Joel	The Hassles
Delbert McClinton	The Ron-Dels
Van Morrison	The Monarchs (and later Them)
Ted Nugent	The Amboy Dukes
Gram Parsons	The Legends
Bob Segar	The Heard
Bruce Springsteen	The Castilles
James Taylor	The Flying Machine
Steven Tyler	The Chain Reaction
Jimmie Vaughan	The Chessmen
Stevie Ray Vaughan	Cast of Thousands
Joe Walsh	The Measles
Leslie West	The Vagrants
Johnny Winter	Amos Boynton and the ABCs
Neil Young	The Squires
Frank Zappa	The Blackouts

Garage Bands Who Made It Big

The Animals (House of the Rising Sun)
The Beatles (Twist and Shout)
The Beau Brummels (Laugh Laugh)
The Box Tops (The Letter)
John Fred and the Playboy Band (Judy In Disguise)
Tommy James and the Shondells (Hanky Panky)
The Kingsmen (Louie Louie)
The Kinks (You Really Got Me)
Manfred Mann (Do Wah Diddy)
The McCoys (Hang On Sloopy)
Paul Revere and the Raiders (Just Like Me)
The Rolling Stones (Satisfaction)
Mitch Ryder and the Detroit Wheels (Jenny Take A Ride)
The Sir Douglas Quintet (She's About A Mover)
Them (Gloria)
The Troggs (Wild Thing)
The Who (My Generation)
The Yardbirds (I'm A Man)
The Young Rascals (Good Lovin')
The Zombies (She's Not There)

Here are some details on the above bands.

The Animals

Eric Burdon (vocals), Alan Price (organ), Hilton Valentine (guitar), John Steele (drums) and Chas Chandler (bass). They broke in the states with a rock version of the folk-blues standard *House of The Rising Sun* which though cool and evil sounding, was not a dance tune and was usually ignored by live combos. The Animals made the grunge playlist with their subsequent releases like *I'm Crying* and *We Gotta Get Out Of This Place*.
Baby Let Me Take You Home

House of the Rising Sun
I'm Crying
Don't Let Me Be Misunderstood
We Gotta Get Out Of This Place
It's My Life
Don't Bring Me Down

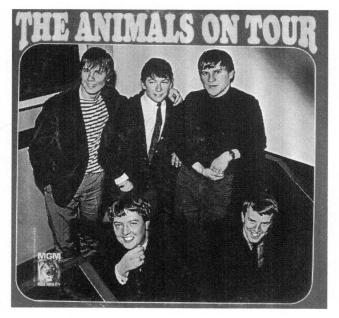

The Beatles

The Beatles had way too many recordings to list here. Only a few of their covers and originals became garage band staples anyway – *Twist and Shout, Money* and *You Can't Do That* being the most played. The Beatles' influence on garage sounds was more of creating an impetus for thousands of young guys to buy guitars and form a band. The actual playlists came mostly from other US and Brit bands.

The Beau Brummels

Softer and folkier than most influences on garage groups, The Beau Brummels had two big hits and one very influential album, "Bradley's Barn". *Laugh Laugh*, their first hit, was a folk-rock song that made garage band lists due to its mean, vengeful lyrical attitude. *Just A Little* scored higher than *Laugh Laugh*, but it was their last big hit. Sal Valentino (vocals), Ron Elliott (guitar) were joined by bandmates Ron Meagher, Declan Mulligan and John Peterson.

1965 *Laugh Laugh*
1965 *Just a Little*
1965 *Don't Talk To Strangers*
1965 *Good Time Music*
1965 *You Tell Me Why*
1966 *One Too Many Mornings*

The Box Tops

From the center of southern soul, Memphis, came this sorta-soul, blue-eyed band which hit big in 1967 with the song *The Letter*. Lead singer and Memphis post-Elvis
legend, Alex Chilton was joined by Tom Boggs, Bill Cunningham, Harold Cloud, Danny Smythe and Gary Talley.

The Box Tops Hits:
1967 *The Letter*
1967 *Neon Rainbow*
1968 *Cry Like A Baby*
1968 *Soul Deep*
1968 *Choo Choo Train*
1969 *Sweet Cream Ladies*

The Spencer Davis Group

This British act arrived on the American scene late in the garage era, in 1966. Nevertheless their three hits influenced the playlists of the last of the garage bands in the U.S. Founder and guitarist Spencer Davis was joined by the amazing voice of the teenaged Stevie Winwood, also on guitar and keyboards. Muff Winwood on bass and Pete York on drums rounded out the band.

1966 *Keep On Running*
1967 *Gimme Some Lovin'*
1967 *I'm A Man*

John Fred and the Playboy Band

This Louisiana road-band led by John Fred were the kings of fraternity row in the East Texas-Louisiana area in the mid-sixties. Though most of their late-sixties single releases don't show it, they were a fun, garagatic, frantic frat band in person. Check their album cuts for their true toga-party roots.

1968 – *Judy In Disguise*
1968 – *Hey Hey Bunny*
1968 – *Agnes English*

Tommy James and the Shondells

Their first hit, *Hanky Panky*, came three years after it was recorded, when the band no longer existed. Although a hit locally in his hometown of Niles, Michigan in 1963, the song took off nationally in 1966. Tommy quickly recruited another group of Shondells and hit the charts regularly for several years. The group he chose was The Raconteurs from Pittsburgh where the song had taken off belatedly. Other than *Mony Mony*, most of the later hits were more psychedelic and modern rock, but *Hanky Panky* continued as a garage band "must-play".

FOUR GARAGE BANDS THAT MADE IT BIG

Top: The Spencer Davis Group (Stevie Winwood far right)
Middle: John Fred and His Playboy Band, The Box Tops
Lower: Tommy James and the Shondells

The Kingsmen

They've been called the first true garage band, but in their section of the Northwest (Portland, Oregon) they were just one of a bunch of bands playing frat parties, clubs and battles of the bands. However, they did become the first true national garage band upon the breakout of *Louie Louie* in 1963. The recording itself is a lot more famous than the band. Recorded for a reported fifty bucks in a tiny studio, the lead singer Jack Ely had to yell the lyrics into the one microphone strung from the ceiling.

Lynn Easton (then the drummer, soon the lead singer and owner of the Kingsmen name), Don Galluci (the organist who later formed Don and the Goodtimes), bassist Bob Nordby and guitarist Mike Mitchell were also in the studio that day. They cut *Louie Louie* in one take. It sounds raw, unrehearsed and downright sloppy because it was all of that. A second take might have polished it up, but it also might have polished it off. The rugged rawness of the song is much of its appeal.

A second appeal for teens and bands of the sixties was the rumor that the lyrics to *Louie Louie* were dirty. Wild and contradictory conclusions as to the actual words led to thousands of bands singing the dirtiest possible lyrics you
can imagine. It became such a famous filthy song, that the FBI spent a ton of taxpayers' money trying to decipher the lyrics on the record by The Kingsmen. They couldn't understand any of it. Had they

discovered the truth, I'm sure they would have been devastated – the song was not filthy or even slightly off-color. It was about a sailor who missed his girlfriend. The lyrics were not only clean, but printable in the Sunday newspaper, had anyone cared to know the truth.

According to legend (and the guys who keep track of these sorts of things) *Louie Louie* has been recorded in over 2000 versions. And I bet each recording cost more to produce than the original hit. The Kingsmen continued for years as successful headliners, frat band and eventually on the oldies circuit.

1963 *Louie Louie*
1964 *Death Of An Angel*
1964 *Little Latin Lupe Lu*
1964 *Money*
1965 *Annie Fanny*
1965 *The Climb*
1965 *Jolly Green Giant*
1966 *Killer Joe*
1966 *Louie Louie* (re-release)

In addition to the singles above, The Kingsmen released two "live" albums (Vol. 1 and Vol. 2) which set the blueprint for local band playlists.

The Kinks

Ray Davies (rhythm guitar, vocals, songwriting), Dave Davies (lead guitar), Pete Quaife (bass) and Mick Avory (drums). The meanest sounding of all the British beat bands, The Kinks played really loud and really fast. Almost any song from their first two albums was an acceptable garage band tune. Album cuts *Beautiful Delilah* and *So Mystifying* became standards, and their single hits would always fill a dance floor.

1964 *You Really Got Me*
1965 *All Day And All Of The Night*
1965 *Set Me Free*
1965 *Tired Of Waiting For You*
1965 *Who'll Be The Next In Line*
1966 *Well Respected Man*
1966 *Dedicated Follower Of Fashion*
1966 *Sunny Afternoon*
1966 *Till The End Of The Day*

The Kinks – Peter Quaife, Dave Davies, Mick Avory and Ray Davies in the front.

The McCoys

From Indiana, this high school combo hit the big time with a series of chart songs, kicked off by an all-time garage classic Hang On Sloopy. The band featured Rick Derringer (Zehringer), Randy Zehringer, Bobby Peterson, Dennis Kelly and Randy Hobbs.

1965 *Hang On Sloopy*
1965 *Fever*
1966 *(You Make Me Feel) So Good*
1966 *Come On Let's Go*

1966 *Don't Worry Mother, Your Son's Heart Is Pure*
1966 *Up And Down*

The McCoys

The Outsiders

A midwest frat-style band had a huge hit with *Time Won't Let Me* in 1966. They followed it up with a frat-version of the Isley Brothers' song *Respectable* and had another respectable hit. Also known for a more minor hit, *Girl In Love*. Members included Ricky Baker, Bill Bruno, Sonny Geraci and Merden Madsen.

Paul Revere and the Raiders

This northwest frat band recorded *Louie Louie* in the same studio, virtually at the same time as The Kingsmen, but were outsold by the tons by the raw energy of The Kingsmen version. The Raider version is much truer to the Richard Berry original and lacks the crazed garage lunacy of The Kingsmen recording. Early albums and singles by The Raiders were pure garage band sounds, but they eventually accepted the safe teen

stardom that was offered them, and their wild stage antics and grungy songs were left behind. Leader Paul Revere (his real name) and singer Mark Lindsay were the mainstays of the group, joined by Drake Levin (guitar), Mike Smith (drums) and
Phil Volk (bass). In keeping with their band name, they wore flashy versions of Revolutionary War outfits including weird, pointy hats which became a short-lived fad among local bands. They may have missed on *Louie Louie*, but Paul and the boys did OK later on with a string of national hits like *Just Like Me* and *Steppin' Out*

1965 *Steppin' Out*
1966 *Just Like Me*
1966 *Hungry*
1966 *Kicks*
1966 *The Great Airplane Strike*
1967 *Good Thing*
1967 *Him Or Me - What's It Gonna Be?*
1967 *I Had A Dream*
1967 *Peace Of Mind*
1967 *Ups And Downs*
1968 *Cinderella Sunshine*
1968 *Don't Take It So Hard*
1968 *Too Much Talk*
1969 *Let Me*
1969 *Mr. Sun, Mr. Moon*

The Rolling Stones
Mick and Keith and the guys started as Little Boy Blue and the Blue Boys, then became Brian Jones and the Rolling Stones, and eventually became simply The Rolling Stones, the world's greatest rock and roll band. Super rhythm section: Charlie Watts on drums and Bill Wyman on bass.
Singles

1964 *Not Fade Away*
1964 *It's All Over Now*
1964 *Tell Me (You're Coming Back)*
1964 *Time Is On My Side*
1965 *(I Can't Get No) Satisfaction*
1965 *Get Off Of My Cloud*
1965 *Heart Of Stone*
1965 *Play With Fire*
1965 *Last Time*
1966 *19th Nervous Breakdown*
1966 *As Tears Go By*
1966 *Have You Seen Your Mother, Baby, Standing In The Shadow?*
1966 *Lady Jane*
1966 *Mothers Little Helper*
1966 *Paint It Black*
1967 *Dandelion*
1967 *Let's Spend The Night Together*
1967 *Ruby Tuesday*
1967 *We Love You*
1968 *In Another Land*
1968 *Jumpin' Jack Flash*
1968 *She's A Rainbow*
1968 *Street Fighting Man*
1969 *Honky Tonk Women*

Influential albums of the Rolling Stones:

1964 The Rolling Stones
1964 12 X 5
1965 Out Of Our Heads
1965 Rolling Stones Now
1966 December's Children
1966 High Tides and Green Grass
1966 Aftermath
1967 Between The Buttons

1967 Flowers
1967 Got Live If You Want It
1968 Their Satanic Majesties Request
1969 Beggars Banquet
1969 Let It Bleed

Many a garage band standard came not from their hit singles but from individual cuts from their albums. *Around and Around, I'm A King Bee, You Can't Catch Me, Mona, She Said Yeah, You Better Move On, Honest I Do,* all of which were covers of American R&B songs – many we'd never heard until The Rolling Stones recorded them.

Mitch Ryder and the Detroit Wheels

A lot of bands tended to name themselves for a town other than where they were actually from, but some bands, including this one, were proud of their hometown. From Detroit, they hit with hard rocking frat-feasts like *Jenny Take A Ride, Devil With A Blue Dress/Good Golly Miss Molly,* and *Sock It To Me Baby.* Their album – "Take A Ride" – is a garage band classic.

Sam The Sham and the Pharaohs

From Dallas. Domingo "Sam" Samudio (on vocals and keyboards) with Butch Gibson, David Martin, Jerry Patterson and Ray Stinnet. They began as The Tom Toms, the house band at the Guthrey Club.

1963 *Betty and Dupree*
1963 *Haunted House*
1964 *The Signifyin' Monkey*
1965 *Wooly Bully*
1965 *Ju Ju Hand*
1965 *Ring Dang Doo*
1965 *Red Hot*
1966 *Lil' Red Riding Hood*
1966 *The Hair On My Chinny Chin Chin*
1966 *How Do You Catch A Girl?*
1966 *Oh That's Good, No That's Bad*
1967 *Black Sheep*
1967 *Banned in Boston*
1967 *Yakety Yak*
1967 *Old MacDonald Had A Boogaloo Farm*
1968 *I Couldn't Spell #%*!*
!

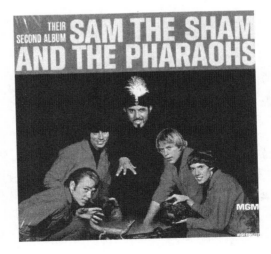

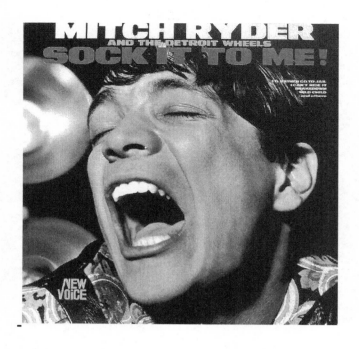

The Sir Douglas Quintet

From San Antonio, Texas, this Tex-Mex ensemble scored a few big hits and a couple of influential albums in the mid-sixties. Led by Doug Sahm on guitar and vocals, the band included Augie Meyers, Frank Morin, Harvey Kagen and John Perez. Their biggest hit was *She's About A Mover*.

1965 *She's About A Mover*
1966 *The Rains Came*
1969 *Dynamite Woman*
1969 *Mendocino*

Them

Van Morrison was the number one single influence on garage band singers. His classic "swollen tongue" vocals were imitated by teen boys from across the states. Almost every song by this band found its way to garage playlists somewhere in the country. From Ireland, they began recording in England in 1964. Playing and recording mostly hard-edged bluesy rock, they benefited from the presence of Jimmy Page (future Yardbird and Led Zep) as a session guitarist. A few hits and two great albums later they were finished, with Morrison continuing as a very successful solo artist.

1965 *Baby Please Don't Go*
1965 *Gloria*
1965 *Here Comes The Night*
1965 *Mystic Eyes*
1966 *Gloria* (reissue)
LPs: "Them" and "Them Again"

The Troggs

The Wild Things themselves. This British band featured Reg Presley, Ronnie Bond, Chris Britton and Peter Staples.

1966 *I Can't Control Myself*
1966 *Wild Thing*
1966 *With A Girl Like You*
1968 *Love Is All Around*

The Who

They began in the states with *My Generation*, a true garage anthem if there ever was one. One of the few "mod" bands with big influences on US frat-garage groups, as The Who's songs became more complicated and artsy, the garage bands

375

looked elsewhere. Pete Townshend (guitar), Roger Daltrey (vocals), Keith Moon (drums) and John Entwistle (bass) made up this exciting band. As well known for their destructive stage behavior as their cool songs, they hit big on both sides of the Atlantic. Townshend's power chord innovations paved the way for the power trios of the late sixties and seventies. Moon's maniacal drumming was unequaled among rock percussionists. Until 1967 when they began to go a more arty direction, The Who was a major influence on American garage groups.

1965 *I Can't Explain*
1966 *My Generation*
1966 *Substitute*
1967 *Happy Jack*
1967 *I Can See For Miles*
1967 *Pictures Of Lily*
1968 *Call Me Lightning*
1968 *Magic Bus*
1969 *I'm Free*
1969 *Pinball Wizard*

The Yardbirds

Tough enough. This group moved from mean blues (with Eric Clapton) to edgy r&b-garage sounds (with Jeff Beck) to early psychedelic guitar-based rock (with Jimmy Page). With constant personnel changes, they eventually morphed into Led Zeppelin when Page looked around and realized there wasn't one original Yardbird left on the stage. The original line up included Clapton, Keith Relf (vocals, harmonica), Paul Samwell-Smith (bass), Chris Dreja (rhythm guitar) and Jim McCarty (drums). Eric was replaced by Jeff Beck who was replaced by Jimmy Page.

For Your Love
Heart Full Of Soul

Shapes of Things
I'm A Man
I'm Not Talkin'
The Train Kept A Rollin
Still I'm Sad
Mr. You're A Better Man Than I
Over Under Sideways Down
Happenings Ten Years Time Ago

The Yardbirds

The Young Rascals

They were the basis of the Joey Dee backup band, The Starlighters (*Shout, What Kind of Love Is This*) before emerging as one of the northeast's best club bands. They began their string of hits with the garage classic *Good Lovin'*. Featured Felix Cavaliere, Eddie Brigati, Gene Cornish and Dino Danelli. On their later hits they were billed simply as "The Rascals".

1966 *Good Lovin'*
1966 *Come On Up*
1966 *I Ain't Gonna Eat Out My Heart Anymore*
1966 *You Better Run*
1967 *A Girl Like You*
1967 *Groovin'*

1967 *How Can I Be Sure*
1967 *I've Been Lonely Too Long*
1968 *A Beautiful Morning*
1968 *It's Wonderful*
1968 *People Got To Be Free*
1969 *A Ray Of Hope*
1969 *Carry Me Back*

The Zombies
Slightly jazzy, a little moody-dark in attitude, Colin Blunstone's breathy vocals and the cool, choppy rhythms made this band England's most rainy-day sounding musical import. Rod Argent was the keyboardist and musical director of the band.
She's Not There
You Make Me Feel So Good
Tell Her No
I Love You
Time of The Season

Above: The Zombies

Although we (Kenny and the Kasuals) didn't play all of the songs above, or even songs by all of the above bands, those listed were the most important influences on our band and every struggling rock band of the sixties.

Greatest Garage Band Song Title Awards
"The Ragged, The Raw and The Terribly Twisted"

A disclaimer right up front: *"For the purposes of literary license, we refer to many bands in this book with terms like 'wild, insane, raw, dangerous, crazed, out-of-control' and words to that effect. Well, don't sue us. We don't mean the actual guys in the band were any of the above, we're talking about the sound, the attitude and often the subject matter of the songs. In fact most garage band players were average teenage guys who went to school, had dates and wore ties to church on Sunday. Insurance salesmen of the future and the pillars of the community."*

There, we're covered. Now let's talk trash about some twisted titles that would have scared the bee-jeebers out of any sixties-era parent had they been aware of their existence. Please vote for your favorites and send the results to: "Who Cares What You Think, General Delivery, Anytown, USA".

Category One
Dangerously Anti-Social Song Titles:
Freakout USA – The Communication Aggregation
Night of The Sadist – Larry and the Bluenotes
Nightmares – The Fairviews

379

Paralyzed – The Legendary Stardust Cowboy
Psychotic Reaction – The Count 5
I'm A Living Sickness – The Calico Wall
Psycho – The Swamp Rats
Scream Mother Scream – Sur Royal Da Count and the Parliaments
Evil – The Backdoor Men
Public Execution – Mouse and the Traps
Please Kill Me – The Mops

Category Two

Song Titles From Mars

Elephant In My Tambourine – North Atlantic
    Invasion Force
Kocka-Mow-Mow – The Dinks
The Orange Rooftop of My Baby's Mind –
    The Livin' End
Boots Are Made For Talking – The Nite Owls
Hey I Saw You Walkin' Up That Wall –
    The Rain Kings
Like A Dribbling Fram – The Race Marbles
Diamonds, Rats and Gum –
    Christopher and the Souls
Uncle Wiggly's Airship – The Shadows of Knight
Get Off My Roof – Jerry and the Landslides
Why Does My Head Go Boom – The Group
Don't Send Me No Flowers I Ain't Dead Yet –
    The Breakers
Prune Growing in June – The Oxpetals
Your Woman Is Ugly – Oganookie
My Soap Won't Float – The Regiment
Your Heart Is Too Big For Your Head – The Inferno
Stinking Peanut Butter – The Movement
Painted Air – The Remaining Few

Amphetamine Gazelle – Mad River
Chrome Plated Yabby – The Wild Cherries
Dorplegank – Revelation
Discomboober – The Fairviews
I Stole The Goodyear Blimp – The Book of Changes
Music to Smoke Bananas By – The Elopers
You've Got Your Head On Backwards – The Sonics
Brains In My Feet - Purple Canteen

The Dinks of "Kocka Mow Mow" fame

Who'd a thunk that a nice looking group of lads like
Christopher and the Souls could have come up with
"Diamonds Rats and Gum"?

Category Three
Bad Attitudes
You Can't Make Me – The Montels
Problem Child – The Four More
I Gotta Fight – The Bed of Roses
See If I Care – Ken and the Fourth Dimension
I Couldn't Care Less – The Run-A-Rounds
Who Cares? – The Unknown Kind
I Don't Care – Gord's Horde
Don't Tread On Me – Kit and the Outlaws
I'm A No 'Count – The Scotchmen
I'm No Good – The 5
Can't Tame Me – The Benders
She's Ugly – The Eccentrics
I Can't Win – The Monocles

CAN'T TAME ME/GOT ME DOWN

The Benders

BIG SOUND NO. 206

Category Four
Best of Show

When it comes to weird band names and weirder song names from the mid-sixties, one band holds both records. The band was called The Driving Stupid and they were from New Jersey, although they recorded out west. The amazing thing about this band is that they anticipated the insane stage of psychedelic weirdness by years. No one else was recording songs like these in the mid-sixties, the height of frat-band-mania. Here are several of The Driving Stupid's song titles from 1966:

Green Things Have Entered My Body Gladys
My Mother Was A Big Fat Pig
The Reality of (Air) Fried Borsk
Horror Asparagus Stories
Hide The Lobsters
We've Come To Take The Earth Away
I'm Gonna Bash Your Brains In
Water My Doing Here?
Girl's Got A Turtle

And, The Creative License "Greatest Teen Title" Award Goes To:

Linda Laine and the Sinners for *"Low Grades and High Fever"*

383

WARNING! INFORMATION OVERKILL!

What follows is a massive, unnecessary and overwhelming listing of way, way too many garage bands. Every North American combo that we have ever even heard of. And you would have to multiply this list by ten or twenty to get some idea of how many bands there actually were. Note: We're going to make the following type face smaller, in order to save pages and the trees that died to make them.

The Northeast (including New York, Connecticut, New Jersey, Pennsylvania etc.) The Age of Reason, The Arkay IV, The Balloon Farm, The Barbarians, The Baskerville Hounds, The Baker Street Irregulars, The Beaten Path, Beep Beep and the Roadrunners, Danny Belline and the Rich Kids, The Bends, The Bentleys, The Blue Chips, The Blues Magoos, The Blues Project, The Bridge, The Brigands, The Buggs, The Calliope, The Centurys, The Changin' Times, Chips and Co., The Coachmen, The Cobras, The Colors of Night, The Confederate Society, Creation's Disciples, The Darelycks, The Denims, The Driving Stupid, The Druids, Dry Ice, The Ebb Tides, The Edge of Darkness, The Emeralds, The Energy Package, Eric and the Chessmen, Faine Jade, The Falcons, The Fifth Generation, The Flowers, The Fonograf Four, Lance Fox and the Bloodhounds, The Friedles, The Fugitives, The Gay Blades, The Grasshoppers, The Groupies, The Hatchet Men, The Id, The Idols, The Inmates, The Innkeepers, The Insane, The Jelly Bean Bandits, The King Bees, The Knickerbockers, The Landlords, The Legends, London and the Bridges, The Loose Enz, Lord and his

Barons, The Loved Ones, The Magicians, The Malibus, The Mauve, The Mojo Hands, The Mojos, The Morning After, The Motts Men, The Moustache Wax, The Mustangs, The Myddle Class, The Mystic Five, The Mystic Tide, The Nightrockers, The No-Mads, The Nocturnes, The North American Invasion Force, The Original Sinners, The Outside Inn, The Oxpetals, The Plagues, The Primates, The Psychopaths, The Remanes, The Retreds, The Rising Storm, The Roadrunners, The Rouges, The Rubber Band, The Sands of Time, The Sapiens, Saturday's Garbage, The Scholors, The 7th Cinders, The Shadows Four, The Shags, The Shames, The Shandells, The Shapes of Things, The Sheep, The Shillings, The Shires, The Strangeloves, The Tallysmen, Teddy and the Pandas, The Teddy Boys, Terry and the Testars, The Tidal Waves, T.P. and the Indians, The Traits, The Tremblers, The Triumphs, The Trophies, The Vacels, The Vandals, The Vikings, The Warlocks, The Wee Four, The Werps, The What Fours, The What Nots, The Whether Bureau, The Young Rascals, Richard and the Young Lions, The Vagrants, The Young Rascals, Yesterday's Children, The Young Monkey Men, The Zipcodes.

The Northwest (Oregon Washington, etc.)

The Accents, The Adventurers, The Artesians, The Bag, The Bandits, The Bards, The Beachcombers, The Bellingham Accents, The Bootmen, Brave New World, The Bumps, The Bunch, The Ceptors, The Chambermen, The Changes, The Chargers, The Checkers, The City Lights, The Counts, Lord Dent and his Invaders, The DeVilles, The Dimensions, Don and The Goodtimes, The Dynamics, The Eccentrics, The El Caminos, Jack Ely and the Courtmen, The Emergency Exit, The Express, The Feelies, The Frantics, The Galaxies, Gentleman Jim and the Horsemen, The Heirs, The Herbs, The Hi-Fives, Jack Horner and The Plums, The Impacts, The Imperials, The

Jams, The Jesters, The Jet City Five, The Jolly Green Giants, The Juveniles, The Kingsmen, The Legends, The Lincolns, LittleJohn and The Monks, The Live Five, Magic Fern, The Mercy Boys, The Misterians, Mr. Clean and the Cleansers, Mr. Lucky and The Gamblers, The Moguls, The Navarros, The New Yorkers, Night People, Noises and Sounds, The Nomads, The Nu-Dimensions, The Page Boys, The Pastels, The Purple Gang, The Raymarks, Paul Revere and the Raiders, Rockin' Robin Roberts, The Rock-N-Souls, Rocky and the Riddlers, The Rooks, Merilee Rush and the Turnabouts, The Scotsmen, Sir Raleigh & The Clip-Ons, The Sires, The Sonics, The Spindle, The Statics, The Talismen, The Tempests, Tom Thumb & The Casuals, The Trolley, Tyme's Children, The Untouchables,The Unusuals, The Viceroys, The Volk Brothers, The Wailers, George Washington & The Cherry Bombs, The Wilde Knights, The Yellow Balloon.

The Southwest (Arizona, Colorado, New Mexico, Nevada etc.) The Astronauts, The Axis Brotherhood, The Bassmen, The Bitter Sweets, Burgundy Run, The Caravelles, The Ceeds, Chob, The Clashmen, The Coachmen, The Dearly Beloved, The Elastik Band, The Elopers, The Era of Sound, The Fe-Fi-Fo Four Plus2, The Five of Us, The Frantics, Grass, The Grodes, The Horde, The Human Beings, The Intruders, The Keymen, King Richard_and the Knights, Kreeg, The Last Word, The Lewallen Brothers, The Lidos, Lincoln Street Exit, The Lollipop Shoppe, The Mile Ends, The Missing Links, The Monocles, The Moonrakers, The Movin' Morfomen, Nobody's Children, The Occasionals, Our Gang, The Outer Limits, The Plague, The Poor, Possum, The Quinstrells, The Rainy Daze, The Reasons Why, The Ric-A-Shays, King Rock and the Knights, The Sidewinders, The Soothsayers, Sotweed Factor, The Soul, The Stumps, The Tongues of Truth, The Topsy Turbys, The Travelers, The Trolls, The Tuesday Club, The Viscount V, The Viscounts, Whose Who, Ye Court Jesters, The Young Men.

The Aardvarks, The Accents, The Alarm Clocks, The Amboy Dukes, The Ascots, The Avanties, The Bad Experience, The Bad Omens, The Bandits, Band X, The Baroques, The Baskerville Hounds, The Basooties, BEAT Ltd, The Beaubiens, The Beaux Jens, The Bed of Roses, The Bedford Set, The Bedlam 4, The BelAirs, The Bells of Rhymney, The Benders, The Berries, The Black and Blues, The Blokes, The Blue Things, Blues Company, The Boss Tweads, The Brakmen, The Breakers, The Camel Drivers, The Canadian Lady Bugs, The Cannons, The Castaways, The Catalinas, The Challengers, The Chancellors, Cherry Slush, The Chessmen, The Chevrons, The Choir, The Chylds, The Citations, The Coachmen, The Cobblers, The Converts, The Cords, The Corvets, The Countdowns, The Couriers, The Crystal Rain, The Dantes, The Dawks, The Dawnbreakers, The Deacons, The Deadlys, Dearborn City Limits, The Decisions, The Defiants, The Del Counts, The Denims, Detroit Riots, The Deveros, The Devilles, The Dinks, The Dynamic Hursemen, The Eags, The Echoes, The Electras, The Emblems, The Endless, The Epics, Eric and the Norsemen, The Esquires, The Eye Zooms, The Fab Four, The Fabulous Depressions, The Fabulous Flippers, The Fabulous Thunderbolts, The Fabulous Trippers, The Faros, The Ferraris, The Fifth Order, Fink Munx 4, The Forums, The Four O'Clock Balloon, The Fugitives, The Galaboochees, The Gallows, Joey Gee and the Come Ons, The Gestures, The Gillian Row, The Gonn, Gord's Horde, Symon, Grace and the Tuesday Blues, The Grapes, The Grasshoppers, The Great Imposters, Dale Gregory and the Shouters, The Grifs, The Group, The Harrisons, The Hazards, The Headlyters, The High Spirits, The Hinge, House of Commons, The Illusions, The Impalas, The Innsmen, The Intruders, Jack and the Beanstalks, The

Jades, The Jammers, The Jeans, The Jerms, The Jesters of Kansas, Juliettas Valiants, The JuJus, Kama Del Sutra, The Kandells, The Keggs, The Kinetics, King Midas and the Mufflers, Kings Court, The King's English, The Kyks, The Lee VI's, The Legends, London Fog, Love Corporation, Love Society, The Lynchmen, The Madhatters, The Marauders, The Marlins, The MC5, The McCoys, The Medallions, The Mersey Men, The Messengers, King Midas and the Mufflers, The Mid-Knighters, The Minutemen, The Missing Lynx, Moby Dick and the Whalers, The Mod 4, The Monuments, The Monks, The More-Ticians, The Mornin' Glories, Lord Beverly Moss and the Mossmen, The Motor City Bonnevilles, The Music Explosion, The Mussies, The Mustard Men, The Mystic Number National Bank, The Mystifying Monarchs, The Night Crawlers, The 9th Street Market, The Noblemen, The Novas, The Olivers, One Eyed Jacks, The One Way Streets, The Onion Rings, The Only Ones, Jerry and the Others, The Outcry, The Outsiders, The Pacesetters, The Pack, The Pagens, The Panicks, The Pastels, The Penetrators, Pepper and the Shakers, The Pictorian Skiffles, The Pied Pipers, Plato and the Philosophers, The Possums, The Premiers, The Princetons, The Psychotics, The Quests, The Questors, The Raging Winds, The Rain, Billy Rat and the Finks, The Rationals, The Rats, The Rave Ons, The Red Dogs, The Restless Knights, Robin and the Three Hoods, The Saharas, Rod and the Satelites, The Sanchers, The Satisfactions, Scott and the Esquires, The Secrets, Bob Seger and the Last Heard, The Senders, The Serfmen, The Seven Dwarfs, The 7 Legends, The Shades, The Shadow Casters, The Shandells, The Shags, The Shaprels, The Sheppards, The Shy Guys, The Skeptics, The Skunks, The Soothsayers, The Soul Benders, Sounds Like Us, The Spacemen, Spider and the Crabs, The

Squires, The Statesmen, Stillroven, The Sting Rays, The Sultans 5, Sweet Cherry, The Teardrops, The Tempests, Those of Us, The Thyme, The Tidal Waves, Tiffany Shade, Tony and the Bandits, The Tornadoes, The Travelers, The Trees, The Tree Stumps, The Tremors, The Trolls, The Tulu Babies, The Turn Ons, The Trademarks, The Twilighters, The Unlimited, The Unbelievable Uglies, The Undecided, The Underbeats, The Underdogs, The Unrelated Segments, The Untouchables, The Vaqueros, The Victors, The Vondells, The Voyagers, Wanderer's Rest, The Wanted, The Warlocks, The Warner Brothers, The Wheels, The Wild Things, The Woolies, The X-Cellents, The X-Men, The Young Lords, The Young Savages, The Zoo.

Chicago and Illinois

The Abandoned, The American Breed, The Apollos, The Apaches, The Banshees, The Berries, The Boys, The Buckinghams, Buzzsaw, The Cave Dwellers, The Children of Darkness, The Circus, The Cobras, The Daggs, Danny and the Other Guys, The Delights, The Del-Vetts, The Edges of Wisdom, The Eighth Day, The Enchanters 4, The End, The Factory, The Family, The Flock, The Foggy Notions, The Furniture, Gary and the Knight Lites, The Group Inc, The Haymarket Riot, The High Numbers, The Huns, The Ides of March, Infinite Pyramid, The Knaves, The Lemon Drops, The Little Boy Blues, Lord and the Flies, The Lost Agency, H.P. Lovecraft, The Malibus, The Mavericks, The Misty Blues, The New Colony Six, The Nickel Bag, The Nite Owls, Nobody's Children, The Omens, Oscar and the Majestics, The Pattens, Pride and Joy, The Reasons Why, The Revelles, The Rovin' Kind, Saturday's Children, The Screaming Wildmen, The Seeds of Reason, The Shadows of Knight, The Shady Daze, The Sweet Nothings, The Todds, The Trojans of Evol, The Trolls, The Troys, Truth, The Underprivilged, The Untamed, The Vydels, The Warner Brothers, The Wanderin' Kind.

California – Los Angeles and California south

The Agents, The Allies, The Ambertones, The Avengers, The Beckett Quintet, The Beefeaters (later The Byrds), The Bees, The Brothers Grim, Byron and the Mortals, The Caretakers of Deception, The Cavaliers, The Children, Children of the Mushroom, The Cindermen, The Cloudwalkers, The Coachmen, The Colony, The Crumpets, The David, The Dirty Shames, The Dovers, Evergreen Blues, The Everyday Things, The Fairviews, The Fantastic Zoo, Fenwyk, The Fire Escape, The Giant Sunflower, The Gigolos, The Good Feelings, The Grains of Sand, The Green Beans, The Grim Reapaers, The Gypsy Trips, The Hogs, The Humane Society, Hunger, The Hysterics, Thee In Set, Jefferson Handkerchief, The John Does, The Last Word, The Leaves, Limey and the Yanks, Love, Love Exchange, The Lyrics, The Mal-Ts, Mark and the Escorts, The Missing Links, Mom's Boys, The Music Machine, The Mustangs, The Nervous Breakdowns, The New Breed, The Nightwalkers, The Novells, The Painted Faces, The Peanut Butter Conspiracy, The Perpetual Motion Workshop, The Premiers, Primrose Circus, Rain, The Nooney Rickett Four, The Rogues, The Rumors, Sean and the Brandywines, The Second Helping, The Seeds, The Sixpence, The Smoke Rings, Sons of Adam, Souls of the Slain, Sounds Unreal, The Spats, The Standells, The Starfires, The Tangents, Their Eminence, Things to Come, The Tikis, The Togas, The Truths, The Velvet Illusions, The Whatt Four, The Wooly Ones.

San Francisco and California north.

The Answer, The Avengers, The Au Go Go's, The Beau Brummels, The Bees, The Brogues, The Brymers, The Charlatans, The Chocolate Light Bulb, The Chocolate Watch Band, The Chosen Few, The Everpresent Fullness, Family Tree, The Golliwogs (early Creedence Clearwater Revival), The Grapes of Wrath, The Knightriders, The Mojo Men, The Mourning Reign, Odds and Ends,

The Other Half, The Other Side, The Stained Glass, The Satans, Teddy and the Patches, The Toads, The Vejtables, Wildflower.

The Deep South

Alabama, Georgia, Kentucky, Virginia, Carolinas, etc — The Aliens, The Alphabetical Order, The Amoebas, The Apollos, The Banana, The Bandits, The Barracudas, The Bassmen, The Beachnuts, The Beau Havens, The Beethoven 4, The Beggars, The Big Beats, Billy Joe and the Continentals, The Chadwicks, The Changin' Tymes, The Chaps, The Checkmates International, The Chimes, The Citations, The Coachmen, The Continentals, The Counts IV, The Creatures Inc., The Creations, The Culls, Dave and the Stalkers, Days of the Week, The Dedications, The Del Prix, Dennis and the Times, The Destinations, The Deuces Wild, The Distortions, The Drag Kings, The Dutch Masters, The Egyptians, The Escorts, Evil Enc, The Executioners, The Fabulous Pharoahs, Famen, The Fallen Angels, The Five, The Five By Five, The Flight Patterns, The Fly-Bi-Nites, The Flys, Fox and the Huntahs, The Fugitives, The Gang of Saints, The Gaunga Dins, The GeeTees, The Gremlins, The Hackers, The Hard Times, The Hazzards, The Heart Attacks, The Horde, The Illusions, The Impacts Ltd., The Individuals, The Invaders, The Jerks, The Journey Back, The Judges, The K-Otics, The K-Pers, The King Bees, The Knights of Darkness, The Kool Kuzzins, The Light Brigade, Little Phil and the Nightshades, The Londons, The Lost Chords, The Mach V, The Mad Lads, The Malibus, Merging Traffic, The Miller Brothers, The Minutemen, The Mishaps, The Mixed Emotions, The Mod VI, The Mojos, The Movement, The Moxies, The New Direction, The New Things, The Nightwalkers, The Nite Beats, The Omen, The Oxfords, The Outlets, The Panics, The Steve Peele Five, The Phantoms, The Piece Kor, The Preachers, The Precious Few, The Proverbial Knee-Hi's, Sir Walter Raleigh and the Tampa Jewels, Randy and the Holidays, The Reactors, The Rites of Spring, The Road Runners,

The Rockin' Rebellions, The Rogues, Rogues Incorporated, The Romans, The Rondels, The Roots, The Rugbys, The Rysing Sons, The Satelites, The Sceptors, The Seeds of Time, The Shandels, The Shadows, The Sherlocks, The Smacks, Something Else, Soul Incorporated, Sound on Sound, The State of Mind, The Stowaways, String and the Beans, The Sweet Acids, The Swingin' Lamplighters, The Swingin' Machine, The Tempos, The Terrifics, This Side Up, The Tories, The Torquays, 24 Karat Five, The Unknowns, The Uprisers, The Vendors, The Versatiles, The Very-Ations, The Vigilantes, The Vikings, The Village Outcasts, The Weejuns, The Week-Enders, The Wild Cherrys, The Wild Vybrashons, The Wylde, The Yardleys, The Younger Brothers.

Tennessee – The Box Tops, The Breakers, Danny Burk and the Invaders, Butterscotch Caboose, The Castels, The Changin' Tymes, The Coachmen, The Escapades, Flash & the Casuals, Joe Frank and the Knights, The Goodees, The Guilloteens, The Jades, The Jesters, The LeSabres, Load of Mischief, Los Angeles Smog Division, The Memphis Blazers, The Memphis Nomads, The Merits, The MidKnights, The Ole Miss Downbeats, The Percusssions, The Ponees, The Rapscallions, The Rapids, The Ravin' Blue, Ricky and the Rainbows, The Riots, The Sants, Shadden and the King Lears, The Shades, The Torquays, The Uncalled For, The Village Sound, The Villains, The Yo-Yo's.

Louisiana – The Alliance, The Back Alley, The Bad Boys, The Bad Habits, The Bad Roads, The Basement Wall, The Beltones, The Better Half Dozen, Billy John and the Continentals, The Castaways, The Countdowns, Dr. Spec's Optical Illusion, The Echoes of Carnaby Street, The Fugitives, The Gaunga Dyns, The Glory Rhodes, Ron Gray and the Countdowns, Jimmy and the Offbeats, The Little Bits, The Mersey Sounds, The Moon Dawgs, Neal

Odom and the Group, The One Way Street, The Palace Guards, The Persian Market, The Playgue, Randy and the Rockets, The Roamin' Togas, The Satans, The Souls of the Slain, The Spectres, The Surrealistic Pillar, Threshold of Sound, The Tiaras, The Tyrannies, The Young Men.

Florida — The Barons, The Berkley Five, The Birdwatchers, Blues Messengers, The Burgundy Blues, The Burlington Squires, The Busy Signals, The Calientes, The Canadian Rogues, The Cavemen, The Cellar Dwellers, The Chain Reaction, The Clefs of Lavender Hill, The Cosmic Camel, The Dalton Gang, The Dark Horsemen, The Dead Beats, The Deep Six, The Dirt Merchants, The Echo, The Echoes Of Carnaby Street, The Emotions, The Epics, The Esquires, The Fewdle Lords, Flower Power, The Generation Gap, The Go-Mads, The Gray Things, The Group, The Hungry I's, The Hustlers, The Illusions, The Inner Thoughts, The Invaders, The Jackson Investment Co., The Jesters IV, Lost Generation, The Magic Circle, The Malemen, The Mammals, The Maundy Quintet, Me and the Other Guys, The Members, The Minority, The Missing Links, The Mixed Emotions, The Mods, The Montels, The Moondogs, The Mor Loks, Mouse & The Boys, The Mysteries, The Mystics, Neighborhood Of Love, The Night Crawlers, Noah's Ark, The Novas, The Outsiders, The Painted Faces, Plant Life, The Plastic Blues Band, The Powers of Purple, The Purple Underground, The Rare Breed, The Ravens, The Rockin' Roadrunners, Ron and the Starfires, The Rovin' Flames, The Saxons, The Senders, The Shades Inc., The Shy Guys, The Souldiers, The Soul Trippers, Sounds Unlimited, The Split Ends, The Stops, The Surprize, The Swaydes, The Tasmanians, The 31st of February, The Tropics, The Twelfth Night, Dr. T. & The Undertakers, The 2/3rds, The Villagers, The Waveriders, We The People, Little Willie and the Adolescents.

Texas – The Actioneers, The American Blues, The Argyles, The Bad Habits, The Bad Seeds, The Bards, The Barking Spyders, The Barons, The Beefeaters, The Basic Things, The BCs, The Bearfax, The Believers, The Blox, The Blue Things, The Bourbons, The Boys, The Briks, The Brimstones, The Brutes, Bubble Puppy, The Buccaneers, The Buckle, The By Fives, Carrolls Mood, The Cast of Thousands, The Cavemen, The Celtics, The Changin' Times, The Chapparals, The Chayns, Chaz and the Classics, Jimmy C and the Chelsea Five, The Chessmen, The Chevelle 5, The Cicadelics, The Coachmen, The Coastliners, The Conquerers, The Conqeroo, The Continentals, The Cords, The Cosmic Tones, The Countdown 5, The Crabs, S.J. and the Crossroads, The Crowd + 1, The Cult, The Cynics, The Debonairs, The Demolitions, Derby Hatville, Destiny's Children, Don and the Demons, The Driving Wheel, The Eccentrics, Eli Shadrach and the Streetcar, Endle St. Cloud, The Esquires, The Excels, The Exotics, The Fanatics, The Feathers, The Felicity, The Five of a Kind, Neal Ford and the Fanatics, The Four More, The Fronts, The Fugitives, The Gs, The Galaxies, The Gator Shades Blues Band, The Green Fuz, Greta Spoone and Her Magic Moustache Band (aka: The Gretta Spoone Band), The Headstones, The Heard, The Heartbeats, Hysterical Society, The Iguanas, Infinite Staircase, The Intruders, The Jackals, The Jades, Just Us Five, The Karats (with Jimmy Rabbit), Kempy and the Guardians, Kenny and the Kasuals, The Kidds, Kit and the Outlaws, Knights Bridge, The Kommotions, Kubla Khan, Lady Wilde and The Warlocks, Larry and the Bluenotes , Lavender Hour, Lemon Fog, The Livin' End, Lost and Found, The Lost Generation,The Love Flowers, The Madison Revue, The Madras Men, Mankind, The Menerals, The Minds Eye, The Mods, The Morticians, The Moving Sidewalks, Murphy and the Mob, The Mystics, The Night Crawlers,

The Noblemen, Nobody's Children, The Nokounts, The Novas, The Outcasts, Oxford Circus, The Pandas, The Passions, ThePendulums, The Penthouse 5, The Perils, The Pirates, The Rafters, The Rain Kings, The Redcoats, The Red Crayola, The Reddlemen, Reekus the Rat and the Rubber Ducks, The Rel-Yeas, The Remaining Few, The Revolvers, The Roks, The Roots, The Runaways, The Salados, The Sands, Satyn's Children, The Sensors, Seompi, The Shades, The Shaydes, Shivas Head Band, The Six Pentz, S.J. and the Crossroads, The Smokin' Bananas, The Snowmen, The Society, Christopher and the Souls, The Spades, The Sparkles, The Sweetarts, The Terra-Nauticals, These Few, Those Guys, The Tiaras, The Trackers, The Trolls, The Undertakers, The US Britons, The Venetian Blinds, The Venturas, The Venture 5, The Visions, The Wanderers, The Warlocks, George Washington and the Cherry Stompers, The Wig, The Wild Ones, The Wilshire Express, The Wind, The Wry Catchers, The X-Tremes, The Y'alls, Yesterday's Obsession, Zachary Thaks.

The Garage Girls – female or female-led bands
Aletha and the Memories (Los Angeles), The Bad Girls (Texas), The Bandettes (Texas), The Baxterettes (Texas), The Beas (USA), The Beatle-Ettes (New York), The Beatle Maids (USA) Kay Bell and the Tuffs (California), The Belles (Miami), The Bermudas (USA), The Birdies (USA) The Bittersweets (Cleveland), The Bomb Shells, (Texas), The Bootles (USA), The Brazen Hussies (Texas), The Cake (Los Angeles), The Canadian Lady Bugs (Canada), The Chimes of Freedom (New York), The Chymes (Los Angeles), The Continental Co-Ets (Minnesota), The Cupons (Los Angeles), The Darby Sisters (USA), Daughters of Eve (Chicago), The Debs (USA), Denise and Company (US), Pat Downey and the Vistas (USA), The Fatimas (USA), The Feebeez (New Mexico), Friday and the Girls (Texas), The Girls (Los Angeles), The Heartbeats (Texas), The Honeybees (USA), The Id (USA), The

Indigos (Kentucky), The Joy Sisters (USA), The Ladybugs (Virginia and Los Angeles), Linda Laine and the Sinners (USA), The Loved Ones (USA), The Luv'd Ones (Michigan), Lynn and the Invaders (Michigan), The Majorettes (California), The Mama Cats (Detroit), Kathy McDonald and the Unusuals (Northwest), The Models (USA), The Nightingales (USA), The Occasionals (Arizona), Patti's Groove (USA), The Pleasure Seekers (Michigan), The Puppets (Michigan), The Pussycats (New York), Merrilee Rush and the Turnabouts (Northwest), The Sanshers (Ohio), The Shaggs (New Hampshire), The Shamettes (Texas), The She's (USA), Society's Children (Chicago), The Southern Belles (South) , The Starlets (USA), Sunday and the Menn (USA), The Sweet Nothings (Chicago), Tammy and the Bachelors (Minnesota), The Termites (USA), The Tone Benders (Ohio), The Tremelons (Michigan) , The Uncalled Four (New York), The Venus Flytrap (San Jose), The Weekends (USA) The What Four (New York), The Whims (USA), The Whyte Boots (USA), Lady Wilde and the Warlocks (Texas)

The Tremelons from Michigan

Top: The Daughters of Eve. Below: The Belles

Canada

Chad Allen and the Expressions (early Guess Who), The Astro Nuts, The Beaumonts, The Berries, The British Modbeats, The Checkerlads, The Cheshyres, The Chessmen, The Collectors, The Cryptics, M.G. & The Escorts, Esquires, Expedition to Earth, The Fiends, The Frat Kings, The Great Scots, The Gruesomes, The Haunted, The Mike Jones Group, Just Us, The King-Beezz, The Lords of London, The Midnight Angels, Mock Duck, The Mongols, The Munks, The Naughty Boys, The Night Stalkers, The Nocturnals, Don Norman & The Other 4, The Northwest Company, One Way Street, Our Generation, The Pacers, The Paupers, Satan and the D-Men, The Shadracks, The Sherlocks, The Shockers, Simple Simon & The Piemen, The Skaliwags, The Smugglers, The Surfdusters, Bobby Taylor and the Vancouvers, William Tell and the Marksmen, The Ten Commandments, The Treblemakers, The Ugly Ducklings, The Vindicators, The Worst, Dee and the Yeomen, The Aristos, The Aristocrats, The Asteks, The Atomes, The Baronettes, The Beaumarks, The Chancelliers, The Chantels, The Chosen Few, The Copains, The Dabsters, The Daloos, The Develons, The Differents, The Faucons, The Gamines, The Heritiers, The Impairs, The Intimes, J.B. and the Playboys, The Lincolns, The Loups, The Luths, The Merseys, The Million-Airs, The Napoleons, The Rabble, Les Sextants, Les Sinners, The Spectres, Les Sultans, The Talismans, The Valiants, The Versatiles, Les Vampires, The Ardels, The British Modbeats, The Canadian Squires, The Last Words, The Liverpool Set, Luke and the Apostles, The Mynah Birds, The Spasstiks, The Bossmen and The Trip, The Descendants of Time, Jerry and the Mongrels, The Painted Ship, The Seeds of Time, The Shaggs, The Shondells, The Squires and The Trippers.

If we left your band out, it's probably because we don't like you personally and never really have. So there.

JUST BECAUSE YOU'VE NEVER HEARD OF THEM DOESN'T MEAN THEY WEREN'T GREAT

Top to bottom: The VooDoos, The Torques, The Empires

Top to bottom: The Riots, Rick's Continentals, The Colonials

The Last Word
From Kenny Daniel

I was a teenage rock star. Or something very, very close to it. That period just seemed to go by me so fast, as life usually does. One doesn't stop to consider or take time to care what's happening when his life feels like that of a rock star. The first era from 1963 to 1968 was simply surreal — like a dream more than anything else. I went to bed each night smiling and woke up smiling, as it seemed to me that my life was perfect. To be honest, the "drugs, sex and rock and roll" legend is overstated. There were way too many drugs around, and rock and roll was my life, but sex was not as prevalent as you might think. It was certainly not one long non-stop orgy. It was a more innocent time. Most of my musician friends were married or had steady girls to whom they were faithful. I'm sorry to disappoint you, but that's the way I remember it.

The stories that we've told in this book are all true...as far as I can remember. Some names were left out on purpose. Some others were forgotten over the years. If we left out you and your favorite stories of the time, I apologize.

Being born and raised in Texas, I have always loved the state, Texas music and the people associated with it. Whether I was playing country, folk, rock or punk, I never wanted to anything else but make music. I'm still doing that. And now more than ever I want to sing and play the kind of songs that tell stories that ring true. Songs that reflect my life - the heartbreaks, the wild times, the laughs, the kids, the wives, the lovers. The people I've met, the players I've shared the stage with. The tears I've shed, the smiles I've smiled, the guys I've hung out with. All things considered it's been one heck of a great life. Just like a song.

Love is the answer to all things. It's all that matters in this life.

Postscript

Kenny, as described above, is still in the music business as a singer, guitarist and songwriter. He also owns and operates a recording studio in the Dallas area and occasionally finds good use for his commercial real estate license.

Tommy Nichols joined the Navy after leaving the Kasuals. Upon returning from service he became a television video engineer before moving into the video editing industry on the west coast. He continues to be a successful video editor to this day.

Lee Lightfoot became a successful commercial artist in Dallas and now owns the company with which he began. They specialize in package design and have several national and regional clients. One of Lee's favorite memories from the band days is when Cher sat on his lap for a photograph.

After college Paul Roach started a production company renting organs and pianos for tours with major recording artists. Some of his clients included The Rolling Stones, Paul McCartney, The Beach Boys, Chicago, The Eagles and many more top acts. After fourteen years he sold his share to his business partner and helped to start Blockbuster Videos. After successfully participating in the introduction of that company, Paul joined the computer technology industry.

David "Bird" Blachley went on to college and received multiple degrees. As mentioned in the book he is a "double doctor" (MD and PhD) and practices medicine in Dallas.

Richard Borgens – From rock and roll guitar hero to the world of academia and research. Dr. Richard Borgens is the Mari Hulman George Professor of Applied Neurology in the School of Veterinary Medicine at Purdue University and the director of the University's Center for Paralysis Research. His work in researching spinal cord injuries and biomedical engineering has brought him extensive recognition.

Rollie Anderson - Rollie was a guitarist in Kenny & The Kasuals from 1987 to 2000 when he retired from the rock and roll scene. A published children's book author ("Teardrops to Rainbows") and playwright ("The Christmas That Almost Wasn't"), he continues to remain active in various creative endeavors. A born-again Christian, he is also very involved in his church's praise music and Celebrate Recovery ministry.

Denny Freeman, Jimmy Herbert, James Anderson and Tim Cooper are all still active in the music business.

"Whatever sounds good...is good."
John Lennon

Kenny and the Kasuals – 2007. L to R: Kenny, Lee, Jerry, Paul and Bruce Surovic

As a trio, performing at The Balcony Club, Dallas. Gregg Daniel, Kenny and Boom Howard.

Acknowledgements and Credits:

Thanks to The Kasuals: To Kenny for all his memories. To Paul Roach who was instrumental in balancing out the story with his memories and near-total recall. To Tommy Nichols who was a big help in reconstructing the earliest days of the band.

Thanks to Kenny's other bandmates especially Rollie Anderson for his amazing memory, great stories and wonderful photos.

Additional appreciation goes to Jamie Bassett (of The Chaparrals), Tim Cooper (of The Diminshuns) and James Goode (of The Excels) for stories from the era.

Credits

Thanks to the various songwriters and publishers for allowing us to use quotes from song lyrics owned by them:

"Rock and Roll is Here To Stay" – Written by David White, published by Arc Music / Golden Egg Music, BMI

"Louie Louie" – written by Richard Berry and published by EMI Longitude Music, BMI.

"Good Times Bad Times" – written by Mick Jagger and Keith Richards (as "Nanker Phelge") published by Abkco Music, Inc., BMI

"Thunderbird" – written by The Nightcaps, published by Vandanburg, BMI

Photo Credits

Thanks to garagehangover.com for allowing us access to their archive of photos of bands and records. Certain photos of The Chessmen, The Gentlemen, Kit and the Outlaws, Jimmy C and the Chelsea Five, The Five of a Kind, Christopher and the Souls and other bands came from this site. For detailed accounts of many of the Texas bands mentioned in this book, visit their website.

Thanks to 60sgaragebands.com Archives, Jim Jones and Gary Carpenter for use of the photos of Jim Jones and the Chaunteys and The Jades. Part of Richard Parker's chapter on the history of The Rain Kings appeared originally on the 60sgaragebands.com website.

Thanks also to the Big D 60s, The Texas 60s Music Refuge and The Trinity River Music websites for help with photo clearance and for their incredible work in documenting the era. Visit their sites to see an amazing library of photos and memorabilia of local bands of the '50s, '60's and '70's.

Author's note: This is a true story, but the recollections and opinions of the individual band members and others interviewed are theirs alone and do not necessarily reflect those of the authors.

About The Authors

Richard Parker spent his career writing advertising, corporate communications and magazine articles for dozens of firms and publications. His work has appeared in The Dallas Morning News, Goldmine, Broadcasting Magazine, Keep Rockin' and The Dallas Observer among other publications. Richard has won over 30 awards for creativity in writing. He also has written two other books about Dallas – "The Twerp Generation" and "A Time Traveler's Guide To Dallas". He is semi-retired and lives in New Mexico. His first "real date" was to a dance in 1963 where the band was Kenny Daniel and The Illusions.

Kenny Daniel is a singer, songwriter and musician from Dallas, Texas. It's his adventures in the music industry that are chronicled herein. So if you want to know more about Kenny, read the book!